Property Portfolio Management

Property portfolio management can be a highly-specialized business. The wide variety of possible land interests, the fact that property has no central market place as an investment medium, and the high level of secrecy that often surrounds property deals ensure that investing in property is very risky for the unwary and untrained.

In such an unpredictable area, the value of a thorough introduction to the essential elements of investment property cannot be overstated. With this in mind, Nigel Dubben and Sarah Sayce have produced this first introductory text on property portfolio management, focusing specifically on the investment context of property transactions. Analysing methods of appraisal, creation, risk, and returns for both individual investments and full portfolios; examining the involvement of major investors in the property market; exploring various strategies for managing investment property; and discussing trends in both national and international arenas, *Property Portfolio Management* will be invaluable to those who seek to maximize return and minimize risk in this uncertain environment.

The comprehensive coverage of *Property Portfolio Management* makes it an ideal text for students of Estate Management and related courses at both diploma and degree level. In addition, with its concise comparisons of options available to the investor, the book will be of undoubted value to chartered surveyors, investment analysts, and practising accountants wishing to benefit from the authors' wide practical and theoretical knowledge.

Nigel Dubben is currently a director of Grosvenor Waterside, plc, a subsidiary of ABP. He has previously worked as a development surveyor, a project management consultant, and as a lecturer at Kingston Polytechnic.

Sarah Sayce specialized in property management and valuation as a chartered surveyor before joining Kingston Polytechnic where she is now Head of the School of Surveying in the Faculty of Design.

Property Portfolio Management

An Introduction

Nigel Dubben and Sarah Sayce

London and New York

First published 1991
by Routledge
11 New Fetter Lane, London EC4P 4EE

Simultaneously published in the USA and Canada
by Routledge
a division of Routledge, Chapman and Hall, Inc.
29 West 35th Street, New York, NY 10001

Typeset by Selectmove Ltd, London

Printed and bound in Great Britain by
Mackays of Chatham PLC, Chatham, Kent

British Library Cataloguing in Publication Data
Dubben, Nigel, *1949* –
    Property portfolio management: an introduction.
    1. Real property. Investment
    I. Title II. Sayce, Sarah, *1950* –
    332.6324

ISBN 0–415–05123–1
        0–415–05124-x(Pb)

Library of Congress Cataloging-in-Publication Data
has been applied for

Contents

Figures

Tables

Abbreviations

CALUS	Centre for Advanced Land Use Studies
CAPM	Capital Asset Pricing Model
DCF	Discounted Cash Flow
DF	Discount Factor
DTI	Department of Trade and Industry
ENPV	Expected Net Present Value
FRI	Full Repairing and Insuring
FRV	Full Rental Value
GDY	Gross Dividend Yield
GRY	Gross Redemption Yield
IPD	Investment Property Databank
IRR	Internal Rate of Return
JCT	Joint Contracts Tribunal
MLR	Minimum Lending Rate
MPT	Modern Portfolio Theory
MWRR	Money Weighted Rate of Return
NPV	Net Present Value
OMV	Open Market Value
PMA	Property Market Analysis
PUT	Property Unit Trust
RICS	Royal Institution of Chartered Surveyors
RPI	Retail Price Index
TWRR	Time Weighted Rate of Return
USM	Unlisted Securities Market
YP	Years Purchase

Acknowledgements

We should like to express our thanks to the many people who helped and encouraged us whilst we were writing this book.

In particular our gratitude is due to the many property advisers who replied to our surveys on risk, return and leasing patterns, to Kingston Polytechnic for the use of its facilities, and to Conspectus Project Management.

The individuals who helped us are too numerous to list but we would like to record our thanks to the following: Nicola Banfield for her work on the Case Study; Patrick Hooper, British Airways Pension Fund Trustees, for allowing us to use their property for our case study; Eleanor Rivers for her advice and encouragement; Patrick McCabe and Dr Paul Auerbach for their help with Chapters 6 and 7; Carrie Howell, Helen Rose and Sally Watkins for typing the manuscript; and last, but by no means least, our families for their invaluable and enthusiastic support.

Nigel Dubben
Sarah Sayce

Chapter 1

The investment media

INTRODUCTION

The aim of this book is to provide a general introduction to the principles which do, or should, concern all those who hold property, whether for the motivation of pure financial return or for occupational or other reasons.

As a study area in its own right, Property Portfolio Management is still in its infancy, despite man's involvement with land ownership throughout history. Many texts have been written on the appraising and price fixing of property investments (Baum and Crosby 1988, Fraser 1984, Darlow 1983, Baum and Mackmin 1989), whilst others have concentrated on the day-to-day operational management (Scarrett 1984, Stapleton 1986).

The intention of this book is to place the management of property in its investment context. This cannot be done without at least a rudimentary knowledge of the principles of investment and of the investment choices open to any investor. Only then can property be viewed as part of the investment spectrum and its qualities and deficiencies analysed.

In this chapter we seek to outline the nature of investment generally and provide a brief introduction to the options available to any investor, together with a note of their comparative qualities. The consideration of property as an investment is left until Chapter 2, but it must be seen within this overall context. At all times it must be remembered that property is competing for funds with other investment media. Investors will therefore look at the options available to them and place monies where they will achieve the maximum utility. Generally the more money available within the economy for investment the more buoyant the property market will tend to be.

This chapter and Chapter 2 should be considered as introductory in nature and readers with some property and investment knowledge may wish to proceed straight to Chapter 3.

THE NATURE OF INVESTMENT

Investment can be defined as the act of laying out money now in order to receive financial recompense in the future. This recompense or reward may be received in the form of future flows of income or by the receipt of a single capital sum. It may or may not be a guaranteed return; equally it may or may not involve the investor in further action to obtain the return.

The essential factors are thus only two, namely a money outlay and future money receipt/receipts. Apart from these common ingredients investments differ in their characteristics, rendering some media more suitable for particular investors than others. The first prerequisite of successful investment is the choice of investments that are appropriate to the requirements of the investor, that is to say, investments should display the qualities most sought after. In addition to looking at the individual investment opportunity, the effect of that investment upon the entire portfolio must be considered. Baum and Crosby (1988) state that 'a good investment is one which produces high levels of return [from income, capital and psychic income] in comparison with the price paid'. However, these characteristics are only some of those which may be identified and it is the overall 'package' of qualities which any potential investor should consider.

INVESTMENT QUALITIES

Capital security

Will the capital sum remain intact, such as with an investment in a building society or high street bank account, or is there a chance that the whole sum spent will never be recouped such as the placing of a speculative wager? In general, capital security is a quality regarded as a high priority for most investors. Whilst it is easily achievable in money terms, government fixed interest stock being a classic example, security in real terms, that is allowing for changing money values, may be difficult to achieve.

Capital growth

It flows from the paragraph above that capital growth is a desirable quality but frequently difficult to achieve. Few investments offer a guaranteed capital growth in real terms: many purporting to offer capital growth guarantee it only in money terms, which may or may not provide a net growth in real terms. In a non-inflationary environment the distinction between real and money return is eroded, but when future money changes are anticipated the investor must take this into account. It has been the proven ability to achieve long-term capital growth which in the eyes of many investors is the most attractive quality of property as an investment. However, over the last years of the 1970s and throughout the early 1980s these prospects for capital growth remained largely unfulfilled, which led in turn to a net disinvestment in the property sector by many large investors such as pension funds. In later chapters the reasons for this are described in more detail. Readers are also referred to Fraser (1984 and 1985).

Income security

Some investment media produce no income at all. A collector of antiques may purchase a fine piece of furniture which over time may yield a high capital return but will not produce an income. Other investments, indeed the majority, produce income, either constant as with gilt-edged securities, or variable such as bank deposit account interest. Index-linked gilts produce an income that is secure in real terms being linked to the cost-of-living index. With property the degree to which income is secure will depend, among other factors, upon the quality of the tenant: is he reliable and has he the financial resources being the first questions a letting agent should answer.

Income growth

As with capital growth, income growth is often more illusory than real. To find an investment offering guaranteed income growth in real terms is difficult if not impossible. Property, if let at a rent below its full rental value (see Chapter 2), may afford a good opportunity for income growth in real terms. Rental growth is realized only at rent review commonly every five years. Between the reviews income will decline in real terms. The review will restore the income profile to full rental value and this may or may not provide growth in real terms.

The concept of the real value of rents and their decline between reviews is explored more fully in Baum and Crosby (1988). However, it is illustrated in Figure 1.1. This shows a typical property income flow in both money terms (a) and real terms (b). The latter assumes that rents achieved on new lettings (that is, the full rental values) have remained static in real terms, that is, they have moved in line with the rate of inflation.

In reality this may or may not be true; there are many instances where the level of rents on new lettings has risen far in excess of the RPI (the Retail Price Index). For example, office rents in Central London in 1986 rose by over 30 per cent substantially in excess of the general level of price rises. At other times growth in real terms may be negative with rents stationary or declining even in money terms.

Whatever the movement in new letting rents, if an inflationary economy

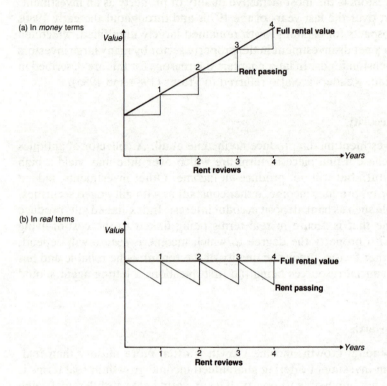

(a) In *money* terms

Value

Full rental value

Rent passing

Years

Rent reviews

(b) In *real* terms

Value

Full rental value

Rent passing

Years

Rent reviews

Figure 1.1 Typical property income flow over time

is assumed, the rent passing will decrease in purchasing power once a letting is effected, until the next rent review.

Income as represented by interest payments on government securities will decline in real terms whilst remaining static in income terms. Dividends payable on ordinary shares, however, are subject to annual alteration, so at best they offer the greatest potential to achieve income growth over a short period, although the income may just as easily decline.

Return

Return is the essential characteristic of any investment. It can take the form of capital or income or a combination of both. Some investors may require their return in the form of capital growth, for example, an individual investing for future retirement or an immature pension fund. Others such as a retired individual or a mature pension fund need high income at the expense of capital growth. The calculation of overall return, that is, taking both capital change and income yield into account, is complex but a full understanding of it is a prerequisite if informed investment decisions are to be made and opportunities compared analytically. Chapter 5 explains in detail the various methods commonly used to calculate return.

Tax treatment

The tax treatment of investments varies considerably. It is important in so far as it is the net of tax or 'after-tax' returns that interest investors. Some media, aimed at individual investors, such as building society accounts, have interest paid at source net of standard rate income tax, thus making them an unsuitable vehicle for the non-taxpayer, but most other investments have income paid gross. At a time when capital gains were treated differently from, and more favourably than, income receipts, there was an incentive to the higher rate taxpayer to opt for investments which showed a low income return but large capital growth. At the current time the two have been brought into line and income tax rates in general have been reduced to a maximum top slice of 40 per cent.

Accordingly the incentive to invest for capital growth for tax reasons has now gone. However, fiscal arrangements are usually short-lived and tax treatment of returns should always be considered when assessing the suitability of an investment.

Grants

The 'flip side' of the tax treatment coin is the presence or otherwise of grants. These may take various forms, such as capital allowances on investment or tax incentives to develop in certain areas, for example, the Enterprise Zones which gave favourable tax treatment to developments within their areas. With property developments the presence or otherwise of grants can be of vital importance.

Timing of receipts

The regularity and timing of income receipts from an individual investment, whilst critical to the small investor, may be of lesser importance to a large institution holding a widely diversified portfolio; however, even the largest institution will need to ensure that income flows are sufficient to meet liabilities, hence the need of pension funds to structure their portfolios in accordance with their known liability to provide pensions.

Dividends from equities and interest on gilts are usually paid half-yearly, whilst property rents are normally paid quarterly in advance. The regularity and exact timing of rental receipts depend on the reliability of the covenant and will affect the overall return that is produced.

Life of the investment

An investment can be of a fixed duration such as a dated government security or a leasehold property, or it can be open ended, that is, it lasts until it is either sold, such as a freehold property, or it wears out such as a car, or it ceases such as a company which goes into liquidation and is wound up. With a fixed life investment it will frequently be possible to determine the end value at the time of initial outlay which may be positive, such as the payback of a coupon value on a government stock, or zero or indeed negative. An example of the latter is where a lease of a property expires and a liability for dilapidations has accrued.

With an open-ended investment at the time of outlay it will not be possible to predict the expiry date nor, in the case of land, the value at the sale date. Thus an investor cannot calculate in advance the overall return that such an investment will yield to him: it is only in hindsight that such a calculation can be made. From the above it does not follow that any investment must necessarily be held until its life end; that will depend on its marketability and most investments are traded. It must be emphasized that it is only where an investment is of a fixed life, with a known end value, that it is possible to be certain, at the time of outlay, of the overall return, and this will only hold if the investment is held for the full period.

In general, the shorter the life of the investment, or the shorter the period over which it is held, the more likely it is that the overall return can be predicted in advance, and indeed the less likely it is that in retrospect the returns achieved will be at variance from those predicted. As the difficulty and inaccuracy in prediction increase so do the risk levels involved. The aim of most investors is to hold an investment for the period which will produce the highest overall return at the lowest possible risk.

Depreciation

Depreciation can be defined as the wearing out of an asset over time. It can be economic, physical or both. Some investments, notably articles for use and property suffer from depreciation whilst paper investments do not, although of course the assets underlying the value of company shares do. Depreciation must therefore be taken into account when considering investment choice and adequate provision made where the investment will depreciate over time. As far as property is concerned, depreciation is given a precise definition in Chapter 2.

Transferability or marketability

The ability to sell an investment is important to most investors, and the lack of marketability is regarded as a serious drawback. Few investments are totally untransferable but some are, for example, certain life policies, and property held on a non-assignable lease. Such investments are only suitable where the investor is certain that he will have no requirement to release his capital before the termination date. Government securities and public quoted company shares are examples of investments sold on a day-by-day, indeed minute-by-minute, basis. Freehold property is readily marketable but has the drawback that transactions normally take a comparatively long time.

Transfer cost

Allied to general marketability and the ability to transfer is the cost of transaction. Obviously the higher the charges incurred the lower the overall return will be. Transfers of government stock and equity shares cost in the region of 1 per cent, whereas the purchase and sale of property is comparatively expensive, amounting to approximately 3 to 4 per cent in many cases. Unit trusts are potentially even more expensive with transfer costs amounting to 5 per cent or more.

Lotting

A consideration important to both institutions and individuals alike is the 'lotting' factor, that is, whether the investment can be purchased in small units, or whether it is available in large lots only. An investment in a bank account, for example, can be of any size, but direct property investment can only be achieved by committing a large capital sum. This can present difficulties when the funds available are limited and a spread of investments is required. Indeed the paper value of some properties is so high that they have very few potential UK purchasers, assuming that purchasers will not be prepared to commit all their funds to one asset.

Risk

The question of risk and uncertainty is taken up in detail in Chapters 6 and 7. It is sufficient here to observe that investors have differing attitudes to risk. In general people tend to be risk averse and require increased returns if they are to be persuaded to accept higher risks. Past wisdom stated that government securities were a risk-free investment and that shares and property, where future income flows are uncertain, were risky. This view is now not universally accepted, with a strong case being

offered that government stock do have risks attached, unless they are held
to redemption (Fraser 1985).

Management and maintenance expenses

With an investment in a building society the cost of management to an
investor are nil. If a work of art is purchased there may be costs of keeping
it in a suitable environment and inevitably there will be costs of insurance.
Apart from this, however, no management expenses are incurred. Property
presents a very different picture: its management can be expensive, often
accounting for 10 per cent or more of the annual income. Even if the costs
are reduced by the transfer of liability for upkeep on to the lessee, the
freeholder still requires skilled management in order to ensure that the
performance of the property is maximized. Unit trusts, too, involve the
investor in annual management costs to reimburse the trustees for their
work in manipulating the underlying investments.

Social effect

To most people the purpose of investing is purely financial: to others wider
considerations, including social implications, come into play. Many people
will not invest in companies based in countries whose political stance they
find unacceptable whilst others refuse to place funds in certain industries
for similar reasons. Until recently such investors wishing to use indirect
media such as unit trusts have found it difficult to reconcile their social
desires with available schemes, but some unit trust managers have now
created unit trusts specifically excluding investment in some products or
countries. Property, too, is an investment which has social consequence.
Not only does the ownership of land bring status, but also it can bring an
element of social responsibility as, for example, residential estates owned
by local authorities.

Diversification and portfolio considerations

The old adage of 'don't put all your eggs in one basket' is one we
examine later in this book. Instinctively most people with funds to invest
wish to dilute their risk by holding a mixture of investments, perhaps
displaying varying qualities in terms of capital/income performance and
investment life. They are then said to hold a diversified portfolio. How
investments can best be combined and the number needed to achieve
effective diversification, will vary from investor to investor.

Hence, when assessing the attractiveness of an investment, its impact on
the portfolio already held must be considered.

Exchange risk

Many investors place money in investments overseas, either directly by, for example, the purchase of foreign assets, or indirectly by holding shares abroad. An additional risk attaches to these investments, namely exchange risk, which can often work dramatically depending on the strength of sterling and the foreign currency. Thus an investor seeking a low risk profile would not normally contemplate placing substantial funds in such sectors.

Psychological value

The psychological value of holding a portfolio of 'paper' investments is of little consequence to most people. The same is not true of property.

The ownership of land and the way it is utilized have been important and sensitive issues throughout history. Status has always been afforded to the owner of land, quite apart from any financial advantage that it may impart. To some individuals the mere ownership of land can be regarded as an end in itself; it is perceived to give personal satisfaction, security and, of course, value. At a corporate level the psychic value of owning a prestigious headquarters building may be of considerable importance. So, too, can the ownership of a portfolio of 'landmark' buildings which can be listed in the annual company accounts. Certain companies, for example hotel chains, have a need to project a corporate image and to them a building which can act as a 'flagship' for the company may have an added value.

INVESTMENT MEDIA

Having decided what qualities are required of an investment, the range of options open to individuals is very wide; to institutions, which themselves are homes for individual investor's monies, the choice is more limited. Recent years have seen an explosion of institutional schemes all trying to attract funds and thereby provide commission for the financial intermediary, be he insurance or mortgage broker, banker or unit trust manager. Recent legislation, notably the Building Societies Act 1986 and the Financial Services Act 1987 have introduced greater freedom for financial intermediaries, albeit subject to the direction of the Securities and Investment Board. Like many other aspects of life, personal investment has become a much more complex issue than it was previously.

The interplay between personal and institutional investment must never be underestimated, as in the final analysis every investment is dependent on the decision of individuals to either forego consumption and save, thus making the funds available to finance other economic activity, or to spend thereby providing the incentive to create further goods for consumption.

The monies spent by the large institutions which have so dominated the property investment market for the last two decades originate to a very major extent from the actions of the individuals, and the returns achieved are likewise so dependent.

Below are outlined the main investment opportunities, other than property, available to investors. A knowledge of these alternatives is essential to anyone seeking to advise on property portfolio matters for the following reasons:

(a) The standpoint taken throughout this book is that investors are essentially logical; they will therefore seek to place funds in the most appropriate medium. It follows that property decisions should be taken in the light of the alternatives available.
(b) If alternative investments are considered, methods of evaluating the likely returns from each must be understood. The measurement and analysis of returns are considered in Chapter 5.
(c) An understanding of the factors which affect the performance and thus the management of investments such as the underlying economic conditions and investor demand assists in the appraisal of property. Appraisal is an activity which is fundamental to the good management of property assets and we refer to this again in Chapters 8 and 9.

Banks and building societies

Essentially these are liquid funds, as monies placed either on deposit in the bank or in a building society are able to be released at very short notice. The income that they produce is normally low in comparison with returns that may be available elsewhere, and it fluctuates depending upon the general movements of interest rates. If the investor is prepared to 'lock in' for a period of, say, three months, the interest rate achievable will normally be slightly higher. In respect of capital they are secure in money terms but not real terms and they have no capital growth. Income from banks is paid gross but at the time of writing that from building societies is paid net of a composite rate of income tax. In that interest on building societies' accounts is normally paid net they are unsuitable for non-tax payers. From 1991 interest will be payable gross, thus rendering them suitable for non-tax payers.

Essentially banks and building societies should be regarded as cash equivalents and are suitable only as homes for funds which must remain relatively liquid. They are unsuitable for anyone seeking long-term capital growth. However their high advertising profile has succeeded in attracting many funds which could almost certainly have produced better returns elsewhere.

Articles for use (chattels)

There is no doubt that many individuals have amassed fortunes by investing in chattels such as paintings, jewellery and furniture. Institutional investors, too, have been known to purchase such items, but how satisfactory are they as investments? They do not usually produce income and, indeed, the costs of security and insurance may well mean that there is a net annual outgoing to the investor. The capital returns may be very large, but they are at best unpredictable and capital loss may be experienced. In addition, the investor who wishes to sell may find it difficult to find a purchaser at any given date. To most investors, therefore, articles for use are only appropriate for inclusion in a fully diversified portfolio due to their lack of income and high risk. After a flirtation with such investments, notably paintings, during the 1970s, pension funds have now mainly withdrawn from the medium.

National Savings

For many years, as part of its borrowing requirements, the government has offered a National Savings scheme, currently comprising National Savings Certificates, Savings Bonds, Ordinary and Investment Accounts and Premium Bonds. Although the schemes are primarily aimed at individuals, some are open to, and used by, institutions. The hallmark of these investments is that they are not marketable, and being government issue they offer total monetary capital security. Here the similarity between them ends.

National Savings Certificates can be either fixed interest, or index linked (these used to be known as 'Granny Bonds' as the first issue was open to pensioners only). They are for a fixed term and there are penalties for early withdrawal. As the interest rates available are often attractive when compared with other 'safe' investments they can be attractive to individuals, especially high tax payers who do not require liquidity, as the returns are free of tax.

National Savings Bonds are similar to Certificates except that the interest paid is variable, and taxable, thus making them of greater interest to non-taxpayers such as charities. As with certificates, there are limits on the amount that any individual may invest in any bond.

Investment in the National Savings Bank is in essence the same as any other bank, that is to say, the longer the notice period on withdrawals, the higher the interest rate that is offered. It should be noted that ceilings exist on the amount anyone can invest.

Premium bonds are mentioned for completeness, but as they only offer a guarantee of Capital Security in money terms, with no income and unpredictable capital return, they are in essence a gamble, rather than an investment.

Guaranteed income and growth bonds

These are issued by life assurance companies on terms guaranteed by the company. They can take the form of guaranteed capital growth or guaranteed income and they last for a specific period typically two to ten years. The guarantee, of course, relates to security in money and not real terms. There are a great many types of bonds on offer at any one time, each aimed at the differing needs of individual investors.

In general the returns offered are higher than those achievable by investment in banks or building societies, and they usually have provision for early redemption albeit with penalties. They are non-marketable and normally there is a minimum commitment (typically £1,000). They are therefore attractive to investors who are in a position to tie up capital for a set period, do not want to undertake high risk, and have medium-sized funds available. They are aimed only at individual investors, not institutions.

Government and public authority stocks

Commonly referred to as 'gilts' the loan stock issued by the British Government provides an extremely important investment medium and one often taken as a 'bench mark' against which to judge other opportunities.

The name gilts originates from the fact that such government loan stock used to be issued on gilt-edged certificates. This practice has long since gone, but the name is taken loosely to refer to not only government-issued loan stock, but other stocks publicly traded on the stock market, namely local authority and nationalized industry issues.

Gilts are issued as a means of raising funds; their attraction to individuals and institutions alike lies first in the fact that default on payment is, to say the least, unlikely. Their second attraction is that they are readily and speedily marketable; indeed the market is so large and active that although small lots may be traded, transactions running into millions of pounds are unlikely to 'flood' the market.

Traditionally the view has been taken that investment in gilts is essentially a long-term activity, but the ease and speed with which they can be traded has led to large investors treating them as cash equivalents rather than a long-term home for funds. The majority of gilts on the market are fixed interest stock and have been issued with a redemption date either totally fixed or fixed between two dates. The issue may be short dated, that is, with redemption within five years; medium term, with a life of between five and fifteen years, or long dated with over fifteen years to redemption. Also available on the market are some undated or irredeemable stock where either no date for redemption was set or where that date was optional and has passed.

Stocks are therefore described by reference to the fixed interest rate that they bear and their redemption date, and their current market prices are listed daily in the financial press, the prices relating to the current value of £100 worth (nominal) of the specific issue. Table 1.1 shows an example for 14 August 1989. On this date government undated War Loan Stock 3.5 per cent was quoted at 38.88. This means that the stock which was issued at £100 could be purchased in August 1989 for £38.88p. The income receivable is £3.50p (that is, 3.5 per cent of the original £100). The stock is thus worth only about one-third of its original capital value. Since the issue of this stock, general levels of interests have risen and been sustained and with it the capital value has fallen so that the investor receives a return in keeping with other returns available. In our example the investor would receive a yield of approximately 9 per cent, in line with the general prevailing interest rates at that date.

The price of gilts moves on a daily basis in line with market trends, prices rising as interest rates fall and vice versa. It should be noted, however, that with short-dated stock the impending redemption date will also affect price; when stock is first issued the interest is fixed at current rates so, for example, new short-dated stock in August 1989 would be issued with a coupon rate of around 9 per cent. At *redemption*, whatever had happened to the price during the intervening period, the investor will receive the face value from the government, and thus as the future redemption date approaches it is the future capital receipt, rather than the interest to be received, which will dictate the market price.

Commonly in the past gilts have been regarded as no risk investments due to their certain returns and capital security. However, unless stock is purchased at issue or below 'par value' and in either case is held to redemption, it is not capital secure, as the capital value of the stock

Table 1.1 Undated stocks prices

Amt (£m)	Stock	Price	Usual dividend	Red Yld
359	Cons 4%	$43\frac{7}{16}$	1 Feb. 1 Aug.	–
1909	**War Ln 3½%**	**$38\frac{7}{8}$**	**1 Jun. 1 Dec**	–
140	Cov 3½%	$65\frac{15}{16}$	1 Apr. 1 Oct.	–
56	Tr 3%	35	5 Apr. 5 Oct.	–
267	Cons.2½%	$27\frac{3}{8}$	5 Apr. 10 Ju.	–
475	Tr 2½%	$27\frac{5}{16}$	1 Ap. 1 Oct.	–

Source: Independent, 14 August 1989.

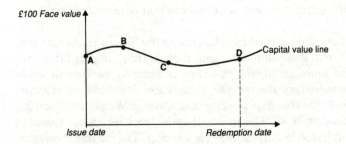

Figure 1.2 Example of gilts price fluctuations

fluctuates daily and may well go down. Figure 1.2 illustrates this point.

In this example an investor purchasing stock at issue (A) and holding it until redemption (D) will incur no capital gain or loss. If, however, after issue the prevailing level of interest rates fall the price will be bid up to say (B). A sale at this moment will give the investor a capital gain. However, if he buys at (A) or (B) and is subsequently forced to sell at (C) a capital loss will be incurred.

It can be seen that only by holding until redemption can the return be calculated with certainty. In addition, only if the purchase is at or below 'par' or issue price will the investor be secure from capital loss by holding to redemption.

It can also be explained numerically: let us assume that £100 worth of short-dated 8 per cent stock is purchased at the date of issue. If this is held until redemption the £100 will be returned to the purchaser and he will have a certain and predicted return, which he could have calculated at the date of purchase. If, however, interest rates rise and he sells one year before redemption, the price of the stock may well only be £90. In this case a capital loss has been incurred. Thus to describe gilts as offering a risk-free investment offering total monetary security is only accurate if the purchaser is prepared to treat them as a non-marketable investment. The price volatility arguably puts them into a high risk category of investment and we return to this point in later chapters.

Another category of stocks are index-linked gilts. With such gilts both the repayment of capital and the payment of interest are guaranteed to move in line with the Retail Prices Index. The coupon rate is very low, typically 2 or 2.5 per cent, but it must be remembered that this represents a return over and above inflation. As with conventional gilts, the price fluctuates. As at August 1989 the majority of such stocks were selling at prices above par, with only long-dated issues selling below, thus reflecting investors' views that over the long term returns greater than 2.5 per cent in real terms could be achieved elsewhere, whereas in the short term a return of 2.5 per cent above inflation looked attractive.

Company stocks and shares

Just as government seeks to raise finance by issuing loans on the gilts market, so businesses too must raise money for expansion and other expenditure. This can be done either by borrowing (debt financing) or by corporate finance, that is, by issuing stocks and shares which are tradable, either through the main stock market or, for less established companies, on the Unlisted Securities Market or third market. The volume of trade is concentrated very heavily on the stock market but, since the reorganization of the stock market in 1986 (the so-called 'Big Bang'), there has been a significant increase in trading on the Unlisted Securities Market.

At this point a distinction should be drawn between the two basic types of investment that may be made in companies: loan stock and equity shares. Loan stock is in many ways similar to government stock except, of course, that there may be a risk of default on payment. Company loan stock is either debenture stock, secured against the assets of the company in much the same way as a mortgage is secured, or unsecured loan stock. The holder is entitled to payments of interest on the loan, normally half-yearly at a fixed interest rate and for a fixed duration. The holders of such stock have no ability to participate in the running of the business, they are merely creditors. Unlike gilts which are always issued at 'par', company stocks are sometimes issued at a premium or more commonly at a discount. 'Deep discount' securities are defined as those where the discount on par value at issue is more than 15 per cent. Where such securities are issued, the coupon rate is normally also low, the attraction to the investor being that the redemption value is at par thus giving guaranteed capital growth. Such issues were popular in the early 1980s when inflation and interest, rates were high, as it enabled companies to raise funds economically whilst higher rate taxpayers benefited from the combination of low income and high capital return investments. Recent tax changes have, however, reduced the attractiveness of such schemes. To summarize, company loan stock has similar qualities as an investment to government stock except that income security may be less, and that schemes are more varied.

The other major way in which individuals and institutions invest in companies is through the purchase of shares, that is, through partial ownership of the company. Share capital itself is divided into preference share capital, and ordinary shares, the latter normally forming the greater section.

Preference shares entitle the holders to a fixed dividend each year, provided that the profits of the company mean that a dividend is payable. Hence the holders of preference shares take 'preference over' ordinary shareholders, and when business is poor it may be that preference shareholders will receive their dividends when ordinary shareholders do not. On the other hand, when business is good, the returns, which are limited to the fixed amount, look poor against payments made to the ordinary shareholders. Preference shareholders, although technically part owners of the company, do not normally enjoy voting rights.

By far the greatest involvement in company financing by investors is by way of ordinary shares which can be bought and sold quickly and relatively cheaply on the Stock Exchange.

A purchaser of ordinary shares in a company has voting rights in the company and the right to share in the profits of the business assuming that there are any. If there is no residual profit no dividend will be declared and the investor will thus receive no income return that year.

In practice, of course, investors purchase shares for two reasons – first the dividend income, and second, in the hope of achieving a capital gain. Any investor in equities must, however, appreciate that a possible outcome could be no income and a capital loss. What determines the capital value of a share at any moment in time is a combination of the performance of the individual company and investors' demand for shares. If demand goes down due to a lack of confidence in the market or in expectation of poor company results, so will the share price. The dramatic speed with which share prices can change was illustrated only too clearly in October 1987 when due to a world-wide confidence crisis, many share prices tumbled by 30 per cent or even more in a few days alone. This does not mean that investors necessarily incurred such capital losses; it is only if they sold at that time having purchased at a stock market high that any loss was in reality experienced. For example, if an investor purchased a portfolio of shares for £10,000 in January 1987 typically such shares may have been worth £14,000 by September 1987. In November following the October slump the value could well have been £8,500. However, by March 1988 the market had recovered in such a way that the value was probably in the order of £11,000. Thus, unless the portfolio was sold in the autumn of 1987, no loss has in reality been sustained, indeed in the example above the investor has seen a 10 per cent capital growth over a year.

The point that we have attempted to illustrate here is that share prices tend to be very volatile, moving as they do on market rumour as well as company performance. It is often the *timing* of sale and purchase of the holding of equity investments and the length of time held that determines the returns experienced. History has shown that the stock market tends to move cyclically, having periods when share prices move either down in real terms or remain static (a Bear market) and periods when prices rise sharply (a Bull market).

In Chapter 2 the mechanics of share price fixing are explained.

Unit trusts

Unit trusts fall into two main categories: authorized and unauthorized. It is the former which make up by far the larger section of unit trust business.

The original aim of unit trusts was to offer to the smaller investor, who lacked the funds and probably the expertise to create his own diversified portfolio of equities, a medium by which he could do just that. In this aim they have to a very large extent succeeded, as evidenced by the great number of schemes in existence. Over a thousand existed in 1987 and some of the schemes have been extremely successful, but others have been distinctly mediocre in performance.

What then is a unit trust and how does it work? As the name implies, unit trusts are legal trusts, in which the money and the investments are held by trustees acting on behalf of the unit holders. Participators in the trust buy 'units' at a price determined by the fund managers who then invest the monies by the purchase of a spread of stocks and shares, mainly on the quoted stock market although a small portion may be invested on the Unlisted Securities Market (USM). The units themselves are tradable, but if the demand for units changes, the trustees can contract or expand the trust by the creation or redemption (buying back) of units, and the purchase or sale of the underlying trust assets as required.

The type of underlying stocks and shares varies from trust to trust; some specialize in buying for high capital growth, some for income and some for a balance between the two. In recent years, funds specializing in, for example, the Far East or high technology have been set up.

In theory whatever the investment qualities required by an individual, it should be possible to find a suitable unit trust, and during the prolonged bull market in equities in 1981–7, unit trusts attracted very substantial funds. However, they do have serious drawbacks; when an investor buys into a fund, there is normally an initial charge which can be in the order of 5 per cent and there is also an annual management charge. This combined with the further charge that is commonly imposed when units are sold, means that in reality their marketability is limited and if they are only held for a short period, the handling charges can have a serious impact on the return achieved. As an investment they should only be considered if a long-term view can be taken.

Another drawback is that their main aim is to reduce investors risk by diversification (see also Chapter 7), yet by creating specialist funds, many of the diversification advantages are being lost; indeed, the performance figures reinforce the fact that returns are often very volatile, varying dramatically from year to year and from fund to fund.

Notwithstanding these drawbacks, units trusts can be beneficial to small investors, and indeed the larger investor who may well perceive advantages in putting some money in the specialist funds that cover areas in which he lacks expertise. To the institutional investor with the funds and managers to create and manage their own portfolio, they are of little real interest.

So far we have only considered authorized unit trusts. To date these are restricted to equities and stocks, although at the time of writing, there are proposals with the DTI (Department of Trade and Industry) to introduce authorized unit trusts directly in property holdings.

Unauthorized unit trusts differ from those authorized in two significant ways – first, unauthorized unit trusts may invest in other media, notably property; second, they are not available to individual investors but are a medium for institutional investors only, for whom they provide a way of investing indirectly in property. Apart from these two factors, they work on the same principle as authorized trusts with an expansion or contraction of demand for units dictating whether the fund managers purchase or sell underlying assets. During recent years they have appeared unattractive relative to equity funds and 1987 saw the demise of two well-known funds (Pension Fund Property Unit Trust and the Fleming Fund), as institutions sought to invest indirectly in property through the medium of shares in property companies, sooner than through the unit trust route. In their favour, it can be argued that they are convenient, offer a spread of risk and they are managed by property professionals, who have become conscious over the last few years of the need for short term performance and active management. One benefit is that the unit holder can realize his money much more speedily than if he owned property directly by simply selling his units back to the managers, who in their turn, will if necessary have to sell the underlying assets. Thus Property Unit Trusts (PUT) provide one way of overcoming the perceived defect of illiquidity of property. It remains to be seen whether they will exert a strong influence on the investment market over the next decade if alternative property vehicles, such as the unitized property market come into being.

Investment trusts

Investments trusts are often considered alongside unit trusts and this is not surprising as they share many similarities, the most important of which is a common aim. In other ways, however, investment trusts are very different. Indeed, the word 'trust' is a misnomer as they are not trusts at all but limited companies set up for the purpose of investing in other companies and whose assets consist almost entirely of shares in such companies. Like unit trusts, investment trusts are specifically designed to offer the investor the opportunity to partake in a widely-diversified portfolio professionally managed by the trust managers. There is also a legal requirement that the monies placed in the trust are invested in a spread of assets; with investment trusts no more than 15 per cent of the total assets may be placed in one holding. This figure is considerably higher than for unit trusts which have a 5 per cent limit.

The tax treatment of both vehicles is similar with no capital gains tax liability within the fund; the liability being borne entirely by the individual investors, who may of course take advantage of any exemptions or reliefs to which they may be entitled.

Whilst most investment trusts invest heavily in equities, they are permitted to invest in other types of assets such as property and unquoted securities. This additional flexibility can result in higher risk, and higher return investment policies being pursued by trust managers.

The major difference between the two lies in the structure of the vehicles. As a limited company, the share capital is fixed so that, unlike the unit trust manager who must constantly buy or sell the assets of the fund, depending on the demand for units, the investment trust manager has a known share capital to invest just as the board of a manufacturing company would. In common with other limited company boards, he can also raise money by borrowing in order to take advantage of rising markets. The degree of borrowing is known as the gearing; a high level of borrowing compared to capital is said to be highly geared.

Gearing, of course, is a two-edged weapon; when markets are rising borrowing leads to potentially higher returns, whereas when markets fall losses are magnified. Example 1.1 will illustrate this point:

Example 1.1

An investment trust is launched with a capitalization of £7m comprising:

£2m	debenture stock
£5m	£1 ordinary shares
£7m	total capitalization

If over a three-year period the issued capital is invested and at the end of that time the portfolio is worth £12 million, the effect is as follows:

Value of portfolio	£12m
Less debenture stock	£2m
Assets attributable to the ordinary shares	£10m
Therefore net asset price per share	£2.00

If on the other hand the portfolio does not prosper and at the end of the period its value is £6m, the effect is:

Value of portfolio	£6m
Less debenture stock	£2m
Assets attributable to the ordinary shares	£4m
Therefore net asset price per share	80p

The net asset price per share will be one factor that will determine the market value of the shares, but it will not be the only one. The level of demand for shares will move up and down in line with the general expectation of the stock market, just as it does for any other company. Whether the shares will outperform the market depends on investors' confidence in the investment trusts manager's ability to handle the portfolio as well as the portfolio's composition.

In practice, investment trust shares normally trade at a discount to their asset value due in part to the high management costs of administering the portfolio. If the discount becomes too large, it is always possible that the entire trust company will be the subject of a take-over or buy out by a pension fund or other institutional investor who sees the opportunity to obtain the underlying assets cheaply.

In theory, the investment trust is a means of achieving risk reduction and enabling the small investor to participate in the equity field in a way he otherwise might not. In reality their performance has often been lacklustre and they are generally perceived to be relatively high risk. It is this latter reason that has probably been the key factor in the undoubted supremacy in recent years of unit trusts as a preferred investment medium.

Other options

In addition to the types of investment outlined in brief, new vehicles are constantly being devised by the professionals involved in financial asset management. In particular, much interest has been shown in off-shore fund investment, and in the whole field of future traded options and commodities. It is outside the scope of this book to discuss the merits and risks of these. Of the media so far detailed, it can be seen that whilst the choice for the individual investor is extremely wide, the larger the investment funds available the narrower the effective choice, so that for the institutions, stocks and equities are the major possibilities apart from property which is discussed in the next chapter.

THE BALANCED PORTFOLIO

Any investor holding a portfolio will need to arrange its composition in such a way that it displays the characteristics that he requires. This may entail holdings in just one medium but more commonly a spread of investments is undertaken to provide a balanced portfolio. For individuals whose capital resources are restricted a spread may be achieved through investing in, for example, unit trusts. For the institutions, however, it implies a mix of government stock, company shares, property, liquid funds and overseas investment.

Table 1.2 gives an example of how a typical institutional investor allocated its funds in 1989. It will be seen that the emphasis is on equity type investments which provide potential income and capital growth. In general such investments have a higher degree of risk involved than is totally acceptable to institutions, so a balance is achieved by investing in guaranteed high income assets such as government stock which are regarded as lower risk.

Property offers growth but may have liquidity and management problems and the size of investment in this sector will often depend on its current performance compared with that of other equity investments.

Hence at a time when share prices are rising, and returns are high, new funds will tend to be channelled to that sector. If on the other hand property returns are running at levels above those obtainable in other sectors, investment in property may be expected to increase.

The reasons for the diversification can therefore be seen to relate to differing qualities displayed by each sector and in particular the way in which they react differently to changing economic circumstances. The price of government stock is closely related to the prevailing level of interest rates, shares on the other hand react to investors' confidence in the management and likely future performance of the company concerned. We examine the factors affecting property's performance in Chapter 2.

At a time when one sector is experiencing poor performance, the allocation of funds may be switched out of that sector and placed elsewhere. An example of this was seen in 1987–8 when, following the sudden fall in stock market prices in October 1987, institutional investment funds into property increased substantially (Figure 1.3).

Table 1.2 Typical institutional portfolio analysed by sector split 1989

Type of holding	% in value
UK equities	55
Overseas equities	22
Gilts	12
Property	8
Cash and other	3
	100

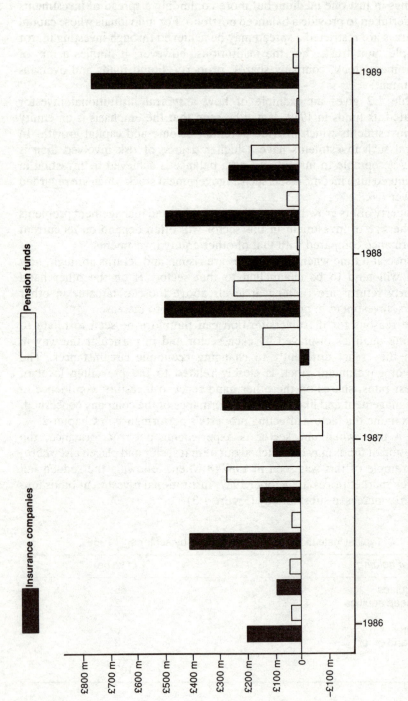

Figure 1.3 Insurance companies and pension funds, net property investment

Source: Debenham, Tewson and Chinnock (1989)

Obviously the above is an oversimplification of the way in which portfolio allocations are made; it serves just to introduce the concept. Later in the book we analyse the needs of institutional investors.

SUMMARY

In this chapter we have introduced the concept of investment and described in outline the various channels for investment funds which compete with property. The essential requirement of any investment is that it must produce a return. However, the size of that return is not, or should not be, the sole criterion on which decisions regarding the allocation of funds are made. Any financial or property manager will consider not only the potential return offered by each opportunity but will also consider the other characteristics it offers. These will include its risk profile, saleability, management requirements, together with fiscal considerations. Lastly it is important that the interreaction of investments is considered so that a portfolio suitable to that particular investor is constructed.

In the next chapter we will look at property and its investment characteristics in more detail.

Chapter 2

Property as an investment

INTRODUCTION

In Chapter 1 a definition of investment was given together with a description of the various qualities exhibited by different types of investment. Whilst return is a very important criterion to an investor, it must not be viewed in isolation; an appreciation of other factors such as marketability, risk, life of the investment, to name but a few, are crucial and it is here that the concept of investment comparison becomes crucial.

In this chapter the nature of property interests is set out and the factors affecting the evaluation of such assets as investments are described.

While this book is concerned primarily with the management of property as an investment like any other commodity, property is unusual in that it is frequently held for purposes other than investment. This affects the working of the investment property market as some participants make choices and evaluate worth on principles that are not purely financial.

Apart from the investment prospects the main motivation for the purchase of any property is for occupation, or, in the case of companies, as a unit of resource. To this must be added the elements of psychic value, status and prestige. Throughout history there are instances of status being afforded to the owner of land. For example, voting rights were at one time restricted to those who held land. Power, too, has long been associated with land ownership. To some people the mere ownership can be regarded as an end in itself; it is perceived to give personal satisfaction, security and, of course, value. To say all this is, however, only part of the story; the motives behind any property purchase are often complex, but it is important that they are identified as it is the motivation of the purchaser that will, to a large extent, dictate how the asset is managed when purchased.

Undoubtedly the two principal reasons for buying property are for occupation and for financial return. Although often regarded in isolation the two are in reality frequently linked. Every homeowner will to some extent regard his house as an investment as well as a shelter. Likewise businesses are increasingly aware of the bricks and mortar value of their premises even to the extent that many large companies have formed separate property divisions or holding companies to manage their assets on an investment basis. Examples of this are Dixons, who has its own property development division, and Sainsbury, who has set up a joint company with London and Edinburgh Trust to identify older stores for redevelopment. Ownership for occupational purposes must be dictated by specific needs as to the type, size, standard and location of the property required. The choice of tenure is, however, something which is not normally need-related but decided on other criteria such as finance and availability. Ownership for financial reasons can itself be subdivided – the principal aim can be to derive income or it can be to obtain capital growth. The latter can be achieved through development including refurbishment and redevelopment, or by the purchase of reversionary investments.

Throughout this book we are concerned principally with the financial motivation for property ownership and the management of property so held although, as already stated, this motivation may be tempered by other considerations such as psychic wealth.

DEFINITIONS

Estate management

Stapleton (1986) defines estate management as 'simultaneously a generic description of a broad range of activity and a specialist discipline'. For the purposes of this book the term 'estate management' is taken to mean the management of a large number of properties, probably of differing types, held by an individual or single organization such as a company or local government authority, probably for a variety of motives. For example, it could refer to the management of a company's property holding comprising a headquarters building, production and distribution units, and trading outlets, or a local authority with a portfolio of offices for occupation, council housing, schools and other units used for statutory purposes together with investment lands. In the latter cases the manager will be trying to balance the financial and social needs of the local population. The keynote in each case is that the properties tend to be disparate in type, tenure, and ownership motivation. They may or may not be concentrated geographically.

The term 'estate management' is therefore very wide and the manager will need to possess many skills from man-management to investment expertise to fulfil his function satisfactorily.

Building management or property management

Whereas estate management must of necessity encompass a large degree of 'overview', building or property management is concerned with the minutiae of management; it is dealing with the day-to-day matters that arise from the occupation of land. As such, a detailed knowledge of structure and law may be required, together with an ability to deal with tenants in occupation. The building or property manager is not specifically concerned with the performance of the property as an investment; his interest lies in the physical maintenance of the unit and compliance with contractual and statutory constraints.

Facilities management

The expression 'facilities management' has only recently come into use. It is taken by the authors to mean the management of a building from an 'end-user's' viewpoint. Hence a facilities manager is concerned with the landlord and tenant relationship if the user is a lessee, but in particular with issues such as costs in use, services, and information technology provision. In comparison with the building or property manager, the facilities manager is likely to require a greater expertise in technical building matters from the impact of design criteria to the control of costs-in-use.

Property portfolio management

A portfolio is by definition a list of investments. Thus property portfolio management is concerned with the management of property held for investment purposes. It is contended therefore that it is a subject in its own right, different from building or estate management. The owner of a property portfolio is interested primarily in its financial return, although prestige and status considerations may be influential. As the motivation is financial, although the minutae of management cannot be ignored as they have an effect upon the financial return, the portfolio manager requires a knowledge of other investment media in order that comparisons may be made. At all times he will be seeking to take action to ensure that the assets are showing satisfactory investment qualities.

In this chapter we examine the qualities of property as a medium competing for investment funds. Such investment can be undertaken either directly through the purchase of a property holding, or by equity participation in a development scheme, or indirectly through the purchase of property bonds, property company shares, mortgages or in the case of the institutions, property unit trusts.

At the time of writing there are proposals to introduce a new type of direct property investment: the unitized property. This, it is anticipated, will enable investors to purchase tradable units in a single property. Various routes to unitization have been proposed and these are described in more detail in Chapter 12.

CHARACTERISTICS OF THE PROPERTY MARKET

The nature of the property market is so different from other markets in which investments are traded that no real understanding of property investment is possible without an appreciation of its characteristics.

Economists often refer to the concept of the perfect market which they define as one in which there are many buyers or sellers, an homogeneous product, perfect knowledge of transactions that occur by people in the market, and the inability of one supplier to affect price.

Although no market-place probably fulfils all these conditions, the property market is remarkable in its level of imperfection. The following may be regarded as some of its important distinguishing features:

(a) **No central market-place**:   transactions take place through a series of submarkets, divided by property type, location and according to whether it is being traded for owner-occupation, investment or development.

(b) **Lack of knowledge**:   it flows from the lack of a central market-place that there is a lack of knowledge of transactions. Despite increasing use of public auction as a method of marketing property, a good deal of secrecy surrounds most deals. Even where prices are published, the full facts are seldom known, and without these a full analysis cannot be undertaken. For example, the basic published details will not reveal the condition of the building, the exact lease terms and whether any special relationship existed between purchaser and vendor or lessor and lessee, yet such factors can have a profound effect upon the price realized.

(c) **Fixed supply**:   although over time the supply of land (within a given location) for any use can increase, subject to planning consent, within the short term it is fixed. This can result in monopoly power amongst vendors and lessors (see section on investment characteristics of property, pp.56–69).

(d) **Complexity**:   unlike most other markets, transactions in the property market are often dependant upon complex finance agreements so that one may involve several parties, each of whom has a different legal interest. Inevitably this means that the time taken to complete any deal can be lengthy and cause additional expense. A beneficial side effect of this is that the market is less volatile than the stock market, for example, where transactions are quick and easy to effect.

(e) **Variety of interests**:   whilst most markets deal with the transaction of homogeneous products, the property market deals with many types of interests in land. These are outlined briefly below.

The nature of property interests

Although people refer to the 'ownership' of land, in theory what is owned is not the property but a legal interest, either freehold or leasehold, in land. Freehold in possession is the highest estate in land that can be owned under English law and it confers on the freeholder full rights over the land subject only to legal constraints such as planning. It is possible to have freehold interests which have restrictions on their titles such as restrictive covenants preventing the owner from undertaking some activity (typically a particular form of development) or easements, rights of way, or rights of light or support, all of which reduce the freeholder's ability to deal with his land as he might wish. Such restrictions are normally imposed either at the time that the interest is created (for example, when a parcel of land is sold with a restriction on it in favour of land retained by the vendor) or they may arise out of long usage (for example, a right of way over a field).

Out of the freehold interest lesser interests may be created: leases and tenancies. These are in essence legal contracts between individuals and the terms that they contain will depend upon negotiation between the parties, although in many cases parliament has intervened to affect one or both of the parties. Examples of such intervention are the Landlord and Tenant Acts 1927 and 1954 which give to most lessees of business premises rights regarding security of tenure and compensation for tenants' improvements. In addition the 1927 act implies certain conditions in typical lease covenants. Lettings of residential property are affected by a complex array of legislative provisions, mainly detrimental to the investment performance of the unit. In Chapter 8 we consider the terms of a typical modern commercial lease and its implications for property management. Unless the lease specifically forbids it, under common law any lessee is free to transfer his interest for value if he so wishes, although most modern leases place at least a qualified prohibition upon such transactions.

THE VALUATION OF PROPERTY INTERESTS

Although the subject matter of this book is not property valuation, there being many good texts available on that subject, no consideration of portfolio management can be undertaken without regard to the price-fixing mechanism of such investments. In this section we explain the mechanics of the market-price fixing mechanisms for property and other competing media.

Initial or all risks yield

The term initial or all risks yield is frequently used to describe the initial return obtainable from a property investment. The usual way in which it is expressed is in annual terms as follows when a property is rack rented:

$$\text{initial yield} = \frac{\text{annual full net rental income}}{\text{purchase price of investment}} \times 100$$

If, for example, a property investment was purchased for £2,500,000 including all transaction costs and the rental income in the first year under the lease was £150,000 net, the initial yield would be calculated as follows:

$$\frac{£150,000}{£2,500,000} \times 100 = 6\%$$

It will be readily appreciated, however, that the term initial yield is a crude method of measurement. The calculation can only be regarded as accurate if the property investment could be purchased and the total annual rent received on the same day. Rental increases payable under a lease are normally received per quarter in advance on the usual quarter days. Therefore, an investor might pay £2,500,000 on say 1 March and one quarter of the total annual rent would be received on 25 March, a further quarter on 24 June and similar amounts on 29 September and 25 December. The initial yield, expressed in the above example as 6 per cent, takes no account of the cost to the investor of foregoing tranches of income. If all the year's income had been received on 1 March it could all have been reinvested whereas, in fact, this is not the case.

For the purposes of performance measurement more sophisticated techniques are necessary, but it is interesting to see that most of the property data published by the major firms of chartered surveyors refer to 'prime commercial property yields' in this way. Investors using this information are not ignorant of its deficiencies and its drawbacks are well understood so that for comparison purposes it can be considered a helpful tool.

Years purchase

The term 'years purchase' is generally understood to be the multiplier by which a full rack rent received annually is converted to the capital value of the income-producing investment. It will be appreciated that initial yield in respect of a rack-rented investment assumes that income will be received annually in perpetuity. Similarly, the years purchase or YP in perpetuity will give the present value of the right to receive income at the end of each year in perpetuity at a given rate of interest. Using the above example, if an investor were willing to accept a 6 per cent initial yield from rack-rented property investment, then the value of the investment to him would be:

$$150,000 \times \frac{100}{6} = 2,500,000 \text{ (where 100 years is taken to be perpetuity)}$$

The YP in this instance is 16.66, and it can be seen that yield and capital value are inversely related. It is important to understand that valuers of property investments apply the years purchase formula in perpetuity to income on the assumption that it will be received annually in arrears. When 'initial yield' is discussed no element of discounting is assumed and income is assumed to be received in advance.

Gross dividend yield

The term 'gross dividend yield' is applied to equities and is quoted daily for each stock in the *Financial Times*. It has already been said that equities do not have a predictable return, unlike a property investment which has a rental income fixed normally for a five-year period. The gross dividend yield is therefore calculated using historic data. The latest annual dividend is used and this will be a percentage of the market price of the share at the time of measurement. In the columns of the financial press, dividends are calculated net of tax (assumed to be 30 per cent) whereas property investment data normally expresses yield gross of tax. To be comparable with property yields, gross dividend yields have to be converted to a gross of tax basis. The calculation is as follows:

$$\text{Gross dividend yield} = \frac{\text{net dividend per share}}{\text{market-price of share}} \times \frac{10}{7} \times 100\%$$

It is customary for many companies to pay dividends half-yearly and this is entirely at the board's discretion, although final dividends must be approved by the Annual General Meeting. It might be assumed that initial yields as related to property, and gross dividend yields are similar concepts, but investors would not be well advised to make this assumption. In the case of a property investment, which is rack rented, there is certainty of income flow within a definable spectrum of risk.

In the case of yields from equity investments, the value of a company should not be assessed by using the gross dividend yield and multiplying it by a 'years purchase' factor, as is the case with a property investment. The company in question might be reinvesting earnings in research or acquisition of plant rather than distributing earnings to shareholders. There may also be hidden value in the company in terms of the value of its assets for purposes other than the company's trading activities.

Institutional investors are faced with a choice of investments, and property investment compared with gilts and equities is often seen as a clear choice. This will not be the case when investment is made in a company owning substantial property assets which are currently underutilized. A company may have been trading unprofitably for a number of years, but if the value of the assets owned shows the potential for greater profit generation, the share price may still be high. This reflects the attitude of investors who will speculate and take a low initial return in terms of dividends in the hope of greater earnings in the future. This type of situation is roughly comparable with investment in a reversionary investment property and the way in which returns from reversionary property are analysed can now be re-examined.

Reversionary yields

We have already seen that, when rack-rented property investment is valued, a 'YP' figure is applied to the income flow and the resulting figure is the value of the right to receive that income in perpetuity annually in arrears. In reversionary situations income is not receivable at its current level in perpetuity but is receivable for a number of years only. Thus if an income of £100 is receivable for four years only and annually in arrears, some allowance must be made for the deferment. This is achieved by assuming that interest payments are foregone on income that is not receivable immediately and the income receivable in the future is reduced, or deferred, by the notional amount of interest that is lost. To take the example of an income of £100 per annum that is only receivable for four years, the right to receive £100 at the end of the first year would be a sum less than £100 depending upon how much earning power has been lost by not receiving the £100 immediately. If we assume that the investor could have earned 12 per cent return on the £100 every year, the right to receive £100 at the end of the first year is

$$\frac{100}{1 + 0.12}$$

Similarly, if £100 is receivable at the end of the second year, the present worth of that tranche of income is

$$\frac{100}{(1 + 0.12)^2}$$

For £100 receivable for four years annually in arrears the computation will be as follows:

$$\frac{100}{(1+i)} + \frac{100}{(1+i)^2} + \frac{100}{(1+i)^3} + \frac{100}{(1+i)^4}$$

This geometric progression can be summed to

$$\frac{1 - \dfrac{1}{(1+i)^n}}{i} \quad \frac{1}{i}$$

and this is the formula for 'Years purchase'. For a period where the income receipts go on for a very long time or into perpetuity, the

$$\frac{1}{(1+i)^n}$$

tends to zero, reducing the formula to the already familiar $1/i$ or the YP in perpetuity.

At the end of the fourth year it is assumed that our property investment is subject to a rent review which increases the income flow. If full rental value at today's date is, say, £150, then, in monetary terms, one would assume that this rental figure would be higher in four years' time. It would perhaps have risen to £200. Property valuations using conventional methods assume, however, that increased income receivable in the future will only be, in monetary terms, the same as the full rack-rented value at today's date. In valuing income receivable in four years' time, what is valued is the right to receive a certain income, based on today's full rental value, in perpetuity but after a given number of years.

We have already seen that for rack-rented investments the YP in perpetuity is used, which is the reciprocal of the initial yield. The formula is

$$\frac{1}{0.12}$$

where 12 per cent is the initial yield. For increased incomes receivable in the future, this value is deferred by means of an appropriate factor in the same way as increases for a certain number of years only are valued. After four years the value of an increased sum will be reduced by a factor of 12 per cent compounded for four years. This is expressed as

$$\frac{150}{(1 + 0.12)^4}$$

where 150 is the full rental value at today's date. The full computation is

$$\frac{1}{0.12} \times \frac{1}{(1 + 0.12)^4}$$

and this multiplier will be applied to the £150 income. The multiplier in valuation parlance is known as the 'years purchase of a reversion to a perpetuity'.

Property investment valuations therefore seek to apply multipliers to income received at present or in the future to arrive at a capital value for one investment property. If the property has development potential then the net value of the site is taken as a capital sum in the future and deferred as if it was one tranche of income receivable at that time.

Earnings yield

Gross dividend yields cannot be compared with property yields as they do not reflect the full earning capacity of a company, whereas rent from property does represent its earning capacity. The multipliers used seek to value this earning capacity in different ways depending on when the property will earn its full rental value. A more useful way of reflecting the real value of a company's present and prospective earnings is by use of the 'earnings yield'. Dividend payable is not used but instead a company's full earnings, net of corporation tax, are taken as a percentage of the market price of the shares according to the following formula:

$$\text{earnings yield} = \frac{\text{full earnings per share}}{\text{market price of share}} \times 100$$

To make this comparable with property yields, which are usually expressed gross of tax corporation, tax would first be deducted at a standard rate and then any allowances would be added back. The full earnings yield will provide a guide to the value of the company based on the level of earnings unaffected by the management's retention policy on dividends. It does not, however, give an indication of the wealth of the company in terms of underlying assets but instead assumes that profits from the business are the only potential for earnings. It does therefore ignore potential capital returns.

Price earnings ratio

A further way of expressing company returns is given by the price/earnings (P/E) ratio which relates the earnings per share to the market price of the ordinary share according to the formula:

$$\text{P/E ratio} = \frac{\text{market price of share}}{\text{net earnings per share}}$$

The price/earnings ratio can be seen to be the reciprocal of the earnings yield. It is likely that the higher the price/earnings ratio the more highly the share is rated by investors. Investors will be willing to accept low earnings per share and maintain market demand and a high share price if growth prospects are good and risk low.

A return from a property investment in terms of future and present income flows determines the value of the investment. Investors can be expected to value the potential and present income flows as precisely as possible to arrive at their bid figures. In the same way that investors in equities will take low yields in terms of dividends or earnings if growth prospects are high, property investors will take low returns initially if the prospects for rental growth are high. There is a link between levels of growth and initial yield in terms of property investment (see the section on yield determinants below, pp.45–56) and various formulae have been devised to relate annual growth rates in rent to level of initial yield. In the absence of bidders in a market-place, any valuation contains an element of risk and it is in this area that analysis of property and shares differs. Government stocks and company shares are valued on the stock market every minute of every working day. At any time an investor will know the price that he can sell or buy for. What he does not know is what the price will be the next day or week. It can be said that the nature of the market in which property and stocks and shares are traded determines investors' attitudes to yields. Although it is true that the stock market 'values' shares, much of this value is produced from investment decisions which are not based on long-term analysis but on short-or medium-term speculation. Stocks and shares are easy to trade, earnings potential is not constrained by legislative interference, and a company's shares can be highly valued as a result of short-term economic factors. Property investment, although more predictable, is not as susceptible to the type of entrepreneurial trading which can achieve spectacular returns in the equity markets. The reasons for this are expressed more fully in the section on investment characteristics of property (pp.56–69).

Equivalent yield

The method of yield calculation mentioned above, namely, initial yield, gross dividend yield, and earnings yield, seek to present one picture of 'return' based upon quantifiable annual earnings. Property investments subject to reversionary increases in rent can be valued by applying 'years purchase' figures to the rental flow. Equivalent yield formulae seek to value both present and reversionary income flows at the same rate. If a property which is not let at full rack rent is valued, then the full rack-rental flow is valued with a suitable deferment. Using Parry's Valuation Tables this would be as calculated below in Example 2.1.

Example 2.1

A property investment is let under lease at a current rent of £10,000 per annum. Full rental value is estimated to be £11,000 and there is a rent review in four years' time.

Rental income	£10,000	
YP for 4 years at 6%	3.465	
		£34,651
Reversion to full rental value	£ 11,000	
YP in perpetuity		
deferred 4 years at 7%	10.8985	
		£119,883
Capital value		£154,534

It is conventional in 'term and reversion' valuations of this type to increase the capitalization rate for the reversionary income to take account of the investor's attitude towards risk. This would result in the rate of return required from rents to be received at some future date being higher than from rents currently payable. If the same rate is applied to both term and reversion such a rate can be found by iteration which gives the same capital value as that obtained by taking different rates for term and reversion. Unless the reversion is very many years distant, and the term rent is very low in comparision to the full Rental Value (FRV), the rate used to capitalize the income flow will approximate to the rate used for the reversionary element. Below we set out a valuation of Example 2.1 using the same rate for both term and reversion and the rate used is known as the equivalent yield. It will be seen that the resultant capital value is approximately that achieved before.

Example 2.2

Rental income	£10,000	
YP for 4 years at 6.96%	3.3902	
		£33,902
Reversion to full rental value	£11,000	
YP in perpetuity		
deferred 4 years at 6.96%	10.9775	
		£120,752
Capital value		£154,654

Thus the equivalent yield is seen to be approximately 6.96 per cent. The use of the equivalent yield is widespread in property valuations as it reflects investors' attitudes to both current rents and future increased income flows. In monetary terms, the figures used for future income are expressed in present-day figures with no increases valued. This may seem illogical as rents from property have reliably risen in the past. It is the use of discounted cash flow (DCF) techniques which allow for future inflationary increases to be valued by explicitly including them in the income flow projections.

Equated yield

All valuations of property interests are calculated upon the basis of discounted cash flow, that is, the valuation represents the sum of the expected future income flows discounted back to today. Traditional valuations, such as we have outlined above, are based on the premise:

(a) That values will remain at todays level.
(b) That income is received annually in arrears.

Although neither of these premises can be defended logically as they are blatantly unrealistic, the justification for so using them is that the market operates satisfactorily upon that basis. Recently such arguments have been rejected by many academics and property analysts. Starting with the Greenwell Report of 1976, the Royal Institution of Chartered Surveyors (Trott) report (1980), Fraser (1984), Enever (1986), and Baum and Crosby (1988) investigations of other more logical methods of evaluation have been proposed. In Chapter 5 we deal in detail with the measurement of returns from property, as distinct from property yield. Here it is necessary to introduce the concept of the 'equated yield', which strictly is a return and not a property yield in order that we can then look at the comparision between property and other investment yields.

An appraisal of a property using an equated yield is a valuation which builds into the calculation expected increase in rent explicitly. We will look at an example here demonstrating the method, but further explanation and a critique of it is reserved for Chapter 5.

Example 2.3

An investor has the opportunity to purchase a property for £500,000. The property is let at £30,000 per annum with rent payable annually in arrears. The current full rental value (FRV) is £40,000 and there is a rent review in two years' time. It is expected that by the date of review the rental value will have increased to £50,000 and that the property can be sold in five years' time for £650,000.

The equated yield for this investment will be that discount rate at which the sum of the expected future inflows exactly equals the current outlay. This can be expressed algebraically or set out in a Discounted Cash Flow (DCF) table as below:

Year	Payment	Receipts	Discount factor at 11.3%	Discounted cash flow
0	£500,000	—	1.000	− £500,000
1		£ 30,000	0.898	+ £ 26,954
2		£ 30,000	0.807	+ £ 24,217
3		£ 50,000	0.725	+ £ 36,264
4		£ 50,000	0.652	+ £ 32,583
5		£650,000	0.585	+ £380,572
				+ £ 590

This shows that at price of £500,000 and a discount rate of 11.3 per cent the investment will show a very slight positive return. In other words, the actual return that an investor will receive, given that the cash flows are realized as estimated, will be approximately 11.3 per cent. It is this return that is known as the equated yield or internal rate of return (IRR). Its importance and use as a measure both of actual return and as a decision-making aid is growing.

RENT AND RENTAL GROWTH

The price that an investment property will command on the open market is a product of the rent passing, the rental value if that is different, and the yield determined by the operation of the market. Accordingly, it is necessary to consider what are the factors which affect rent and rental growth. In the section on yield determinants the effect on yield is considered (pp.45–56).

Rental value

Rental value has been defined as 'the annual rent that the property can reasonably be expected to command, if offered on the open market, on the terms on which properties of the same type are normally rented' (Darlow 1983). The chief determinant of the level of rental value is the interreaction of the supply and demand for the particular property. These considerations and some of the other factors which affect the amount that a prospective tenant would be prepared to pay are considered below.

Occupational demand

In the final analysis the rental value is dependent upon occupational demand. As Fraser (1984) says, this depends 'principally upon the expected surplus from carrying on the business activity that is appropriate to the property'. Thus rent is in essence a surplus; no tenant will be prepared to pay more in the way of rent than he can do without making his occupation unprofitable. It follows therefore that the rental value will be determined indirectly by the potential profitability of the occupation undertaken in the premises, and this, of course, is a product of general economic conditions. With some types of property, notably leisure and agricultural units, the relationship is clearly demonstrated as rents are frequently negotiated with reference to the actual trading accounts of the occupier or, in the absence of accounts, by the estimation of the turnover of the 'hypothetical tenant'.

To say simply that the economic rent a tenant can afford to pay for a property will determine the rent is too simplistic. No tenant will be prepared to bid up to this level unless he is forced so to do. Frequently, where there are few potential tenants for a particular property, due to one of the factors considered below, for example, a tenant may be able to secure the tenancy or lease by bidding a rent below that which he could afford.

Another element of occupational demand is the relationship between price and demand for land. If a small change in the price of a good results in a change in demand that is proportionally higher, such a good is said to be 'price sensitive'. If on the other hand the demand is or comparatively unaffected by a change in price asked then the good is said to be inelastic in demand.

In that the demand for any property relates to the underlying demand for the product with which the occupation is linked, so the effect on demand for any property or type of property occasioned by a change in price required will to some extent be determined by the relative elasticity for the good underlying the tenant demand. It follows therefore that property used for the manufacture of staple products, such as farmland or primary industrial units, should have a less elastic, and hence more constant, demand than land used in connection with luxury or non-essential items, such as leisure property and fashion shops. Following from this, it can be expected that rental values of units used for stable demand items are less prone to fluctuation. Unfortunately these relationships cannot be observed closely in the market due to other constraints. For example, legislation surrounds the letting of farmland such that the supply is artificially restricted and there is in fact a domination of owner-occupation of primary industrial units. However, the tenant demand for leisure property does tend to be more volatile than that for other sectors, although data on this sector of the property market are scarce.

Finally, it should be noted that in most cases rent represents only a small proportion of the total business costs for many tenants so to that extent demand can be expected to be relatively unaffected by rental change.

Supply

Ultimately the supply of land is fixed, other than in the very long term when factors such as erosion and other geographical change can come into play. The supply of land should be considered in terms of property type, use and location. Any potential occupier will be constrained to a greater or lesser extent by his needs relating to these factors. Whilst some occupiers may be comparatively 'footloose' with regard to location, for example, a mail order business in comparison to a high street retailer, very few can be totally flexible. The constraints of the nature of the business and the planning laws will determine what type and size of unit is suitable.

For all practical purposes the supply of land is fixed only in the very short term. Over time the demand, subject to planning constraints, will encourage the provision of additional stock. The longer the term that is considered, the greater the degree of elasticity of supply. However, even in a relatively short period supply can change significantly. This is because in most sectors of the market the supply is largely comprised, not of newly-constructed units, but of existing stock. Hence, if the demand for a particular class of property falls and tenants seek to vacate, then the supply will increase. As supply increases the incentive to developers to create more units will reduce, until a point is reached when supply and demand are once more in equilibrium.

Physical factors

Among the physical factors that will affect the level of rent for a property are the size and design of the building, its construction and its susceptibility to obsolescence (see pp.56–9 on durability). In addition to its condition, the quality of the services, fittings and fixtures are all relevant factors to the tenant, particularly if he is responsible for the cost of maintenance, or the lease is for a long term and the tenant will be liable for any deterioration of the building. To some tenants a building's potential for improvement or expansion or indeed redevelopment is also significant.

Under the heading of tenure the tenant must consider first the terms of the lease or tenancy being offered. If the term is short and he has little or no security of tenure thereafter, his flexibility regarding the use of the building is impaired and his rental bid will be adversely affected. This is of particular note to tenants who may have very high fitting-out costs or who need the security of a long term in order to establish their business. The nature of the other covenants such as to repair, to insure, to pay service charges and to comply with statutory obligations will all affect the occupation costs of the tenant and hence his ability to pay rent. To the direct contractual terms agreed between the landlord and tenant must be added any restrictions placed on the property such as the presence of easements, rights of way and of light, and so on. Any item which either increases the occupational costs or restricts the tenant's ability to use, alter or otherwise deal with the property, has a potentially downward affect on rent.

Legislation

Legislation can have either a direct or indirect effect on rental value. Under the Rent Act 1977, rents of some residential properties are restricted to a 'fair rent' (Rent Act 1977, s.70) which specifically requires that the rent must assume that supply and demand are in equilibrium, whether that be the case or not. The Landlord and Tenant Act 1954, however, which controls most commercial relettings, contains no such restriction but allows for rents to be set at a market level. However, it goes on to exclude from consideration, under certain circumstances, improvements carried out by the tenant which, under the operation of common law, would revert to the landlord. Examples of Acts which can have an indirect effect on rents are, *inter alia*, the Fire Precautions Act 1971, the Offices, Shops and Railway Premises Act 1963, and the Occupiers Liability Act 1957.

Also under the head of legislation must be mentioned the planning Acts which govern the ways in which a property can be used and developed. Frequently a property may be physically capable of a use more valuable than that allowed by the planning regulations. Hence there is often scope (see Chapters 8 and 9) to increase value by obtaining planning permission or change of use or development.

Location

It has often been said that the three most important words in connection with the valuation of property are 'location, location and location'. Whilst this may be regarded as an exaggeration and distortion, the importance of location on rental value is undoubtedly great. How far it will affect values depends on the type of property.

With retail units the difference in value between a unit in a 'prime position' in the main shopping street and one maybe only yards away, which fronts a side road and is thereby secondary, can be very marked. A reduction in value of 50 per cent or more would certainly not be unusual. A prime retail location in any settlement is one which enjoys the maximum pedestrian flow, thereby maximizing trading opportunity. Frequently it is associated with the presence or proximity of one of the major multiple retailers such as Marks and Spencer, British Home Stores, Boots and W. H. Smith.

Offices, too, are very location conscious with marked rental value differences evident over small geographical areas.

Other properties, for example, warehouses, may be less sensitive to location.

Rental growth

It has already been remarked that one of the chief attractions of property as an investment is its potential to provide income growth over time. The factors that cause rental growth are therefore of paramount importance to investors. Rental growth may be purely money-change related, or it may be growth in real terms. It is with the latter that the investor is most interested. What then causes rents to rise over and above the general level of price rises? As with rental value, several factors are at play, most of them interlinked. They can best be considered under the heads of demand factors and supply factors.

Demand factors

Over time the demand for any particular property or type of property may change relative to the market in general. Tenant demand may increase as a result of improvements in the underlying economy resulting in a demand for the tenant's product, be it a manufactured good or services. Allied to this is the level of people's personal disposable income or wealth. In the last forty years a steady rise in incomes has seen increased spending on items such as consumer durables. This consumer spending 'boom' associated also with the very substantial increase in personal credit availability, has led to substantial rises in retail rents. Property indices, published by many of the leading firms of property agents and analysts (for example, the Jones Lang Wootton Property Index, the Investment Property Databank Index and the Michael Laurie/Morgan Grenfell Index to name but three) all substantiate the comparatively large increases in the level of retail rent

Table 2.1 Rental growth by sector

(June 1977 = 100) (June 1967 = 100)	Office FRV	Shop FRV	Industrial FRV	Agricultural FRV
June 1967	28 (100)	47 (100)	48 (100)	37 (100)
June 1968	31	52	49	–
June 1969	32	52	53	–
June 1970	36	59	56	46
June 1971	47	60	62	48
June 1972	55	69	66	48
June 1973	68	83	73	53
June 1974	85	97	84	69
June 1975	95	99	93	79
June 1976	99	100	98	92
June 1977	100	100	100	100
June 1978	103	115	116	106
June 1979	118	131	129	125
June 1980	122	155	152	137
June 1981	133	185	175	152
June 1982	147	192	176	159
June 1983	147	206	174	169
March 1984	148	215	178	179
June 1984	150	217	177	180
Sept. 1984	150	219	180	182
Dec. 1984	150	225	181	183
March 1985	151	230	181	186
June 1985	151	234	181	187
Sept. 1985	153	239	182	186
Dec. 1985	157	242	182	186
March 1986	159	248	183	188
June 1986	160	257	182	187
Sept. 1986	165	261	187	189
Dec. 1986	170	268	191	187
March 1987	172	284	192	186
June 1987	179	290	195	187
Sept. 1987	189	299	197	187
Dec. 1987	197	313	206	188
March 1988	209	337	211	191
June 1988	215	366	218	191
Sept. 1988	223	392	225	191
Dec. 1988	242	414	243	181
March 1989	257 (909)	431 (919)	255 (533)	172 (460)

Source: Jones Lang Wootton Property Index.

rises over other property sectors during the 1970s and early 1980s. Table 2.1 shows comparative income growth between property sectors over the period 1967 to 1988. At the time of writing, however, with high interests acting as a break on consumer spending, the level of retail rental growth has slowed so that some analysts are currently predicting very little, if any, rental growth in the next year.

In contrast to the retail sector, rental growth in offices tends to be cyclical and localized. The factors affecting tenant demand are more closely correlated to the local economy. So, for example, during the period 1986–7 City of London office rents rose steeply due to demand from companies wishing representation in the City following the deregulation of the Stock Exchange – the so-called 'Big Bang'. At this time, too, the financial sector was experiencing very high levels of profitability. However, office rents in other parts of the country were relatively unchanged. Further reference to this is made in Chapter 7 when the theory of portfolio diversification is discussed. The cyclical nature of office rental growth relates more to the supply situation than demand, and is considered below.

Rental growth in the industrial sector, too, is a product of the state of the economy, but in this case the influence of the UK overseas trading position is greater. As imports are at a high level, and manufacturing industry is adversely affected, rental growth will either be limited or non-existent.

In addition to the economic factors underlying rental growth that we have briefly outlined above, there are other factors which help determine the level of growth experienced. These include:

(a)   Locational change

The relative attractiveness of a location may change over time. A shop unit which was in a prime position may become 'off-pitch' due to the construction of a new shopping centre some distance away or the whole centre could be adversely affected by an out-of-town centre. Alternatively, locations can improve with, for example, the construction of a motorway nearby improving accessibility, adding a fillip to industrial and warehouse rents.

(b)   Structural or use change

On a micro level the rental value of an individual property may increase as a result of either improvements or alterations carried out to the premises or as a result of a change of use. Whilst the former necessitates further capital injection, the latter may not, although in practice the mere right to change the effective use of a property must be accompanied by some physical alteration, however minor. Some investors whose priority is in achieving rapid rental growth will actively seek to purchase properties where the opportunity exists to produce value change by these 'active management' methods and we refer to this again in Chapter 9.

(c)   Aesthetic and design considerations

We have already noted that design and occupation costs of a building will affect the rent that a tenant is prepared to pay. Over time these considerations will impact upon investment performances, and buildings of poor structural design which result in high running costs, and those which are inflexible in design perform comparatively poorly in terms of rental growth (see Salway 1986). Another factor is the the aesthetic appeal or fashion of the building. A 1960s office building, quite apart from any consideration of use suitability, looks very dated in 1990, whereas a building with a classical façade has proved to retain appeal over time. These factors will again affect the level of rental growth achieved.

(d)   Legislation

Legislation can have an affect on rents: it can affect rental growth, either directly by preventing increases being realized, or indirectly by affecting the operation of the market, on either the demand or supply side. An example of direct intervention was seen in an extraordinary way in 1973 with the Counter Inflation Act which 'froze' all rents of commercial buildings whenever they had been agreed, even those maybe forty or fifty years old or more. This, of course, is an extreme example, not repeated since, but it demonstrates that interference with the workings of the property market is always a political option.

More frequently the action is indirect. The impact on rents of, for example, the uniform business rate, and optional VAT on rents, remains to be clearly seen. What is evident already is that these taxes will have a differential effect, increasing the outgoings for some occupiers compared with others. For example, in the retail sector which, as has been noted, has seen the highest levels of rental growth over the period 1973–88, the new rate will produce increases well above that for commercial occupiers as a group. Within this sector it is the town centre shops of the prosperous areas of the south-east which will bear the heaviest imposition. Over time this may affect the level and distribution of rental value growth.

Other fiscal measures such as the level and structuring of income, corporation and capital taxes, will affect the demand for property as they affect potential profitability.

Supply factors

Although in the short term supply of a particular type of property in a given location is fixed, we have already noted that this is not true over time. In order for supply to change in response to demand certain conditions must be able to be fulfilled:

(a) There must be the physical potential to create the supply. An address in London EC3 may be crucial to some potential tenants; however, this is a small physical area and at some point physical saturation could be reached.

(b) A sympathetic planning policy is required. If there is not, however strong the effective demand, supply cannot alter significantly.

(c) There must be developers or others prepared to create the required product. This will only happen if there are sufficiently attractive financial rewards to be had as a result. If there are punitive rates of taxation payable on gains arising from the development of land, then land will not be brought forward for development.

(d) Supply may be most quickly increased if tenant demand falls, so that units are vacated. If therefore there is an increase in tenant demand, the amount of property coming forward on the 'second-hand' market, which comprises the bulk of transactions, may diminish.

(e) Lastly, the time-lag in terms of construction will vary from property type to type. For example, the development period for high quality offices is much greater than that for simple industrial units.

From the above it can be seen that the ability of the market to increase supply will vary between both location, as evidenced by different planning policies, and property type. Where supply cannot alter swiftly, the highest levels of rental growth are likely to occur.

YIELD DETERMINANTS

In the section on the valuation of property interests (pp.28–37) we introduced the concept of property yields, and in particular the all risks yield which is the price-fixing mechanism applied in the market to rack-rented property investments. The price at which any property freehold rack-rented property is exchanged depends on two elements, the rent or rental value and the all risks yield. In the section on rent and rental growth (pp.37–45) we examined the factors which will affect both the rental value of a property and its potential for rental growth.

In this section we look at property yield patterns and seek to identify the factors which determine the yield and thus the multiplier or YP.

Table 2.2 displays the yields applicable in 1989 to rack-rented prime property. At this time yields on gilts were in excess of 11 per cent. From this it can be seen that investors are prepared to pay higher prices, relative to income, for property as against government stock. There is also

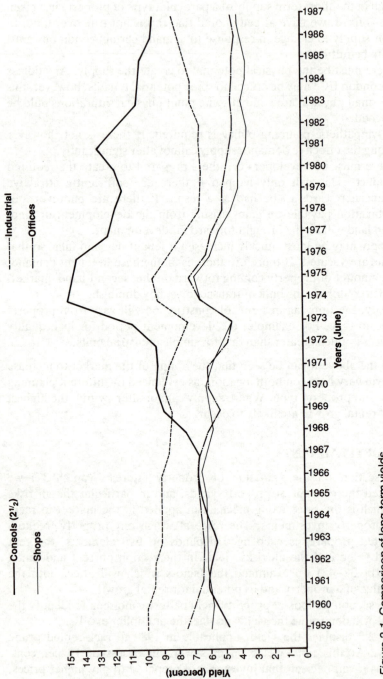

Figure 2.1 Comparison of long-term yields

Source: Jones Lang Wooton Consulting and Research

Note: 1: Prime yields – Jones Lang Wooton internal records

2: Consols are undated government stock yielding a fixed coupon

Table 2.2 Yield comparisons by sector

Food stores	7.5%
Retail warehouses	7.25%
Industrial warehouses	7%
Mixed use business space	6.25%
Central London offices	5%
Provincial offices	6.25%
Shops	4.75%

Date: December 1989

Source: Healey and Baker Research.

a wide difference between yields relating to property of different types. The current relationships of yields have not always held; until the 1960s the pattern was very different, with government stock yielding the lowest, with prime equities and property showing yields somewhat higher (see Table 2.3 and Figure 2.1).

What then has caused the pattern of relative yields to change over time and indeed why are investors prepared to accept such low initial returns from some properties?

Table 2.3 Investment yields and inflation, 1950–83

Year	UK ordinary shares %	Bank rate MLR %	Consols 2.5%	Retail prices inflation %	Prime shops %	Prime office %	Prime industrial %
1950	5.5	2.0	4.5	2.4	5.5	6.5	n/a
1951	6	2.5	4	12.2	5.25	6.5	n/a
1952	5.5	4	4.25	6.1	5.5	6.5	n/a
1953	7.25	3.25	4	1.5	5.5	6.5	n/a
1954	7	3	3.75	3.5	5.5	7	n/a
1955	6.25	3.5/4.5	4.5	6.2	5.5	7	n/a
1956	6.25	5.5	4.75	3.4	5.5	8	n/a
1957	7	5/7	5	4.3	5.5	7.5	n/a
1958	7	5.5/4	5	1.7	5.5	7.5	n/a
1959	7	6/4.5	5	0.0	6	7.5	10
1960	5	5/7	5.25	1.8	5.5	7	10
1961	4.75	7/6	6.25	4.6	5.5	7	10
1962	5.5	6/4.5	6.25	2.3	5.5	6	10
1963	5.75	4	6	2.1	5.5	6	10
1964	5	5/7	5.5	4.8	5.5	6/7	10
1965	5.25	7/6	6	4.6	6	6/7	9
1966	6	6/7	6.5	3.5	6	6.5	9
1967	6.5	6/5/8	6.75	2.3	6.5	6.5	9
1968	5.75	8/7	8	6.0	7	7	9
1969	4.5	8	9	4.6	7	6.5	8/9.5

Sources: Investment yields – Allsop and Co; Retail Prices Index – Central Statistical Office; but taken from McIntosh and Sykes 1985.

The reverse yield gap

In a world of low or non-existent inflation and low interest rates an investor will be principally concerned with the security in money terms that an investment offers. It is only when money values are eroded by reduced purchasing power that an investor becomes concerned with the ability of the investment to retain value over time in real terms. During the first half of this century inflation was not a major consideration for investors and interest rates were generally low. Therefore government fixed interest stock, with its regular half-yearly payments and no default risk, was perceived to be an attractive investment medium compared to both equities where the income flow fluctuates annually, and property with its attendant management problems and possible risk of tenant default. Table 2.3 shows the prevailing level of yields for the period 1950 to 1969. From this it can be seen that a 'yield gap' existed between the rates realized for government stocks and for equity shares and prime property.

It was during the late 1950s that inflation began to occur. Interest rates began to rise and with it investor awareness of the potential attraction of equity investments. In the early 1960s a 'reverse yield gap' emerged with yields on gilts rising significantly. At times since then the gap has narrowed, but with inflation an ongoing economic reality, and real growth in company profits and property demand being sustained, the reverse yield gap is now an established part of the investment spectrum.

Interestingly, over the long term the movement of yields has taken place largely within the market for gilts, not that for property. Baum and Crosby (1988) trace the pattern of gilts and prime shop yields over the period 1946–60. In that period they found that property yields moved by only 1 per cent from 5 per cent to 6 per cent, whilst gilts moved from 2.6 per cent to 6.4 per cent. By the latter half of 1989 the yield on gilts had risen further and was in the region of 10 per cent, whilst that on prime shop property remained around 5 per cent (Edward Erdman Research 1989). The yield gap as between property and company equity shares has varied over time, with the relative performance of shares and property dictating whether the all share index shows a lower yield than property or vice versa.

At this point it must be stressed that whilst any rational investor will be aware of the differences in yield obtainable between sectors and, further, that this may be a very important issue in his ultimate choice, comparison between all three is rendered difficult for two major reasons:

(a) With gilts the published data, the gross redemption yield, is the return that the investor will receive. With equities and property this is not the case. The published yields (the price/earnings ratio for equities and the initial or all risks yield for property) do not represent the investors' required or anticipated return.

(b) In each case the method by which ultimate returns are measured differs, and in the case of property the nature and timing of income flows is quarterly rather than half-yearly.

We expand the implications of these problems in Chapter 5.

Whether the reverse yield gap as it is currently understood will remain in the future cannot be known. What can be said is that it will obviously change, and within the property sector yield patterns between uses will alter. Before we look at some of the factors which affect the movement of property yields it is useful to recap on the main reasons for the reverse yield gap. These are:

(a) In an inflationary economy, investments whose income is fixed in money terms become unattractive by comparison with those in which income growth can be achieved.

(b) It flows from (a) above that as gilts became less attractive the prices fell, or put another way, yields were forced to rise.

(c) Many investors, it is thought, still require a higher overall return from equities and property than they do for gilts, due to the perceived additional risks attaching. Conventional wisdom states that a 2 per cent premium is appropriate for property. Despite this the overall returns obtainable are such that prices are consistently bid down to a level whereby the yield is often only half that obtained from fixed interest stock.

Readers wishing a more detailed examination of the impact of gilts yields on property investment yields are referred to Fraser (1984) and Baum and Crosby (1988).

Prospects for rental growth

We have outlined above the factors that affect the prospects for rental growth and sought to explain the relationship between property and other investment yields. It has been stated that it is the prospects of obtaining rental growth that will determine very largely the level of attraction to investors and hence the all risks yield of any particular property. In Chapter 5 we examine how the overall returns for investments can be measured and the difficulties in so doing. It is sufficient here to reiterate that the greater the expected level of rental growth, the greater will be the overall return at any particular investment.

An example will illustrate the point:

Example 2.2

Two properties have just been let at £5,000 p.a. with the rents fixed for the next five years. In five years' time a review will take place to the then open

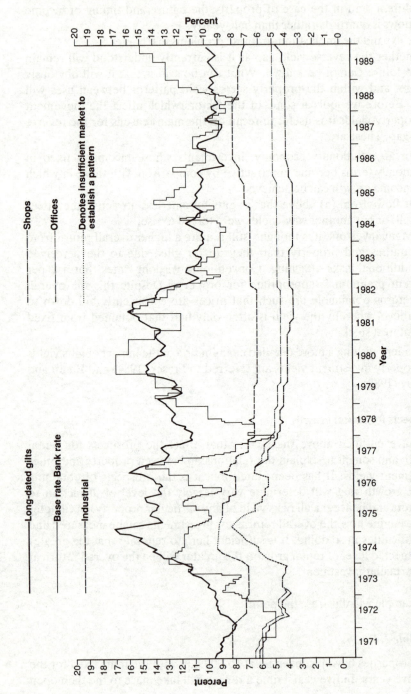

Figure 2.2 Healey and Baker prime commercial property yields, 1971–89

Source: Healey and Baker

market rental value. Property A is expected to achieve a rental growth of 10 per cent p.a., but Property B is expected to achieve only 2 per cent.

If the growth targets are achieved in five years' time, Property A will have a rental value of £5,000 compounded at the rate of 10 per cent p.a. which is:

$$£5,000 \times (1.1)^5 = £5,000 \times 1.61051 = £8,052.$$

Property B on the other hand will have a rental value in five years' time of only:

$$£5,000 \times (1.02)^5 = £5,000 \times 1.1041 = £5,520.$$

If one then makes the admittedly unrealistic assumption that upon review both properties could be sold at the same all risks yield, let us say for illustrative purposes 8 per cent, Property A would sell at £100,000 approximately and Property B for only £69,000. To any rational investor the worth of Property A must be substantially above that of Property B.

We can now take the example further and ask, given the figures above and assuming that in both cases the investing purchaser requires an overall return on his money of 15 per cent p.a., what is the maximum price that he should be prepared to pay for each? The calculation required is to find the net present value to him for each upon the assumptions that we have made. This can be done as follows:

Property A

The value is the sum of each of the income flows discounted at his required rate of return (15 per cent) for the period until review and then the capital value of the asset following the review:

$$\frac{£5,000}{(1.15)} + \frac{£5,000}{(1.15)^2} + \frac{£5,000}{(1.15)^3} + \frac{£5,000}{(1.15)^4} + \frac{£5,000}{(1.15)^5} + \frac{£100,000}{(1.15)^5} = £66,459$$

Property B

The investment worth of B can be found in exactly the same way:

$$\frac{£5,000}{(1.15)} + \frac{£5,000}{(1.15)^2} + \frac{£5,000}{(1.15)^3} + \frac{£5,000}{(1.15)^4} + \frac{£5,000}{(1.15)^5} + \frac{£69,000}{(1.15)^5} = £51,052$$

The purpose of this example was to demonstrate how the level of rental growth can affect the amount that a property is worth to an investor. It was of course an unrealistic example in that the YP or all risks yield achievable on sale following the review will not be the same in both cases. The property with the continuing prospects for rental growth will sell on the basis of a lower yield to reflect this inherent growth potential. Table 2.2 which shows the prime property yields prevailing in summer 1989, reflects that, taken over a long term, investors are building into their appraisals of property more optimistic estimates of growth for the retail sector than for industrials with offices lying between. The relationship between the all risks yield for a property, its expected growth on an annual basis, and its overall internal rate of return is a mathematical one that can be expressed by a formula. The formula has several different notations but all are mathematically the same. It can be expressed as:

$$\text{All Risks Yield} = \frac{e\left[(1+e)^n - (1+g)^n\right]}{\left[(1+e)^n - 1\right]}$$

where e = the equated yield or overall return required,
$\quad\ g$ = the expected annual growth, and
$\quad\ n$ = the period between rent reviews.

For a full explanation of this formula, readers are referred to Enever (1986), Baum and Crosby (1988) or Baum and Mackmin (1989).

Whilst the prospects of rental growth demonstrably affect the market yield of any property, there are other factors which are important too.

Investment quality

The expressions 'prime' and 'secondary' investment are often used to describe the overall quality of an investment when viewed from an institutional viewpoint.

Investments which are considered to be prime will command the highest demand from potential purchasers and hence have the lowest yields. Secondary properties are of less attraction to the major institutions but are none the less important avenues of investment. Prime investments can be considered in terms of their location, sector, structure, tenure and possibly most importantly, covenant.

Location

The importance of location to rental value and growth has already been outlined. As far as yield is concerned, certain locations are regarded as prime, that is, they are ones for which the level of tenant demand is high and is likely to remain so for the foreseeable future. Certain types of property, notably retail and office premises, tend to be more 'location conscious' than do others. However, what is regarded as a desirable location may change over time due to factors such as new adjoining developments, population movements, employment trends and changes in transport patterns.

Sector

For institutional investment purposes the property sectors that are currently acceptable are retail, office, industrial, warehousing and some of the 'hybrid' uses which have recently emerged. The residential, agricultural and leisure sectors are ones which currently do not attract such funds to a significant degree. In Chapter 3 we look at each property type in more detail.

The property sector or use of a property is one of the most important factors affecting the yield that is achievable (see Table 2.2). The reasons for the different achievable yields relate, as before, to the differing levels of rental growth, themselves products of the underlying economic conditions. Over the last twenty years it has been the increase in consumer spending and personal wealth that has underpinned the growth in the retail sector and sustained the low level of yields. Had this spending been associated with UK manufactured goods, then a corresponding growth in industrial units might have been expected. However, as much spending has been associated with imported goods, the industrial sector remained comparatively unattractive. During 1988 and the first part of 1989 a change has been noted with rental growth in the retail sector slowing, as a response to higher interest rates, but high rental growth being recorded for industrials in the wake of the stimulation of that sector of the economy. However, it must be remembered that all published data relates in the main to transactions of prime units. Thus whilst statistics may show a yield of say 5 per cent for high street shops and 6 per cent for offices as a generalization, individual units will frequently change hands on the basis of very different yields.

Structure

In Chapter 3 we describe structures in relation to each property type. The effect that structure will have on yield pattern relates to its durability and susceptibility to obsolescence (see the next section on investments characteristics of property, pp.56–69). A property whose structure is such that substantial sums are required either to repair or maintain it will increase the costs of ownership or occupation and management. This in turn reduces purchaser attraction. For a property to be given the label 'prime' the structure should not only be sound but of good and flexible design and thus likely to sustain tenant demand.

Tenure

Under tenure we include both the type of tenure under which the investor holds the premises and the terms of any lettings or sublettings which provide the income flow. Obviously any defect on title will have an adverse effect on the price that can be obtained for the unit and, for example, the presence of rights of way or easements which potentially restrict the use enjoyment or redevelopment potential will result in a higher yield than would otherwise be appropriate.

Many investors have a policy of investing in freeholds only; to others leasehold interests are considered acceptable, although the market will normally determine a higher yield to reflect the higher risk nature of a leasehold, the potentially onerous covenants attaching and the essentially depreciating nature of the interest.

With regard to occupational lets there is a strong institutional presumption in favour of lettings on the basis of a full repairing and insuring lease preferably for a term of twenty-five years. There is also a dislike by many institutions of properties that are multi-let as these increase the requirement for management involvement. If a property is so let and the landlord retains liability for the costs of repairing and maintaining the building not only will necessary deductions need to be made to the rental flow, but the yield will normally be pushed upwards by at least 1 per cent. We refer to this point again in Chapter 8.

As we have said above, most commercial property leases build in five-yearly rent reviews. If a property is subject to a three-yearly or even annual rent review, then the attraction to the investor would increase and the yield would be driven down.

Covenant

Whilst the property supplies the needs of the occupier, it is the occupier who creates the income flow and hence creates the value. Accordingly, if the tenant is one who cannot be relied upon to pay the rent and discharge the other covenants, the value of the investment is impaired. The quality of the covenant will therefore be an important consideration to any potential purchaser and a good property let to a first class covenant will sell on a lower yield than a comparable unit whose tenant is not of the same calibre. The importance of the covenant is reinforced by the practice of granting commercial leases of substantial periods, often twenty years or more, and the application of legislation which grants security of tenure to all but the weakest and most unreliable of tenants (see Chapters 8 and 9).

Development/ refurbishment potential

Although undoubtedly the majority of properties change ownership on the basis of their existing use values, many are sold at a price which reflects the potential of the property for either total redevelopment or for refurbishment. When such development value occurs the initial yield at which the transaction is concluded may bear little or no relationship to the income passing or indeed the full rental value of the property in its existing use and structure.

Risk

The whole concept of risk is fundamental to investment choice. In general terms, most investors are 'risk averse', that is, given investments offering equal returns they will choose the one which minimizes risk. Within the property sector those properties which are generally regarded as low risk, such as prime retail properties, have the lowest yields. Properties which are likely to suffer from obsolescence, have an unattractive location or a poor tenant may be regarded as high risk. Investors' perception of what constitutes a high or low risk investment may change over time and with it the pattern of yields will alter. For example, for many years the lowest yields were those relating to agricultural land, the demand for which was thought to be ever present and thus the risks lower than for other property. Events in the 1980s proved this not to be the case with values of vacant land falling in some cases from £2,000 per acre to figures of around £1,000 per acre. The reasons for this we set out in Chapter 3. The result was however, that agricultural yields increased from around 3 per cent in 1980 to 7 per cent or even more in 1986. The nature of risk and its evaluation we return to in Chapters 6 and 7.

Comparative returns

Throughout this section we have endeavoured to show that ultimately the initial or all risks yield is a price-fixing mechanism for investment property. It is therefore determined by the laws of supply and demand. Investors for their part will be prepared to put the highest value on those properties which offer the investment qualities they seek. For this reason the profile of the unit in relation to its likely ability to continue to attract tenants, its risk, and its level of potential rental growth, are the major determining factor.

Not only should investors seek to analyse the comparative attractions of properties, but they should put the likely returns available in comparision to those obtainable from other avenues of investment. Only then does a decision to invest in any particular property become logical. However, in

order to so do it is essential that property can be analysed in terms of return
and risk in the same way as other investment media and this we look at in
more detail later in the book.

INVESTMENT CHARACTERISTICS OF PROPERTY

When considering the particular characteristics of property as an investment, it must be appreciated that each type and tenure of property displays
differing characteristics, which may result in disparate investment profiles.
A short leasehold interest in a high street shop unit with a fixed profit
rent, for example, has arguably more in common with a short-dated
government security than the freehold of an obsolete industrial unit ripe
for redevelopment. Notwithstanding this, it is possible to identify certain
characteristics which are of relevance to most real estate assets. These
are considered below; a more detailed description of the different types
of investment property is given in Chapter 3.

Heterogeneous

It is perhaps a cliché to say that no two properties are the same; nevertheless
it is true in that every property is fixed in location, and location is a
crucial factor in value determination. In addition, not only are there
normally physical differences relating to size, accommodation, structure
and condition, but also tenurial differences relating to the type of lease,
the rent passing and the quality of covenant. The fact that property is
heterogeneous, coupled with the absence of a centralized market-place
(such as is found for stocks and shares) means that it is not normally possible
to objectively and easily evaluate comparatively two property investments
in the way that, for example, shares can be analysed.

Durability

Whilst land itself is in essence durable, despite the risk in some areas of
erosion and subsidence, the buildings on it are not. Building life will depend
upon legal, economic and physical factors. Legally there may be restrictions
on the building owner preventing demolition, for example, if the building is
listed as being of architectural or historical interest.

The economic and physical factors can be grouped together under the
heading of obsolescence. Obsolescence in relation to property has been
defined in the Royal Institution of Chartered Surveyors *Statements of Asset
Valuation Practice* and *Guidance Notes* as follows:

> Depreciation is the measure of the wearing out, consumption or other
> reduction in the useful economic life of a fixed asset, whether arising from

use, effluxion of time or obsolescence through technological or market changes.

copyright RICS

It can be seen that the rate at which a building becomes obsolete is a function both of its physical structure and economic factors. The rate at which physical deterioration sets in will be a function of the design, quality of construction, including the nature of the materials and the level of maintenance and repair carried out. With a building of reasonable specification, adequately maintained, there is normally no reason why the physical life of the building should not be extended indefinitely, as evidenced by much of the UK housing stock.

Economic decline relates to:

(a) *The suitability of the building for occupational demand*, that is, is it still of a type and design compatible with tenant requirements?

(b) *Locational factors* – the quality and desirability of any location may change over time, particularly for retail property, where, for example, the presence of a new shopping centre may shift the centre of retail activity in a town.

(c) *The permitted use may no longer be one for which demand exists.*

The point at which obsolescence has rendered the building and site together worth less than the site alone is the point at which redevelopment or refurbishment takes place. This point is taken up again in later chapters, and readers wishing to look at the question of depreciation in more detail are referred to the Centre for Advanced Land Use Studies *Study on Depreciation in Offices* (Salway 1986), to Bowie (1983) and to Baum (1989).

A simple example will demonstrate the basic principle. With a newly-constructed office building it might be expected that the value of the whole investment may be divided into 66 per cent 'bricks and mortar' and 33 per cent site value. Over time, and assuming no inflation or change in real value, the 'bricks and mortar' element will decline as physical obsolescence sets in until the point is reached where the value of the property is the site value less the demolition costs (see Figure 2.3). It is at this point that redevelopment takes place, assuming that no economic issues are involved. How long this will take may be influenced by the quality of construction and the level of maintenance carried out.

In reality it is economic, rather than physical, obsolescence which is the determining factor. Over time values will generally tend to rise due to inflation; also demand may fluctuate or a change of use to a more profitable use may become possible. These factors will affect the timing of redevelopment (see Figure 2.4)

In Figure 2.4 the line *AC* shows the increase in site value over time, whilst the line *BC* shows the increase in total value. The latter line has a lesser gradient due to the comparative decrease in the value of the building. At point C the value of the site equals that of the site and building together and redevelopment will take place. The more susceptible to obsolescence the shallower the gradient of the AC line. In Figure 2.4 line BC_1 shows a building which suffers from premature obsolescence and thus has a shortened redevelopment cycle. Line BC_2 shows a building of sound structure and design for which demand remains high thus delaying the onset of obsolescence and lenghtening the redevelopment cycle possibly indefinitely.

Over recent years the cycle of commercial property has shortened significantly, particularly for offices and shopping centres where design considerations have undergone rapid change. Further reasons for this are given in Chapter 3. Conversely, residential property has a redevelopment cycle that is much longer, due in part to aesthetic factors leading to strong demand for older property.

Thus the concept of even freehold property as a durable asset must be treated with caution. In the case of leaseholds obsolescence may be a

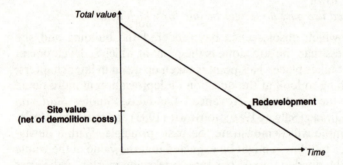

Figure 2.3 Value decline of asset over time

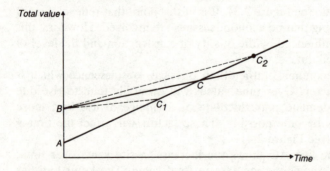

Figure 2.4 Determinant of redevelopment timing

consideration depending on the length of the unexpired term. Quite apart from obsolescence all leaseholds suffer from depreciation over time. Whilst changing money values may disguise this for a time, so that a leasehold can experience value increase, as the term shortens all leaseholds will eventually depreciate until at the expiry date the value is nil or possible is a negative due to a liability for accrued dilapidations.

Lotting

To many investors the 'lotting' problem is the one which debars them from direct property investment. Unlike other investments which can be purchased in lot sizes to suit the investor, property has to be acquired in fixed, inflexible and frequently large 'lots'. Not only is the price of many properties beyond the financial capabilities of all but the institutional investor, but some of the well-located City of London offices, for example, may have values such that only a limited number of investors have funds sufficient to acquire them as part of a diversified portfolio.

To taken an example – A City of London office block of say 5,000 square metres is let at a rent of £600 per square metre. The capital value could well be in the order of £60 million. If an investor has a portfolio structured such that only 10 per cent of funds were to be committed to property and within that sector it was considered inappropriate to devote more than 15 per cent of value to any one property, then the investor would need to have £400 million available for investment in property and a total portfolio size of £4,000 million. How far this lotting problem affects saleability and value is debatable. Unpublished research by Brown (1987) showed that at that time many institutions were making a discount for size deduction on the valuation of large (in excess of £20 million) assets.

Various attempts to overcome this problem have been postulated. Unitization, which is one suggested mechanism is discussed in Chapter 12. At the time of writing the problem has receded slightly as sufficiently large amounts of foreign funds are flowing into UK property often in the form of syndicated loans.

Expense and speed of transfer

It has already been remarked that the costs incurred in the transfer of real property are normally high compared with those for other media. Solicitors, surveyors and agents' costs combined with stamp duty and VAT on purchase make transaction costs on purchase in the order of 4 per cent of the agreed purchase price.

With regard to the time taken to complete a transaction, although this can be very quick, as evidenced by one transaction known to one of the authors which took a total of only two days, the norm is for the whole matter to take weeks if not months. When the market demand is weak it is not unusual for an owner to take in excess of six months to release his capital.

Management

The specific requirement for property to be managed is considered in Chapter 8. It is sufficient here to point out the obvious, namely, that it requires skilled management, the expense of which can vary between approximately 2.5 per cent of rents in the case of commercial property let on full repairing terms, to in excess of 12 per cent in the case of residential investment property.

Uncertain returns

It has already been noted in Chapter 1 that the return on an investment such as government securities can be accurately predicted if the stock is held to redemption but not otherwise as the sale price is not known in advance. With property, return can only ever be calculated retrospectively, although predictions of return are inherent in every purchaser's appraisal.

The reasons for this uncertainty are twofold; first, the capitalization yield may change, thus altering the market value, and second, the income derived from the property will fluctuate over time. Usually rents are fixed upon a five-year rent review pattern with the rent upon review being movable in an 'upwards only' manner so that the initial rent agreed is in effect the minimum guaranteed rent throughout the lease term. However, in the event that rental values go down between reviews a situation will arise whereby the lessee is paying in excess of the market rent. If this happens the risk of tenant default will increase as few tenants will be content to accept such a situation.

The inability to forecast with any accuracy the return that will be achieved could predispose investors with a requirement for a guaranteed minimum return from investing in property.

Long-term status

For the reasons already outlined, namely the cost and time involved in transferring title, property is generally perceived to be a long-term investment requiring a minimum holding period of some years. If held for short periods only the transfer costs may outweigh any capital growth achieved. This is not to say that good short-term returns cannot be achieved. When the market is very buoyant with tenant demand outstripping the availability of units, rents and thus capital values can move rapidly.

Where the opportunities exist for changes of use, or redevelopment, or refurbishment, short-term gains may be realized, although there is always a high level of risk attaching to such activities. It is here that the skills and expertise of property developers come to the fore. In addition, the property market is not a perfect one and opportunities may exist for short-term gains to be realized by the purchase of a unit undervalued due to market imperfections.

As a generalization, however, property is not normally regarded as a suitable home for short-term funds where a high degree of liquidity and high short-term returns are required.

Government intervention

All investments are subject to government intervention in the form of fiscal changes, but property is affected, not only by fiscal changes, but by a whole gamut of statutory measures. Of the fiscal provisions which have historically affected property those worthy of particular note must be the taxation of development gains. Over the last forty years the taxation level of these has varied from a nil level to a punitive 80 per cent under the Development Land Tax Act 1976. At the time of writing the only tax on such gains is under the capital gains tax rules, which taxes gains, after making an allowance for inflation at either income or corporation tax levels. Other taxes having an impact on the performance and management of investment property include VAT, now chargeable upon many land transactions, and some rents and commercial rates.

Other statutory interventions include the landlord and tenant provisions relating to commercial and residential property and the planning Acts. The former type of legislation may affect the freeholder's ability to let land in an unfettered way by granting the lessee certain rights in relation to security, rent control or other covenants entered into between the parties. Planning laws control the use and development of land and can thus be fundamental to the potential return achieved. These legislative factors are considered further in later chapters.

Valuation

Earlier in this chapter a brief introduction to property valuation, or the price-fixing mechanism for investment property, was given. As we explained then, it is very difficult for any valuer to predict accurately the sale price likely to be achieved at any particular date; hence the popularity of auctions as a method of sale. However, most investors require to monitor their investments on a regular basis without actually disposing of them, therefore they want to know with some degree of accuracy what they could obtain on the market at any particular moment in time. Without such knowledge the evaluation of return must at best be regarded as imprecise, as it is based on a hypothetical figure which may or may not be achievable, with or without a significant delay. This point is addressed again in Chapter 9.

Table 2.4 Comparative indexed returns from property gilts and equities, 1967–88

(June 1977 = 100) (June 1967 = 100)	Long-dated gilts	FTA All Share Index	JLW Index
June 1967	61 (100)	36 (100)	26 (100)
June 1968	58	54	30
June 1969	54	51	35
June 1970	58	48	39
June 1971	66	66	48
June 1972	71	83	57
June 1973	70	81	76
June 1974	55	47	66
June 1975	67	62	70
June 1976	81	79	81
June 1977	100	100	100
June 1978	117	119	127
June 1979	133	149	160
June 1980	142	171	185
June 1981	154	213	217
June 1982	188	232	251
March 1983	244	308	252
June 1983	259	346	257
Sept. 1983	265	340	262
Dec. 1983	278	362	268
March 1984	286	410	275
June 1984	270	383	280
Sept. 1984	291	424	285
Dec. 1984	297	472	294
March 1985	300	503	300
June 1985	310	499	307
Sept. 1985	326	513	310
Dec. 1985	330	560	316
March 1986	378	675	321
June 1986	380	683	328
Sept. 1986	352	659	337
Dec. 1986	367	723	349
March 1987	417	883	358
June 1987	420	1,014	374
Sept. 1987	402	1,072	392
Dec. 1987	427	780	413
March 1988	455	812	442
June 1988	445	882	470
Sept. 1988	460	876	496
Dec. 1988	467	868	537
March 1989	481 (787)	1,018 (2,831)	575 (2,180)

Source: Jones, Laing and Wootton & Property Index.

Capital security and growth

Although capital values may go up and down in exactly the same way as do other investments taken over a long period, historically property has shown an ability to provide capital security, and in many cases capital growth. Table 2.4 shows comparative indexed returns from property gilts and equities over the period 1967 to 1988. Whilst property over this period did not produce the highest individual returns, the long-term picture is one of sustained growth.

When the economic prospects indicate a likelihood of significant inflation, making investments fixed in money terms appear unattractive, any investment which gives the opportunity to 'hedge' inflation by an upward revision of income becomes increasingly attractive. Company shares and property are the two major homes for equity funds and, logically, in such conditions, will be preferred to fixed interest stock. However, inflation is also associated with a difficult trading climate for manufacturing and trading companies so dividend income may be at risk. Whilst in the final analysis rent is a function of the occupier's ability to pay, so that an economic downturn should logically reduce rental value, such effect takes longer to be felt and hence rents are 'cushioned' in the short term against economic downturns. Accordingly rental values are more likely to be sustained than dividend income. Demand for property let to sound covenants from investors at such times may well be such that yields are driven down giving rise to capital growth.

To sum up, the historical evidence that investments in good freehold property can provide capital security and growth is one of the major attractions of the sector to investors and the chief reason why they are frequently prepared to accept low initial returns.

Low volatility

Arguably more important than its ability to provide capital growth is property's historically low volatility of return. Fraser (1985) has shown by a fifteen-year comparative study that the annual returns achieved by prime property fluctuate far less than do those of the other major investment sectors. The high annual returns sometimes achieved by equities are rarely matched by property but the chances of experiencing a loss are also far less. This low level of risk is a major attraction to many investors and is a point explored further in Chapter 6.

Security of income

Taking up the point made in the section on capital security and growth above, rental income, whilst not guaranteed in the same way as government stock income, is secured by legal covenant and is not dependent

just on an executive decision as with company dividends. In the event of
tenant default the lessor does at least have the benefit of the physical asset
backing, unlike an investment in a company which fails. Indeed, if a property
is let at a rent lower than the full rental value, as is often the case due to a
general level of value rises over time, a defaulting tenant gives the landlord
the opportunity to obtain a higher rent upon reletting.

However, although a failure by a tenant to pay the rent can be seen to
have some compensating factors, it is normally indicative of some underlying
problem associated with the property or its management. This aspect is
discussed further in Chapter 8.

The degree to which property income can be regarded as secure will vary
with the type of property, its condition, the level of tenant demand, the
quality of the tenant's covenant and to a certain extent the terms of the lease.
To expand on the last point: in the event of a lease being on internal repairing
terms with the lessor retaining responsibility for repairs and possibly other
outgoings, the net rent each year will fluctuate and frequently over time
decline as the costs of outgoings change and invariably rise.

Flexibility

Albeit within legislative constraints such as the planning Acts, the freeholder
of land has great freedom to deal with his land as he so wishes. This gives
flexibility to the investor who can either occupy himself, or let on any number
of arrangements designed to suit his particular investment requirements.
For example, if he owns a property suitable for redevelopment he has
the choice either to carry out the development himself, thereby making
a capital injection, and then letting at a full rent, or to grant a building
lease to a developer at a percentage of the full rental value as developed,
thereby reducing his level of capital commitment yet creating an investment
with 'built in' long-term capital growth.

Typically for any investment property there may be a variety of legal
interests each offering differing degrees of rental security and differing
rental patterns. One submarket that deserves a special mention is the short
leasehold market. Short leaseholds are generally defined as those where the
investor receives a fixed income from the sublessee and pays a fixed head
rent himself. As in such cases the repairing liabilities normally lie with the
occupier (the sublessee), it can be argued that such interests are more akin
to investments in gilt-edged securities than in property, albeit that the risk
of tenant defaults still exists.

In the case study (Appendix A) the creation of a retail property
investment is traced from the identification of a development site lying
within several ownerships through the acquisition and development process
to the time of the first rent reviews. During the process several freehold and
leasehold interests were merged to create a structure of freeholder (the local

authority), a long lessee (a pension fund) and numerous occupying lessees each with potentially marketable interests. The case study demonstrates the quality of flexibility over time that is one of the hallmarks of property as an investment.

Taxation and grants

In Chapter 1 tax treatment, p.5 the point was made that an investor is concerned with net of tax return. As far as property is concerned the general principles of both income and capital taxation apply with taxation levels being determined by the tax status of the individual. A distinction has to be made between owners who are regarded as dealers or traders in land and those who are investors. At the time of writing the distinction in tax rates between capital and income receipts, long an important distinction in structuring property transactions, has been removed.

One important point regarding the taxation of property investors is that many significant investors such as the pension funds are tax exempt bodies. Where they are active in the market there may be instances in which they can afford to outbid other potential investors.

The principal taxes affecting property investors are income tax, with income taxed to schedule A, capital gains tax, inheritance tax and corporation tax.

The scope of value added tax (VAT) has recently been extended to affect some transactions in land including the optional taxation of rents and taxation of transfers including payments for surrender of leases. Another tax of importance to the management of property is the national non-domestic rate, which became effective on 1 April 1990. This tax, based upon the hypothetical letting value of commercial property, falls upon the occupier rather than the owner of land. However, the amount of any outgoing will affect the tenant's ability to pay rent and hence affect rental value. In short, any alteration in taxation regulations may potentially affect value patterns and necessitate changes in management policies.

In the past various legislative measures have been passed which have sought to tax at a penal level gains arising from the ability to carry out development, that is, gains arising as a result of the grant of planning permission. In general these attempts have been shortlived and unsuccessful. They have also, whilst operational, reduced the amount of land brought forward for development. Of these the most recent legislation was the Development Land Act 1976 which at one time had a tax rate of 80 per cent with only a £10,000 annual exemption. Before its final demise in 1984 the level of tax was progressively reduced and the annual exemption limit raised and so the tax became uneconomic to collect. Although there is currently no tax on development other than capital gains tax, it would be a rash investor considering a long-term venture in property who did not contemplate the possible reintroduction of similar legislation at some time in the future.

Grants, in the form of capital building allowances, and rate exemptions, can have a significant impact on the working of the property market with many instances of development only being feasible because of the presence of such grants and reliefs.

It is not within the scope of this book to examine the effects of taxation and grants in any detail for two reasons: first, they are constantly changing, and second, the impact of such measures must always be considered for each individual investment proposition as very minor differences in superficially similar schemes may result in widely-differing tax treatments. Readers wishing for a detailed treatment of taxation are referred to Butterworth's *Tax Guide* (current edition).

Timing of receipts

Whilst income from some properties let on old leases may still be receivable annually in arrears, the norm is for rent to be paid quarterly in advance. In addition, if monies are outstanding, many leases provide for interest to become payable, sometimes at punitive rates. Despite this, property valuation, as distinct from investment appraisal, is calculated upon the assumption that rents are receivable annually in arrears. It is argued that this does not result in an undervaluation as the capitalization rate used is chosen as a result of analysing similar transactions. The point to note here is that the timing of receipts generally differs from, and is more advantageous than, that of other investments where income is generally payable half-yearly in arrears. The impact of this assumption is discussed again in Chapter 5. Readers wishing for a further consideration of the mathematical implications of the use of annual in arrears assumptions are referred to Bowcock's *Property Valuation Tables* (1978) and valuation texts such as Richmond (1985), Enever (1986) and Baum and Mackmin (1989).

Transferability

Mention has already been made (section on expense and speed of transfer, pp.59–60) of the expense and slow speed of most property transactions, these factors being held to be some of property's chief drawbacks by many investors. However, property is generally transferable, albeit that there may be some restrictions on the title which could affect transferability, such as restrictive covenants. In the case of leaseholds the lease will dictate whether the lessee may transfer freely or indeed whether any assignment is permitted. For commercial property the norm is that the lessor's prior consent is required, subject to the caveat that such consent may not be unreasonably withheld. Where a total bar is placed upon the lessee assigning or subletting it may be possible by negotiation to alter the clause but a financial penalty may ensue (see Chapter 8 for further reference to assignment provisions and their implications). It seems unnecessary to point out that such a leasehold has no market value and does not form an adequate security for a mortgage advance, as in the event of default the underlying asset cannot be sold. Despite this one of the authors has come across instances in practice where reputable lenders have been prepared to do just that.

Risk

The subject of risk in relation to property is discussed in Chapters 6 and 7. As an investment some properties have a high-risk profile, others a low one. Much depends upon the definition of risk used and the nature of the property and its letting. Taken as a sector the traditional view has been that property is a higher risk investment than government fixed interest stock and prime equities as it is subject to matters such as tenant default and illiquidity. Hence investors have sought to obtain a 'risk premium' on property returns in the order of 2 per cent; the validity of this wisdom has been questioned in recent years by Fraser (1985) and others.

Prestige and status

In Chapter 1 (p.9) we alluded to the psychic value which land may possess. To some investors the ownership of a particularly prestigious building may give a return hard to quantify in money terms. Many commercial concerns are insistent that their headquarters buildings should reflect the image for the company that they wish to project. Whilst the ownership of such a building may have a non-quantifiable 'comfort' or 'status' value only, to other companies the ownership of certain prominent buildings may have a more quantifiable appeal. Such can be the case with hotels, where the prices at which some well-known London properties have been transferred undoubtedly includes a 'premium' element as the purchaser is anxious to obtain representation in the area. The size of such premiums is difficult to accurately predict, depending as it does on the value of the prestige attaching.

Portfolio considerations

The aim of most investors is to hold a diversified or balanced portfolio. Classically an institutional investor will seek to achieve this by investing in a spread of government gilt-edged securities, equities and property with a proportion of funds being placed in overseas investments or held in cash. In 1989 a typical pattern of investment was as displayed in Figure 1.4.

Property with the qualities already mentioned of long-term growth and low volatility is regarded as a foil to the more volatile sectors of the money market investments.

Any investor should, however, do more than just look intuitively at the spread of investments. He should seek to balance his risk and return profile using an analytical approach. To do so he should consider not only what qualities he needs in individual investments, but in his portfolio as a whole. For example, an elderly retired person may have a need to construct a portfolio with a relatively high income rather than one designed for capital growth; at the same time he will not be able to accept high risk propositions. A younger person on the other hand who has a high earned income and low liabilities may well seek capital growth at the expense of income return. He may also be in a position to accept lower liquidity.

Institutions, too, vary in that a pension fund of a young but fast expanding company will have different requirements from one which is in decline and has a large number of pensioners already. Chapter 5 looks at the characteristics of the dominant active investors in property in some detail.

Whilst the overall objective of the investor's portfolio may be clear, the important question is how can it be achieved? What investments should be undertaken to achieve the right balance and what effect on the portfolio as a whole will result from the purchase of an additional unit. Possible approaches to the answers to these questions are attempted in Modern Portfolio Theory (MPT), which is introduced in Chapter 7. To date this theory and its derivative, the Capital Asset Pricing Model (CAPM), have been applied mainly within the sphere of the stock market, but analysts have for some time been examining its possible application to property portfolios.

Within portfolios comprising property alone, it may be possible to achieve a balance by investing across sectors and within sectors by a geographical diversification. For example, an investor with large property assets will usually choose to invest in a spread between say offices, shops and industrial units as the risk that all sectors will perform badly at one and the same time is less than the risk relating to each of them.

Not every investor will choose to act in this way, some property companies in particular have developed an expertise within a given sector and have made a conscious decision not to diversify to any large extent. Examples of this are Haslemere Estates who specialize in London and South-East offices and Industrials and Slough Estates who specialize in industrial property.

Even within one sector, let us say offices, it may be possible to reduce risk by geographical distribution. This is because rent and value rises tend to peak and trough on a cyclical basis, but not all parts of the country are at the same point on the cycle. Hence when rents are stagnant in one locality they may be moving ahead strongly in another region. By investing in properties lying in different regions it may be possible to reduce, though not eliminate, risk.

The results of a study on this was carried out in 1988 by surveyors Jones Lang Wootton (*The Allocation of Property Assets*).

The whole question of portfolio balance is one that is an essential part of portfolio management and we refer to it again in Chapter 9.

Summary

To sum up, it can be seen that the main advantages of property as an investment lie in its qualities of capital security and growth, its flexibility and, arguably, its low risk profile. However, for many the 'large lot' characteristic and its relatively high cost and low liquidity are such that, as a vehicle for direct investment, it is not possible or appropriate.

For such investors the route of indirect investment may be preferred and these vehicles are now briefly described.

INDIRECT PROPERTY INVESTMENT

Property bonds

The true property bond is a single premium life assurance policy linked to property assets owned and managed by an insurance company. The bonds are tradable through the bond managers in much the same way as any other marketable bond except that repayment, if required, may be delayed to enable underlying assets to be sold. Thus to some degree they suffer from the same problems as direct property investment. When they were first introduced in the 1960s they attracted much public attention, but returns in many cases have not been spectacular, with short-term losses being recorded in some cases. Nevertheless, they do offer a relatively low-risk method of investing in property and as such they have attractions for individuals debarred from PUTs (Property Unit Trusts).

Property company shares

In much the same way as authorised and property unit trusts differ, so do property bonds and property company shares. To purchase shares in a property company enables the investor to share in the returns arising from development, active property management and rises in property values. However, as with all shares, they are subject to double taxation on profits made, that is, taxation of the company and taxation of the shareholder. Property company shares also tend to have high levels of volatility. This is largely because many property companies have high borrowing and gearing, making their profits particularly susceptible to economic and market changes. This point was clearly demonstrated in the autumn of 1987 when the property company sector of the Stock Exchange suffered a reduction of share price in the order of 35 per cent as against a general market fall of approximately 25 per cent. Those companies having a large development programme were particularly hard hit, despite the fact that in many cases the value of the underlying assets had not been adversely affected.

Mortgages and debentures

Whilst often not considered as a medium of property investment, the grant of a mortgage is strictly an indirect property investment.

In recent years the level of loan has presented a problem with prime commercial property as rental yields have been driven down whilst the general level of interest rates has risen. In many cases, therefore, rents have been insufficient to cover the annual interest payments.

An example will illustrate the point:

A building has a capital value of £5,000,000 but a rental value of £250,000. The purchaser wishes to borrow 70 per cent of the valuation, that is, £3,000,000. If the interest rate is taken at even 10 per cent the annual charges of £350,000 cannot be funded from the rent received by the investor. In the event of default the lendor would therefore stand to lose money until such time as the asset could be sold.

To overcome this problem, the normal reaction would be to restrict the size of the loan to a level where the interest charges are covered. One alternative is for the lender to take an equity share in the property. Such mortgage equity schemes are thus a combination of direct and indirect investment in property. This subject, together with other funding methods are discussed in some detail in Chapter 11.

Property unit trusts

These have already been described in Chapter 1 and need no further comment here.

SUMMARY

In this chapter we have attempted to put property into context as an investment. At all times the investor or appraiser of interests in land should be seeking to rationalize the choice within the wider context of investments. However, such comparisions do not come easily. Some of the reasons for this can be summarized as follows:

(a) The property market differs from other markets and reliable information regarding deals is still not always easy to obtain.

(b) Properties display characteristics that are different from other investments and it is not possible to satisfactorily analyse out the effects of each of the characteristics individually to enable exact comparison to take place.

(c) Decisions regarding property are often made for reasons other than pure financial return. In particular occupational requirements, and matters such as prestige and status are inextricably bound up in the decision-making process.

(d) The pricing mechanism for property investments is not comparable with those used for other investments; nor does it reveal the potential or actual return to the purchaser. In order that greater rationality can be introduced into management decisions, other measurement means have to be established, such as the internal rate of return. As data from individual transactions normally relate to yield and not return, the comparison difficulties are compounded.

In the next chapter we look in more detail at individual types of properties before subsequently considering the issues of return and risk evaluation.

Chapter 3

Investment property specification

INTRODUCTION

In this chapter we consider the main categories of property that are held as investments, and the criteria dictating their suitability and value as investments.

The chief criteria that any individual or institution will employ when selecting a property will be:

(a) Do its particular characteristics satisfy the investment needs in terms of security, growth, and so on?
(b) Is the price to be paid reasonable in all the circumstances?
(c) Is the property suitable in respect of portfolio balance?
(d) If the need to alter the portfolio changes, will the property be readily saleable?

This last point has a very large impact on the type and specification that forms the core of the investment property market. Investors are reluctant to purchase property which is not of a type for which there is a substantial market. Thus there tends to be a reluctance, by the institutions in particular, to place funds in innovative developments, where tenant demand may be uncertain and there is little history of rental growth to rely on when projecting likely rents on review.

A consequence of this is that such schemes are perceived as high risk and when developed are less readily saleable than investments of a 'tried and tested' nature. During the 1980s, a period which has seen a reduction in pension fund involvement with property, there has been a fragmentation of the classic categorization of property users and the advent of new subsections such as retail warehousing and high-tech developments. These new types have been partly institutionally funded but since the mid-1980s there has been increasing bank financing in the form of commercial mortgages, including equity mortgage agreements and the provision of bank syndicated loans.

One important influence on the changes and types of development, which have largely been the result of tenant-led demand, has been an alteration in planning controls in the form of the new Use Classes Order 1987. This order lists categories of properties, and within each 'class' it is possible to change use without planning consent. Hence, for example, under the Class B1 a unit currently occupied for a light industrial purpose may be used as offices without the need for permission, unless any external physical alteration is required. Prior to June 1987, any such change needed permission and frequently this would not be forthcoming. Any change between a use falling within one class and another needs specific consent.

The main categories of property which have established investment markets are:

(a) Retail
(b) Offices
(c) Industrial and warehouses
(d) Agricultural and woodland

The agriculture and woodland sector is small in comparison with the first three, but such properties have formed part of many investment portfolios in the past. Residential and leisure properties are sometimes traded as investments and will be considered briefly, although in both these categories the owner-occupier market is predominant.

PORTFOLIO MIX

The question of the balance of properties within the portfolio was introduced in Chapter 1 and is considered again in Chapter 9. A decision to invest in property requires further decisions as to the type and balance of properties acquired. This 'split' will vary between investors depending on, *inter alia*, historical factors, management expertise, expectations of future performance and the nature of the investor's liabilities (for example, whether high income or high capital growth is required). Hence, to take two property investment companies as examples, Haslemere Estates have built up a reputation and expertise for office refurbishment schemes in London and the south-east, whilst Capital and Counties are associated with shopping centre development. Pension funds with a greater need to consider long-term liabilities to shareholders may well adopt a policy of risk reduction through diversification.

Whilst it may be argued that there is no such thing as the 'ideal portfolio' and that in any event over time requirements may change, it is often possible to perceive general trends. These will often track the recent past performance of individual sectors of the market and the performance of other investments. Thus, in the late 1980s a substantial reduction in institutional investment in property, which reached a low point in 1987, mirrored a period when returns from equities exceeded those from property.

Within property during this period the returns from shops exceeded those from other sectors and this may go some way to explaining the results of the *Chartered Surveyors Weekly/Property Market Analysis* survey carried out in late 1986. This survey (see *Chartered Surveyors Weekly*, 20 November 1986) was based on interviews with over 100 fund managers and reproduced the hypothetical 'Ideal Pension Fund Portfolio'. At that time this recorded a preference for approximately 50 per cent retail, 30 per cent office and 20 per cent industrial. Since this survey was published, substantial growth in both offices and industrial at the expense of retail has taken place and in 1989 total returns were:

Retail:	8.8 per cent
Office:	15.3 per cent
Industry:	26.3 per cent

Source: Investment Property Databank, *Annual Review 1990*.

These figures can be compared with the annualized returns per sector over the period 1981–9 of:

Retail:	14.4 per cent
Office:	14.0 per cent
Industry:	13.7 per cent

Source: Investment Property Databank, *Annual Review 1990*.

Within sectors, specialization can take place with some investors preferring to concentrate on opportunities which require proactive management, and others on fully-let prime investments. Geographical preferences are also displayed and again decisions may be taken on pure property grounds or they may be influenced by the organizational structure. Readers wishing for more information on portfolio mix are advised to consult the research publications of the large firms such as Richard Ellis, Debenham, Tewson and Chinnock; and Investment Property Database, all of whom publish annual or quarterly bulletins of returns and investment trends.

PROPERTY TYPES

Retail, offices and industrial properties which, when let, are collectively known as 'business premises' fall within the ambit of the Landlord and Tenant Act 1954 (Part 2) and associated legislation. Under this legislation, the occupying lessee has the right upon lease expiry to be granted a new lease at a market rent, unless the landlord can prove certain grounds for possession, such as redevelopment plans or tenant/lessee breach of contract. The effects of the legislation are considered in more detail in later chapters. In general, the legislation has stood the test of time, is accepted, albeit with some reservations, by both sides of the political spectrum and does not act as a deterrent to potential investors. Except where specifically mentioned, business premises are commonly let on leases of twenty to twenty-five years, with the lessee responsible for repairing, maintenance and insurance.

Retail

Retail investments are often considered to be the jewels in the crown of any portfolio, with yields purchasers are prepared to accept for prime units generally lower than for any other type of property. At times yields have fallen to 4 per cent, or even lower. This implies that purchasers are making assumptions regarding future rental growth: it is in anticipation of future increases in the income stream in real terms that they are prepared to accept an initially low return on their investment (see Chapter 2).

The retail investment market will be considered under several subdivisions:

(a) High street shops
(b) Town centres (purpose-built developments)
(c) Superstores
(d) Retail warehouses
(e) Out-of-town shopping centres

Apart from these, there are many other types of retail outlet, ranging from the station kiosk to the corner shop, to the suburban parade, but these are either owner-occupied or of appeal only to small investors. Shops may also form part only of a structure, for example, a shop with a flat or offices above may present valuation problems and attract poor covenants and hence such units are less popular as investments.

High street shops

The view that the three most important factors determining property value are location, location and location is as true for high street shops as for any other property. An ideal shop property from the investor's viewpoint is one situated in the position of maximum pedestrian flow in the main shopping area of a prosperous town or city with a sound economic base. The investor will consider the past rental growth record and whether there are any factors which could affect this in the future, such as a new competing out-of-town centre, the closure of a large employer firm, and so on. Put simply, what matters is that the trading position is likely to remain popular and profitable to potential tenants in the future and that the town in which it is situated will provide safe trade.

The design and structure of such units tend to be of relatively little importance as most are let on full repairing and insuring leases. However, a purpose-built modern structure of standard size (approximately 6 m frontage and 20 m built depth) or multiples thereof, will be most sought after, as it will have the greatest tenant appeal. Small kiosk units are often let on unusual terms, and although they may be achieving comparatively high rentals, they have limited appeal; large size units (1,500 sq.m upward) may also be more difficult to let. Likewise, multi-storey shops and department stores are of limited appeal and are increasingly the subject of refurbishment schemes for subdivision.

The other crucial factor of high street shops is the quality of the covenant; a unit let to a multiple trader such as Mothercare, Boots or Dixons, where the risk of tenant default is minimal, is more attractive than a unit let to an individual, however good his trading record.

Town centre developments

The history of town centre schemes has been relatively short; they are principally a phenomenon of the 1960s onwards, but it has been a history of rapid change from the early uncovered centres of the 1960s (for example, the Whitgift in Croydon) through to the fully air-conditioned centres of the late 1970s (for example, Eldon Square, Newcastle) and the specialist centres of the 1980s (for example, Coppergate, York).

Most shopping centre developments have involved institutional funds and they provide numerous examples of co-operation between local authorities acting as landowners, institutions providing funds and developers with their technical and market expertise.

It is very tempting to think that a brand new shopping centre, architect-designed and developed by experts, must provide the main equity holder, typically a fund, with a first-class investment, incorporating the best aspects of retail opportunities, namely income security and income growth. Such a thought is misconceived and there are numerous examples of shopping centres which have proved to be difficult to let and subsequently have had management problems. Examples of large developments which have suffered in this way include the Elephant and Castle in south London and the Tricorn in Portsmouth. The latter is now the subject of redevelopment proposals.

What then makes some centres successful and others dismal failures? In our view, the following are essential ingredients needed to produce a sound scheme:

(a) The scheme must be appropriate to the town. If the town is in essence not a regional centre, but caters only for the day-to-day needs of the inhabitants, then to construct a large-scale centre offering the types of facilities usually found in the regional centres is a risky proposition, and will only succeed if the centre can draw on a large population from outside the town. It will therefore need very good transport links, accessibility and adequate parking. An example of a regional centre created in a location previously not associated with large-scale shopping, is Brent Cross in north-west London, though here it could be argued that the development is more akin to an out-of-town centre.

(b) The location within the town is of vital importance. Where it is intended to site a centre within a central area, careful study must be made of the pedestrian flows, position of main stores (unless they have been persuaded to relocate within the centre), car parking, and so on. The centre should be positioned so that it 'marries in' to the existing patterns. It is true that some centres have succeeded in altering the focal point of a town's shopping area, but this can only happen over time, and if the centre has strong 'pulling power' in terms of national retailers, and there has been an under-provision of shopping in the town. An example of this is in Maidstone, Kent, where the Stoneborough Centre, constructed in the mid-1970s, was at the edge of the main retail area, and well away from key traders such as Marks and Spencer and Boots. It proved slow to let, and only after Sainsburys, British Home Stores and Boots had taken space, did the scheme become fully let. Even so, it is the subject of refurbishment proposals at the time of writing.

An earlier centre, built in the 1960s, was Dolphin Square, Weston-super-Mare. This was similarly sited at the end of the main shopping street. It failed to attract any major retailer, and twenty years on the largest unit is a covered market selling low quality goods, whilst the remaining units, though let, have attracted few multiples.

(c) It follows from (b) above, that for a scheme to succeed it must attract good retailers of a type compatible with the market. In general this will be the multiple chains, but where a specialist centre is conceived, the presence of local independent traders can add variety and strengthen the pulling power of the centre. In practice, with many successful schemes, pre-lettings to large space users have taken place, thus reducing the risks to the investor.

(d) The design of the centre is a crucial element. For any centre to succeed it must attract shoppers, and to do this, its appearance must be pleasing and inviting. Once in the centre, the shopper should feel free to circulate to all parts, with focal points provided to draw him in. Traditionally, therefore, 'magnet' stores, that is, those with most 'shopper appeal', have been positioned well within the centre to maximize pedestrian flow past other units.

Changes in design have been dramatic in the last two decades. The 1960s Whitgift Centre in Croydon, a vast two-storey open centre, was constructed with drab grey concrete finishes. Similarly, 'Friars' Square' Centre in Aylesbury is a monument to the 1960s obsession with modernism and concrete. In the late 1980s such appearance is generally regarded as unacceptable. The Whitgift has been the subject of a £10 million scheme to cover part of the centre, reduce mall size and generally improve the aesthetic appearance and shoppers' comfort. Friars' Square, too, will shortly be refurbished.

More recent schemes have been fully enclosed, air-conditioned, with much attention being paid to providing an attractive and relaxing environment, normally with provision of a food court and maybe with childrens' crèche facilities. Full air-conditioning can, however, prove very expensive to maintain, and in the 'Ridings', Wakefield, which was completed in 1983, the scheme makes use of natural light and natural ventilation, with comfort in winter being provided by warm air.

(e) The management of the centre is critical. For any centre to be successful it is not sufficient that the physical factors are right; however well designed and located the centre, and however strong the covenants, if the management is not correctly and imaginatively handled it will not trade to its optimum level. In recent years there has been a growing awareness of the need for centres to be promoted and marketed in much the same way as any other retail product. This has led to the requirement for shopping centre managers to acquire similar skills to those of the individual tenants. Attention to cleanliness and security at one time was regarded as sufficient to ensure that tenants had the opportunity to maximize their trade.

Now the relationship between shopping centre management and the tenants is seen as one of partnership, with both parties having a vested interest in ensuring the success of the centre. In this respect the pattern is following that of the United States shopping centres, where the manager frequently has a retailing, rather than property, background.

To sum up, therefore, the scheme must be designed to link in with other shopping and attract both tenants and shoppers by its layout, aesthetic features and facilities provided. It must also be designed so that its maintenance costs are minimized, thus keeping service charges low. If costs are high, this will adversely affect the rent tenants can pay and, ultimately, the scheme's lettability. Flexibility of design is also

important. Within twenty years, and often less, the schemes hailed as
innovative look sadly dated, and in many cases fail to provide the
environment and facilities demanded by shoppers. The more flexible the
design, the cheaper, theoretically, any subsequent refurbishment will be.
This is discussed further in Chapter 10.

Superstores

Superstore is a generic name to cover large single stores, constructed on
greenfield sites in edge-of-town or out-of-town locations. Associated with
the superstore may be a few small units supplying ancillary goods, but in
general they are 'stand-alone' units, having floor areas typically of between
3,000 and 10,000 square metres. They have evolved as a natural progression
from the town centre supermarket selling basic good commodities on a
self-selection basis. As car ownership has increased, shoppers are able to
carry more bulky goods home. This means fewer shopping trips, so the
size of the stores and their product range has tended to increase, and their
location has changed. An example of this is Sainsburys, which in the late
1950s used to occupy standard or double units in the high street selling
groceries and provisions. Now they tend to locate in large stores on the
edge of town with ample surface car-parking, for example, Guildford, and
also Weston-super-Mare, where, in addition, they have a 'Do-It-Yourself'
(DIY) off-shoot, 'Homebase'. There are exceptions to the edge-of-town
rule. Sainsburys in Redhill, Surrey, is a recent town centre development.
Here the location is acceptable, due to the car-parking available within the
complex and comparative lack of any effective competition.

The design of superstores has also undergone rapid development from
early structures of almost industrial design, to an extensively landscaped and
aesthetically sympathetic developments recently undertaken by companies
such as Tesco (for example, the Gatwick Tesco Superstore).

The essential features in superstore development have always been, and
remain:

(a) A prominent position, well located for access via major roads and
    motorways, to large areas of population.
(b) Adequate site size to allow ample surface parking and room for
    expansion of the trading area if demand increases.
(c) A store designed to meet the occupier's requirements.
(d) Typically a 'stand-alone' store, but maybe incorporating some ancil-
    lary units.

Unlike town centre schemes, superstores in the main have been developed by retailers for their own occupation. Whilst there are examples of
let premises, the developments have been largely initiated and carried out
by retailers. As an investment superstores are perceived to be higher risk

than high street shops because (1) the sites are not in general suitable for other commercial uses, and (2) there are fewer suitable tenants, so tenant demand is less certain.

Retail warehouses

Retail warehouses bear many of the same characteristics as superstores, namely:

(a) They are recent in origin, dating only from the early 1970s.
(b) Their growth derives from the same underlying factor of increased car ownership, town centre congestion but, additionally, income growth and the surge in DIY activity.
(c) They require a prominent location with good road frontage and access and ample car-parking.
(d) The typical store size can be up to or exceeding 4,000 square metres.
(e) Until recently they were dominated by retailer-led developments.

During the 1980s differences between the two sectors emerged:

(a) The construction of retail warehouse units is still along industrial lines, that is, a basic steel- or concrete-frame building with low pitched roof, and brick and sheet cladding. Internal and external finishes, whilst better than fifteen to twenty years ago, are still of a lesser quality than the superstore.
(b) Retail warehouses may be constructed singly or in clusters, but are often developed as retail warehouse parks with total floor areas of up to 750,000 square feet.
(c) With the growth of the parks has come institutional funds and developer-, not retailer-, initiated schemes.
(d) The range of tenants who occupy retail warehouses is wider than superstores. It extends to DIY, furniture, carpets, electricals, home furnishing and motor accessories. With this increase in the number and type of potential lessees comes a decrease in the risk of voids, and this may explain why the institutions prefer such schemes to the single superstore.

Out-of-town shopping centres

Although retail warehouse parks could be described as out-of-town shopping centres, this would be a misnomer. The retail warehouse park offers only a limited range of goods, essentially consumer durables. To the consumer, their advantage is that they offer a convenient way of purchasing such goods and the ability to view a larger range of products than would be possible in any high street store.

The true out-of-town shopping centre, however, aims to provide the full range of products and services that are associated with a town centre. Not only will a full range of retail goods be found, but also services such as banks, crèche, cafe and, typically, leisure facilities such as health centre and cinema. It will have a retail floor area in excess of 100,000 square metres and extensive car parking.

Centres such as this are a new concept in British retailing and therefore involve a much greater risk to the developer than any in-town centre, where the location has usually been established for retail purposes over a long period. The shopper using the centre is mainly car-borne, although the Metro centre in the north-east attracts a large number by public transport. As the shopper's transport costs will be more expensive than if he were to use local facilities, the centre must offer incentives. These are:

(a) Easy car-parking.
(b) A visually-pleasing shopping environment in enclosed malls, with a large range of good quality merchandise offered by multiple traders, including department store traders.
(c) Ancillary services (for example, food).
(d) Leisure facilities to encourage a longer stay within the centre.

It can be seen, therefore, that the essential ingredients are the same as for town centres; the difference lies in the scale of development and the amount of leisure and associated facilities provided, many of which would not be viable as independent developments. The presence of such facilities will increase costs substantially, but justification is threefold.

(a) By increasing the time each shopper spends in the centre, the 'unit spend' is increased, and hence profitability.
(b) They are normally a prerequisite of planning consent, which in any event is frequently difficult to obtain.
(c) Consumers have constantly rising expectations from shopping centres and increased competition between centres make such provision essential.

The out-of-town centre is still embryonic in most cases and there is no proven track record of rental growth achieved at rent reviews to attract investors. This, combined with the very high cost of development, means that funding is usually by syndication to reduce each parties' risk.

The most celebrated scheme to date is the Metrocentre just outside Gateshead, which was opened in stages from 1985. Adjacent to and integrated with the Metrocentre is Metroland, a 'Disney style' leisure complex. Other schemes currently being developed include Lakeside at Thurrock, just off the M25, and Meadowhall at Sheffield, just off the M1.

In summary, retail property in general offers the investor:

(a) A proven track record of rental growth and associated capital growth.
(b) Many opportunities to buy investments where the income flow is generated by reliable tenants.
(c) High street shops are less prone to obsolescence due to building design than, for example, offices and industrial premises. However, shopping centre schemes not only require intensive management, but with rapid changes taking place in the retail industry, need large capital injections at ever-shortening intervals.
(d) An increasing range of investment choices as the retail market fragments.

Offices

With the seemingly relentless increase in service industries that are based on the use of office premises, the continued tenant demand looks assured, and this has been reflected in recent return figures. Yet this is not necessarily the case; although a large proportion of the work-force do work in offices, the pattern of work undertaken is changing, with the advent of computerization, away from the repetitive clerical jobs to more analytical functions. The introduction of microcomputers has transformed the need for many workers to have an office into a requirement for a work station, fully equipped with the latest electronic gadgetry. If this trend continues, it is possible to speculate that a time will come when the need for offices reduces as workers fulfil more of their functions at home, with data being transformed electronically to and from a central data bank, which could be located almost anywhere. This picture is not intended to be in any way a prophesy, but an illustration that design and demand criteria are undergoing such rapid changes that even this traditional stable property sector can no longer be regarded in the way it was just five or ten years ago.

Offices can be of almost any design or structure; they range from the two rooms over a shop, to a converted house, to a 20,000 square metres purpose-built glass-clad block. They are located throughout the country in both town centre and suburban locations, but there is a predominance in supply in south-east England, and London in particular. Rental values, too, vary dramatically with current top rental values of over £60 per square foot in the City of London being up to twenty times those achieved in some parts of the Midlands and the north.

From an investor's viewpoint, the type of office which forms the bulk of the market are those located in central business areas of large towns and cities. Offices are less location sensitive than shops, as pedestrian flows do not matter. What is important is that they have good accessability, including that to public transport. If on-site parking is not provided, the presence of public car-parks or on-street parking is also important. Examples of towns which have developed as areas of strong tenant demand for offices due to good communication systems include Croydon, with its excellent rail links and Redhill/Reigate, which has become popular with the opening of the M25 giving easy access to both Gatwick and Heathrow airports.

The City of London must be mentioned as a special case. Historically, the city has been a centre for all financial services, particularly banking and insurance. Due to a generally strong tenant demand and restricted supply arising from the physical and planning constraints, rents have always been higher than those achieved elsewhere. With the deregulation of the Stock Exchange in 1986, and the explosion in the financial services sector, demand rose, pushing up rents dramatically due to the inability of supply to respond quickly.

The nature of office rental movements tends to be cyclical, following the pattern of economic activity but with a time-lag. As the economy moves into growth so demand for space increases. However, the time taken by the market to provide new space is normally about two years, assuming that the planning environment is not hostile. During the period until the developments are completed, rents will be forced up, and by that time, if the economy has fallen back, oversupply may occur. At the time of writing in Central London offices have experienced a boom and many new developments including the much publicized scheme at Canary Wharf in Docklands are progressing. Whether the economy will retain sufficient real growth that an oversupply will not be experienced when new offices come 'on stream' remains to be seen.

Notwithstanding this cyclical pattern, offices have always been regarded as an important ingredient in any property portfolio, but any institutional investor placing funds in a new office development will wish to know:

(a) How lettable is the building to a good tenant? This will depend on its location, size, architecture, quality, facilities, finishes, and running costs.

(b) How is it likely to perform at first rent review?

   To an extent this is an unanswerable question and will depend on the general office market as well as the particular building. Factors that will tend towards a good settlement at first review include:

   (i) A lease on terms with an unambiguous rent review clause. Commercial lease terms are considered in detail in Chapter 8.

   (ii) The presence of other similar buildings in the locality which will provide good comparable evidence of rental value.

   (iii) An energy efficient building, as the lessee is interested in the total running costs in use of a building, not just the rent; thus the lower the running costs, the higher the rent he can afford to pay.

(iv)   A unit of a size for which there is likely to continue to be strong tenant demand. Any building in excess of 10,000 square metres is likely to have a small number of potential lessees and thus rent at review may be depressed.

(c) Will it be relettable at the end of the lease in twenty to twenty-five years' time?

The last is the most difficult question of the three to answer. The changing needs of office occupiers has already been mentioned and it is a foolhardy man who could hope to predict accurately what tenant requirements will be in twenty years' time. It is a sobering thought that some offices developed in the 1960s and considered to be prime investments with a life-span of at least fifty to sixty years are now the subject of redevelopment. Premature obsolescence is frequently the result of inflexibility of design, and flexibility is now a most important consideration. In order to achieve this, the basic structure is designed to have a physical life of fifty to sixty years, with storey heights sufficient to allow for raised floors and suspended ceilings, so that cabling can be accommodated. Services will have a much shorter life so the building design must allow for easy renewal as required. The new Lloyds Insurance building in the City of London has all service provisions, including lifts, running on the outside of the building so that they can be renewed without disruption to the user.

Internal space should be designed to be adaptable. Whilst some people will argue in favour of a narrow building of no more than 12 to 15 metres depth, which subdivides easily into 'cells' which can be naturally lit, others prefer a deep building of 18 metres or more, built to a 3-metre grid. Such buildings are generally cheaper to construct, but the choice will inevitably be dictated by the site constraints and market requirements.

In addition to designing for maximum flexibility, the ratio between the gross area which determines cost and the net area on which rental is calculated, must be considered.

One recent trend in the office sector has been developments of small, self-contained buildings for onward freehold sale. The desire of companies to own their own accommodation can be seen as a prestige or status factor, linked with a desire to be protected from possible large rent increases.

Industrial and warehouses

Of all the major investment property types, industrial property is regarded as subject to the highest risks, and for this reason investors have demanded higher returns, with initial yields on rack-rented property frequently being in excess of 10 per cent.

The basic reasons behind this view are that:

(a) They are the most susceptible to economic recession.
(b) Associated with (a) above, they have the highest risk of tenant default.
(c) Unless there is very buoyant market letting, reletting may be difficult.
(d) Building structures, although cheaper initially, tend to suffer design and physical obsolescence quickly. Whilst the twenty-year redevelopment/refurbishment cycle is a new phenomenon in the office and retail sectors, it has long been associated with industrial property.

In response to these factors, investors will seek to develop or invest in schemes which demonstrate the following characteristics:

(a) Located in areas which have proved to be more resilient to difficult economic conditions, that is, where unemployment levels are low, employment is predominantly service-based, not reliant on one or two large employers engaged in primary industries such as coal-mining or steel-making. In general this has led to institutional activity in the south and south-east sooner than the traditional industrial heartlands of the Midlands and north.
(b) Well-located for access to vital communication links, in particular, motorways, airports and ports. Thus areas such as the Heathrow/ Gatwick, London triangle and the M4 Corridor have been the subject of much investor interest.
(c) Of optimum size for tenant demand. This will depend on the type of development (that is, industrial or warehousing) but obviously the larger the units the greater the financial impact on any tenants' default.
(d) Modern construction complying to all statutory requirements, and with acceptable standards of finish and floor loading. We refer to this in more detail below.
(e) A prominent site whilst desirable is not always possible to achieve. The site should be developed to no more than 50 per cent cover and preferably less. This means that adequate space exists for parking and possible future expansion.
(f) Not located in areas of special tax treatment unless there are other overriding considerations. Generally speaking, tax incentives, such as Enterprise Zones, are short lived and relate to areas of high unemployment and poor economic growth. Such locations are not likely to be compatible with investor requirements.

Industrial properties may be subdivided as follows:

Heavy industrial
General industrial and light industrial
Warehousing
Hi-tech (B1-users)

Heavy industrial

Properties used for heavy industrial processes inevitably have a high plant and machinery content and must be designed and constructed according to the user's specific requirements. They are therefore not suitable as investment vehicles and are normally owned freehold by the occupier, or at least held on long ground leases, possibly the result of a sale and leaseback transaction.

General industrial

General industrial properties are those which are suitable for a wide range of activities, and are normally constructed on estates. The preferred type of structure is a single storey frame with 4–6 metre eaves height, with good quality cladding offering high levels of insulation. Floor loadings must be adequate (5,000 lb per square metre), and provision of sprinklers, heating systems and 3-phase electricity is also important. Where the use is for light industrial purposes only, floorloadings may be less.

One of the characteristics of these industrial units is the amount of office provision. Typically 10 per cent of floor space was the norm, but today 15–20 per cent may be provided. Where a high content of office provision is made (30 per cent), the units have been dubbed as 'mid-tech'. Here the development aim is to realize higher rental levels, at relatively little increased cost.

Units may be terraced and of varying sizes, from small 'nursery' units of 500 square metres, mainly of light industrial use, to large ones of, say, 2,000 square metres. One important change that has occurred with the development of industrial units over the last decade, has been the increase in standards of finishes, both internal and external, and in landscaping and estate layout. These higher specification developments have achieved higher rentals, and it is considered that their performance over time is likely to exceed low specification estates. With improved landscaping has come increased management responsibility but the costs are largely recouped by way of service charges. As with shopping centres, it has been the experience of some investors that a more 'hands on' style of management, with greater involvement in the day-to-day running of the scheme, has resulted in improved rental performance.

Warehousing

Warehouse units are those which are used for storage and distribution sooner than manufacture, although physically the buildings are very similar to the manufactories.

During the 1970s the 'shed' as it was often named was a very popular investment because:

(a) High tenant demand existing in the wake of changes in industrial and retail patterns. Many manufacturers chose to concentrate production in smaller numbers of locations and distribute the goods via a series of distribution depots, rather than carry out the manufacturing process close to the eventual market. Shop rents rose, thus encouraging retailers to store as much as possible away from the high street shops. It followed that the areas of highest demand tended to be close to airports and motorways and large centres of population.
(b) With high tenant demand rental growth was strong, unlike that for general industrials.
(c) Warehouses are both simple and cheap to construct, thus the time-lag between identifying the demand and creating the supply is less than with other property types, given no planning difficulties or delays.

During the early part of the 1980s, however, following a large increase in the supply of such units, and the advent of interest in other forms of 'quasi' industrial development (for example, hi-tech and campus schemes), developer interest waned, but within the second half of the decade interest has revived as the oversupply has been taken up.

The current standard specification for warehousing is similar to that for light industrials, but the following differences often occur:

(a) Clear height to eaves tends to be greater, as the use is for storage. Frequently 7 metres or more is required by the occupiers.
(b) Consequent on (a), floor loadings may need to be higher, say up to 7,000 lb per square metre.
(c) It is more important that the internal space is clear of stanchions and pillars to facilitate maximum useable space and ease of manoeuvre for forklift trucks. This affects the type of construction, which tends to be steel portal frames, pitched roof, brick cladding to 2 metres and tin above.
(d) Because the use is storage, with few personnel on site, provision of car-parking, offices, toilets and heating can be to a lower specification. Generally 10 per cent office content will suffice.
(e) Internal and external finishes generally are of lesser quality, with lower levels of insulation. In the middle 1980s, with supply outstripping demand in some areas, developers gradually improved finishes to a level commensurate with other industrials.

Warehouse units are generally developed in estates of mixed size units, to maximize tenant appeal. Although the ideal site for a warehouse development is level land in a prominent position, with good accessibility and convenient for major roads and railways, it is seldom that such sites become available. The reason for this is that they will tend to be developed for other permitted uses which have the same locational requirements, but which can yield higher rents. As 'hi-tech' and campus developments generally yield higher rent and yet fall within the same use-category currently, it is not surprising that much pure warehouse development is taking place on backland sites, at least in south and south-east England. To the north of the country there has been less such development.

Whilst the provision of new warehouse units has been the result of developer/institutional activity, there is an active owner-occupier sector. Many large companies with the necessary internal financial resources have chosen to develop their own warehouses and distribution centres, sooner than lease estate units, for reasons partly of corporate image on policy and partly as a reflection of their particular locational and design needs.

Hi-tech and campus developments

Over the last decade new designations of quasi industrial property have appeared seemingly daily. Terms such as hi-tech, science park, research park, business park and campus developments have entered the vocabulary of property people without any exact definitions being offered, at least initially.

Originally such developments came about as a result of demand from potential tenants seeking premises suitable for the service and information-technology-based industries that began to emerge in the mid to late 1970s. For such companies the property requirements were for:

(a) highly-serviced accommodation with the benefits of central heating and air-conditioning required by the computers;
(b) flexible space, which could accommodate manufacturing, assembly showroom and offices within one unit;
(c) an 'up-market image' as the place of manufacture was also the point of sale;
(d) extensive car-parking and good landscaping;
(e) room for expansion in view of perceived business prospects;
(f) accessible and prominently situated buildings located in areas with a pool of highly-skilled, largely graduate, employees.

Not only were the property requirements different physically from those of industrial/warehouse tenants, but the type of lease they demanded was different too. The potential lessees were frequently American offshoots, and had a policy of leasing for not more than five years, or they were young companies again reluctant to take on the full burden of a twenty-five-year full repairing lease in accordance with the institutional norm.

Developers responded to this demand, but it created certain planning difficulties as the product did not fall into either office use class or light industrial. Hence the location of such development tended to be dependent upon the local planning authority's attitude to individual proposals. However, the position has been clarified with the introduction of the Use Class Order 1987, firmly categorizing such properties as 'B1-Business Use'.

This emergent sector naturally experienced initial difficulties, not least those of tenant default, inappropriate design and campus management. Institutions, too, were reluctant to invest in such schemes due to the uncertain returns, and the difficulty of predicting likely performance at rent review.

During the period from 1985 onwards, the sector became more acceptable to institutions as rents experienced real growth and planning uncertainties faded.

What then are the chief considerations that influence the choice of a campus development?

It must be remembered that the lessees of units will be very status conscious, and that the unit is not only their manufactory, but also their office, and, more importantly, their retail outlet. For this reason, the quality of construction and finish is very important, being more akin to offices than industrial, although the basic shell may well be an industrial design. The buildings, which typically are low rise, two or three storeys, with manufacturing at ground-floor level, may be either deep space or traditional 15 to 17 metre depth. Their internal services, that is, heating, reception, toilets, and so on, are based on office specifications but, in addition, industrial requirement for ground-floor loading and 3-phase electricity, must be incorporated.

The buildings will be sited on an extensively-landscaped campus with substantial car-parking provision (one space per 25 square metres is often specified).

The location will often be a greenfield site away from a town centre so the importance of good roads and rail communication systems cannot be overstated. To date, such schemes are mainly confined to the south of England.

Whilst some campus developments are small, some, such as the Poole Business Park, are massive undertakings. In such cases it is important that ancillary facilities are provided for the workers on site, particularly leisure facilities. This together with the need to provided communal landscape grounds has meant that the freeholder needs a very positive management approach.

In summary, campus and B1 developments are still in their infancy as investment vehicles, but as more reach their first rent review, it may be possible to judge their investment performance more adequately. Inevitably, as the sector develops, so it will fragment in the way that the retail sector has, but at the time of writing it appears that it has developed sufficient institutional interest to be considered as a sector in its own right, not merely as an office/industrial hybrid.

Agricultural land

If one of the criteria for investing in property is the avoidance of properties which are subject to government intervention, then agricultural land is a sector not suitable for large-scale investment. The last forty years have seen not only a succession of legislative provisions, the results of which have been to affect the agricultural market substantially, but also a series of changing subsidies and grants which has affected tenant prosperity.

Notwithstanding these factors, during the inflationary years of the 1970s, the newly-emerging institutions invested in farmland to such an extent that a committee of inquiry under Lord Northfield was ordered by the government. The report, published in 1979, revealed that although much buying had indeed taken place, institutions held only 2 per cent of the agricultural land stock. The report predicted that institutions would continue to increase their market share. In practice, the 1980s have seen a reversal of the trend and many large investors have sought to reduce their commitment to farmland, for reasons we explore below.

Agricultural land is classified by the Ministry of Agriculture, Fisheries and Food into five grades, ranging from Grade 1, which is the top quality land, level, fertile with favourable climatic conditions and capable of supporting most types of crop, through to Grade 5 which is land with severe physical and climatic limitations, unable to support anything other than grass and maybe a few cereals.

Grade 1 land accounts for only about 3 per cent of agricultural land and Grade 2 a further 15 per cent, whilst the majority lies within Grade 3.

At the beginning of this century, the freehold of most farmland lay with major landowning individuals and the traditional institutions, such as the Church and educational charities. Some of the land so owned was farmed 'in hand', that is, with a salaried farm manager under the direct control of the landowner, but by far the greatest acreage was let in small units, frequently 100 acres or less, to individual tenant farmers. The letting agreements would be short term and, typically, with the landlord retaining a high degree of repairing liability.

This pattern has changed, not least due to legislation. The Agricultural Holdings Act 1948 was introduced to give tenants security of tenure by restricting the landlord's right to obtain possession to certain specified grounds such as for development requiring planning consent or in the case of 'bad husbandry'. The security provisions were subsequently extended so that a farm tenant was not only effectively in possession for life, but the tenancy could be transferred on death to a spouse or other members of a tenant's family, who was actively involved in the workings of the farm. These provisions have now been withdrawn and, under current legislation (Agricultural Holdings Act 1986), there is now no succession for new tenancies.

The consequence of this legislation has been that freeholders have been reluctant to relet when they have obtained possession or farmed the land 'in hand'. Thus a two-tier market has evolved:

(a) Let land which is valued as an investment, that is, by the capitalization of the income flow.
(b) Vacant possession land, which due to its scarcity has a premium value, currently in the order of 50 per cent.

Any investor seeking to purchase farmland has a choice between buying:

(a) Let land, which in addition to rental income, provides the possibility of a capital gain in the event that the tenant vacates or planning permission for development can be obtained.
(b) Vacant possession land to relet. This option is normally rejected due to the premium value such land possesses.
(c) Vacant possession land to farm in hand, either by employing a manager or contractor, or by entering a share farming agreement. The last course has proved attractive to some investors who see it as a way of retaining more flexibility than is possible if land is let, yet involving less risk than if a manager is employed and very little management involvement.
(d) A sale and leaseback proposition, where an owner-occupier sells the freehold and takes a long leaseback on full repairing terms. This is normally done when the owner has a need to raise capital and the terms of the deal may well not reflect current rental trends.

Of the four options listed above, only (a) and (d) have been the subject of institutional activity. What then are the perceived advantages of farmland as part of the portfolio?

(a) To the owner of commercial property, it represents the chance to diversify into a sector perceived as low risk.
(b) Unlike commercial property, the value of which is largely dependent on the infrastructure and hence is susceptible to obsolescence, the value of agricultural land lies principally in the physical and climatic characteristics, which are stable. It is only with small units (those of less than, say, 200 acres) that the quality of the farmhouse and buildings have any real impact on the capital value.
(c) In the event of tenant default, there is normally a strong demand from other tenants unless, of course, the investor wishes to realize his capital gain.
(d) Over the period to 1980 farmland produced increases in rental and

capital values such that the overall returns looked attractive when viewed against other sectors.

(e) The psychological value of land has been mentioned and there is no doubt that this element is present in the desire of many investors to hold farmland.

(f) The agricultural economy has long been the subject of government subsidies, first from the UK system of guaranteed minimum prices and deficiency payments, and latterly from the EEC under the terms of the Common Agricultural Policy. Under this policy, during the 1970s in particular, British farmers received prices based on the less efficient farming methods generally found throughout the rest of the Community. Thus British farmers, who generally were better capitalized than their European counterparts due to a history of favourable bank lending, subsidies and secure markets, were able to pay increased rents demanded largely due to inflationary pressures.

With such an impressive list of advantages, it is little wonder that the institutions turned to agriculture as an investment medium during the inflationary period of the 1970s.

However, a dramatic turnaround has taken place during the 1980s, with institutional activity seeking to disinvest and yields doubling. The reasons for this are complex, but some of the factors involved are:

(a) The terms of the Common Agricultural Policy have become generally less favourable to British farmers. This, combined with the gradual withdrawal of many subsidies, has reduced their ability to pay increasing rents. Notwithstanding, the economic viability of farms has been under increasing strain.

(b) The very high level of working capital required in agriculture as against many other business ventures means that tenants' borrowings are high. Thus in terms of high interest rates, profits get squeezed.

(c) During this period equities entered a sustained bull market, thus making the sector look unattractive in relative terms.

(d) The agricultural land market is small with very few transactions, compared to the number of commercial deals. It follows that a few isolated transactions can distort the market and lead to a general lack of confidence.

(e) The appearance of surpluses in food production, whether actual or politically perceived, have forced the industry to change its basic direction for the first time since the Second World War. Encouragement is given to diversification, but not all farms have the capability to adapt easily.

(f) The current 'greening' of the countryside, an example of which is the campaign against the use of herbicides, is leading to uncertainty regarding farmers' profit margins.

(g) Agricultural land is no longer the hedge against inflation it was once thought to be.

Current indications are that the investment market has stabilized and institutions are starting to show renewed interest, although pension funds are still disinvesting. Assuming, however, that a decision to purchase let land is taken, what features will be sought?

(a) Generally investors require a very minimum of 300 to 400-acre lots of Grade 1 and 2 land, with good fixed equipment, let to a tenant, considered to be a good covenant.
(b) The farm should have a site which offers good access within the countryside. Proximity to main road and rail connections and centres of population are not crucial, but a farm which is close to an expanding town which offers long-term prospects of development, could hold special attractions.
(c) The presence of sporting potential can be important. Fishing and shooting rights are lucrative and can raise the level of income obtained substantially.
(d) Increasingly, the purchaser will consider the possibilities for diversi- fication. With an oversupply of production having been identified, the possibility of using some of the land, or buildings for 'countryside' activities such as rural crafts, stabling, and so on, can be important. This relates to the increasing interest in leisure mentioned below.

In recent years the performance of agricultural land has moved against the trend of other properties, and now offers higher yields than are obtainable on prime commercial investments. As part of a diversified portfolio, it could be argued that it has a role to play. It must be mentioned in conclusion that the legislative factors and management issues involved with farmland are not the same as with other properties, and the requirement for specialist knowledge to successfully manage it may act as a deterrent to some potential investors.

Residential

At the start of the twentieth century the housing stock in this country was dominated by the rented sector with only about 10 per cent being owner-occupied. Much of the stock was owned by private landowners, although there were large tenement blocks owned and managed by charitable organizations such as the Peabody Trust, as well as estates owned by the Church Commissioners, educational bodies and industrialists.

The situation today is almost a complete reversal with home ownership having experienced a meteoric rise, particularly since the 1950s. This reversal has occurred for complex social and political reasons, ranging from an increasing desire for rising living standards to legislative and fiscal interference by successive governments.

Legislation in the form of Rent Acts, giving control over the maximum rents that a landlord can charge and granting occupiers security of tenure were measures introduced as ways of preventing hardship to tenants in time of housing shortage, such as prevailed after the First World War. Their effect has been twofold: it has starved landlords of the income necessary to justify spending realistic sums on maintenance repair and improvement, and it has deterred landlords who did get possession from reletting. Hence, instead of assisting people wishing to rent, the overall effect was to create a dearth of accommodation at the middle and lower end of the market. The secondary effect has been that the condition of the private rented housing stock deteriorated. Generally, the legislation has not affected the luxury housing market.

The above is, of course, an over-simplification of the facts, but it does go some way to explaining why the sector is one not favoured by institutional investors. Currently the residential market can be subdivided into:

Owner-occupied houses and flats

These form the largest portion of the market. Tax incentives in the form of relief on mortgage payments provide one incentive to purchase; a track record of escalating values is another. Under English law, it is difficult for an individual to own the freehold of a flat as freehold implies ownership from below the soil up to the airspace above the infrastructure. Accordingly, flat-dwellers usually hold a long lease at a low 'ground rent'. The freehold of the block of flats may belong to an investor, but increasingly it will belong to a management company owned by the lessee. Even these arrangements give rise to management problems, and currently there are proposals to introduce a new legal estate, Commonhold, which would effectively give flat-owners a freehold interest. The Landlord and Tenant Act 1987 gives a right to long lessees to purchase the freehold interest in their flats in the event that the owner is neglecting his management obligations.

Private rented houses and flats within the Rent Act 1977

This is a dwindling sector, comprising mainly older units frequently in poor condition and possibly lacking basic amenities. To fall within the Rent Acts, the dwelling must have a rateable value of less than £750 outside London or £1,500 inside London, be let as a dwelling, and not fall within one of the exceptions listed in the Act. Under such tenancies, not only does the tenant have security for his life and his spouse's, but rents under such tenancies are restricted to 'fair rents' under s.70 of the Rent Act 1977. By definition, this excludes any figure for scarcity. Due to the legislation, such houses sell at figures between 30 and 50 per cent less than they would achieve if sold with vacant possession. The attraction of such properties to investors lies not in their income, but in the prospects of obtaining a capital gain if and when vacant possession is obtained. Such investment opportunities are attractive to the small investor, not the institutions, who in any event try to avoid properties which are politically sensitive and/or management intensive.

Private rented houses and flats under the Housing Act 1988

From mid-January 1989, new lettings within these rateable value bands fall within new legislation, namely the Housing Act 1988. Whilst tenants are granted security of tenure, rents will be at a market level. One of the government's aims in introducing this legislation was to stimulate private sector investment in housing. Indications to date are that this aim will not be met as investors continue to be concerned about the quality of an individual's covenant, and the political sensitivity of housing. However, 1989 has seen a downturn in the owner-occupation market, due partially to rising interest rates, and some potential vendors have turned to letting as an alternative.

Luxury residential units

A small part of the market are luxury flats and houses, mainly in Central London, that have rateable values above the Rent Act limits. Such units are generally free from political intervention, but like all residential property, they require sensitive and intensive management. In addition, they are frequently short lettings and thus the continuity of income is not guaranteed. They appeal only to a few specialist investors.

Other private lettings

In 1980 the government introduced different types of letting, namely shorthold and assured tenancies, in a bid to induce private investors to let houses. Shortholds, as their name suggests, were short-term agreements (between 1 and 5 years), and assured tenancies applied only to lettings by registered housing associations and housing trusts. Neither had a large impact on the quantity of units available to rent or make-up of investment portfolios. Under the Housing Act 1988 shortholds have been replaced by assured shortholds, which are broadly similar in effect. The old 1980 Act assured tenancies can no longer be created. In the budget proposals of 1988, further incentives to potential landlords were made in the form of extensions to the Business Expansion Scheme, but at the time of writing, the impact of this measure cannot be assessed. Further exclusions to the Rent Act legislation exist in the form of restricted contracts, lettings by educational bodies, and so on, but again, they form only a very small part of the market.

Council housing and Housing Associations

The first half of the twentieth century saw a large rise in the number of council housing estates, as local councils built to provide low cost accommodation. The Housing Act 1980 has, however, provided local authority tenants with the 'right to buy', normally, at a discount on market value, and the stock so held is declining. As it declines and the ownership of estates becomes fragmented, so the management difficulties faced by owning authorities is likely to rise, particularly in the case of flats where complex service charge arrangements are required.

Housing Association tenants are in some ways in a similar position to local authority tenants except that, in the case of charitable associations, the right to buy does not exist. The investment motivation of Housing Associations is different from those of most other property investors; their purpose is to provide by constructing or improving and managing the housing accommodation. Because of their aims, they do not form part of the general investment market and are therefore outside the scope of this book.

In summary, the residential sector is currently unattractive to all but the small investor prepared to take risks in the hope of achieving long-term capital gains, the high rate taxpayer seeking opportunities with special tax treatment, as under the BES (Business Expansion Scheme) and bodies with special investment aims or statutory obligations, such as Housing Associations and local authorities. Unless the current trend towards a general reduction in government intervention is accelerated, and a commitment to such a policy accepted by both sides of the political spectrum, it is hard to envisage the emergence of a large residential investment market. To this must be added the desire of most individuals to own their own house if the necessary finance is available. As it is difficult to see a reduction in bank and building society activity in the home ownership movement, the re-emergence of a private rented housing sector seems unlikely.

Leisure

In contrast to the residential field, which has seen a great decline, the investment leisure sector is growing rapidly and now attracts interest, if not commitment, by many large investors.

The question of what constitutes a leisure property can give rise to difficulty and confusion. For example, is the food court in a shopping centre a leisure use or a retail one? Again, the farm which advertises 'pick your own' and offers a cafe and children's playground, together with nature trails, may be regarded as being as much a leisure activity as an agricultural one. Apart from the difficulties of deciding whether a particular use is leisure or not, the sector is more fragmented than any other in terms of the type of locational need, infrastructure, leasing arrangement, risk and general profitability.

Some types of leisure properties are:

Theme parks/country parks
Golf courses
Hotels and public houses
Theatres, cinemas, bingo halls and casinos
Squash clubs, gymnasium and fitness centres
Swimming and leisure pools

A common theme regarding all leisure property is that demand for them arises only when people have leisure time. Their commercial viability requires both time and money. Currently leisure provision can be categorized into that which is provided on:

(a) a need basis, such as the local-authority-owned and controlled public park and playground, and the subsidized swimming pool and golf course;
(b) a demand such as the private squash club and gymnasium, the public houses and hotels, and huge leisure complexes such as Metroland.

The first category, the 'need' group, have been supplied, not on a strict investment basis, but on social criteria, and funding has come mainly from government sources, directly or indirectly.

The remaining properties, those which are commercially operated, can again be categorized into owner-occupied, and held for investments. Unlike other commercial units, leisure properties are only just beginning to feature in the portfolios of investors, having until very recently been developed and managed by either individuals or leisure specialist groups, such as the brewery and hotel chains. Why is this, and what is happening to change it?

Traditionally, leisure has been regarded as a high risk area, subject to volatility in profits and susceptibility to changing fashions (the rise and fall of cinema attendances, the brief popularity of skate-boarding). Whereas the value of an office building does not lie in the nature of the business of the occupier, leisure properties have traditionally been valued on the basis of business profitability. This method of valuation, whilst bearing similarity to that used for agricultural land, is at variance with the method used to appraise other commercial investment opportunities and is thought to have acted as a deterrent to investors.

Consequently, when new leisure developments have taken place, these have been gradually undertaken either by local authorities, or other similar bodies on a 'need' provision basis, or by companies who have a fairly high risk acceptance profile and expertise in the business proposed. Finance for such commercial undertakings has been largely internally generated.

The last five to ten years have seen more investor involvement, particularly in the development of leisure schemes associated with other forms of development, (for example, leisure/business parks and leisure/retail centres), but many leisure developers still find funds hard to obtain. For example, the proposals to convert Battersea Power Station into a leisure complex have foundered time and again due to lack of financial backing, despite the developers having a proven track record of successful leisure development.

Some of the key factors giving rise to the change have been:

(a) Planning requirements: because of conditions imposed on planning consent, many developments such as out-of-town shopping centres have only been granted if a leisure element has been incorporated within the scheme.
(b) Developers have seen that leisure elements incorporated within other developments have, if correctly planned, helped in the success of the overall scheme. This has led to a greater enthusiasm to incorporate leisure elements voluntarily.
(c) Joint leisure/office or leisure/retail schemes have the advantage of shared infrastructure such as car-parking, landscaping, servicing, and so on, thus in some cases reducing unit construction costs.
(d) With rising real incomes and increasing leisure time, the market for leisure facilities has grown dramatically. The last few years has also seen an increasing fragmentation of the market, as between age groups (for example, the emergence of the so called 'woopie' or 'well off older people' is leading to the provision of new facilities aimed at the 50+).
(e) Investors have become increasingly aware of the substantial real returns that leisure operators have obtained, although it remains true that many ventures have continued to fail. The possible inclusion of leisure property as a part of a diversified portfolio is thus no longer ruled out.

This does not mean that a landlord/tenant relationship, such as is found with other sectors, has developed. At the moment, the majority of such properties are owned, either on ground lease or freehold, by specialist companies who manage or franchise the business operation, having designed the development themselves. It is only at the funding stage that institutional interest is beginning to be shown. It is believed that unless, and until, the specialist companies change their valuation techniques for leisure properties and start to lease out properties, it is difficult to see the market developing along the lines of the office and other commercial sectors. Additionally, it is thought that a lack of hard data regarding returns and values, such as is readily available for retail, office and industrials, may be a contributing factor. If the current trends continue it remains to be seen whether leisure may become an established institutional development sector.

SUMMARY

In this chapter we have outlined some of the main characteristics of the chief types of investment properties. We have also given some details of the sectors which, whilst currently not in vogue, either have in the past warranted attention from the large investors or may, in our opinion, do so in the future. During the last decade the requirements of investors have remained largely unchanged, that is, they have sought the optimum combination of risk/return, coupled with the maximum possible liquidity. However, the proportion that are now perceived to fulfil such needs have themselves changed. In short, the market for investment properties has matured.

The retail sector, which historically has produced the best returns, is experiencing a downturn, whilst the stimulation and growth of the economy in 1987–8 led to high returns in the industrial sector. However, perhaps the hallmark of the 1980s has been the fragmentation of the markets, and with this, increasing sophistication of investment decisions regarding the placing of funds. This fragmentation, whilst it can be seen on a 'micro' level, cannot easily be detected from published statistics, which mainly produce data divided into the chief use groupings, or possibly subdivided regionally. If a true comparative picture of performance is to be obtained, data must be analysed by subsector, geographical location and lot size. No doubt with further advances in information technology, and the continued growth in property research departments and organizations, this will develop in the 1990s.

Whether the early signs of large investor interest in the leisure sector will develop, and whether data will be published enabling investment comparisons to be made, remains a question for the future. It is an area which demands research.

Chapter 4

Property investment and development, 1945–88

INTRODUCTION

Property portfolio management between 1945 and 1988 can be viewed in a number of ways. First, economic and political forces had an important influence on the policies adopted by the investing institutions and property companies. Second, direct government action affected land availability and the attractions of property as an investment. Third, technological change and innovation combined with changing public sentiment towards the use of buildings has resulted in the end product of property development changing in terms of design and performance. The period can perhaps be best appreciated by dealing with it in a series of short time periods each of which has a distinct character:

(a) 1945–50: the first post-war Labour government and the start of post-war reconstruction.
(b) 1950–64: Conservative governments and the rise of the post-war property millionaires.
(c) 1964–74: the boom years and the property crash.
(d) 1973–74: the collapse of the property market
(e) 1974–79: recovery and the rebuilding of confidence.
(f) 1979–87: the Thatcher government and the second post-war boom.
(g) 1987–88: the October 1987 stock market crash and aftermath.

1945–50: THE FIRST POST-WAR LABOUR GOVERNMENT AND THE START OF POST-WAR RECONSTRUCTION

The history of the first post-war Labour Government has a background of a war-damaged economy, ideological commitment and a tentative approach to a planned economy. The aftermath of the Second World War overshadowed the period but in many areas opportunities were available for the creation of many of the property investments which formed the portfolios of the 1960s and 1970s.

The British economy faced post-war reconstruction with virtual exhaustion of gold reserves and with many foreign assets liquidated to pay for imported goods during wartime. Britain was increasingly dependent on American finance and this is typified by the 'lend lease' policy. The government's policies were not overtly left wing by 1980s standards. For most of the period economic policy resulted in a deflationary budget with surpluses and voluntary pay restraint. This, together with a 30 per cent devaluation of the pound, avoided Keynesian methods of recovery, and although the devaluation did result in stimulation of demand, its main purpose was to reduce the cost of public borrowing. Most of the policies of the government during this period where centred on the management of demand rather than aiming towards an economy where capital provision, savings and demand would all be centrally managed.

The insurance companies and pension funds have grown in dominance from the 1960s onwards mainly due to the increasing number of people being able to provide for their retirement. This phenomenon, stemming from rising real incomes and the growth of occupational pension schemes, has resulted in institutional investors receiving £85bn of investors money in 1981 compared to £7bn in 1957 (Plender 1982). Before and immediately after the Second World War the institutions did not have the financial muscle to play the commanding role which they do today and were interested mainly in lending money on the security of property rather than participating in project control or equity growth.

In the absence of government intervention, and with capital available, the post-war development boom might have commenced before 1950 but a number of factors resulted in development being restricted during the 1945–50 period. In respect of offices in central London, demand was certainly in evidence both from American firms requiring a London base and from an increasing number of government workers employed to adminster post-war social legislation. Government policy resulted in the supply of capital being restricted whilst at the same time ideologically inspired legislation had the effect of reducing confidence in property development. Combined with this the contracting industry did not immediately have the resources to respond to the demand for new buildings and government restrictions in the form of building licences directed construction activity towards the provision of public buildings and repairs of war-damaged buildings. These restrictions had an immediate practical purpose but the post-war Labour Government also enacted legislation which had been proposed by the 1941–2 Uthwatt and Scott committees.

To understand the ideological aspects of government intervention in the land market during the 1945–50 period it is necessary to appreciate the political ideas which gave rise to the legislation. First, there is what is conventionally known as the 'compensation and betterment problem'. Central to the debate about compensation and betterment is the idea that where the state, or the community, creates increases in property values, then the benefits to private individuals should be taxed and returned to the state. The origins of this idea can be traced back to the fifteenth century. In 1427 increases in private property values resulted from public expenditure on sea defence and an Act of Parliament of that year sought to return these increases to the Crown. Political power in the hands of landowners led to recoupment of betterment being largely ignored by legislation during the eighteenth and nineteenth centuries and the 1845 Land Clauses Consolidation Act allowed compulsory purchase by the state for public works, with the landowner receiving full market value plus a 10 per cent addition to compensate him for the compulsion to sell. All betterment in terms of value created by the state's activities would remain with the landowner when the land was acquired.

There are other aspects to the compensation betterment problem. The state's role in the grant of planning consent effectively controls development values in and on the fringe of urban areas. There was, and is, a body of opinion which favours complete development land nationalisation so that the state or community can stimulate building according to its needs in the area where development is required. The Uthwatt Committee considered this and other ideas relating to the compensation/betterment problem and recommended that:

(a) An independent national commission should be created to oversee all planning administration.
(b) Local planning control should be strengthened to allow for comprehensive planning by local authorities rather than small-scale speculation.
(c) Where developed land increased in value as a result of the state's activities, a system of site value rating would be adopted whereby 75 per cent of the increase in value due to public works would be recouped.
(d) For undeveloped land it was proposed that the land should be acquired by the state at existing use value (that is, value on the assumption that no development could take place) and subsequently leased to private developers.

The Committee's recommendations perhaps seem radical in the political atmosphere of the late 1980s but at the time it was seen as a reasonable solution embodying a consensus between the ideas of the three major political parties. The proposals of the Uthwatt Committee were enacted to a degree in the legislation passed by the 1945–50 Labour Government. The 1947 Town and Country Planning Act allowed local authorities to acquire land compulsorily. Furthermore, the Act stated that development could only take place with planning permission from the county or county borough. These authorities would prepare development plans which would predict future acquisition of development land. Landowners would be compensated but would only receive existing use value rather than the value reflecting the prospect of development. The increase in value consequent upon receipt of planning consent would be taxed at 100 per cent. There were some exemptions relating to landowners who wished to develop a single plot of land but the essential point was that all development rights were to be vested in the state and there was no incentive for landowners to bring land forward for development.

This legislation in trying to impose public charges on a notionally free market had little time to become workable before a change of government. However, the essentials of the planning system established at that time survive to modern times and the ideologically inspired taxing of development land values together with state intervention in the provision of development land can be traced through to the 1975 Community Land Act and the 1976 Development Land Tax Act. For the property investment and development industry the period 1945–50 was one of confusion in the land market with the prospect of state intervention, pent-up demand for office buildings which could not be satisfied because of restrictions on the construction industry, and a funding market which was difficult to enter. With the election of the Conservative Governments of 1950 and 1951 the post-war property investment boom proceeded with restrictions largely removed by government.

1950–64: CONSERVATIVE GOVERNMENTS AND THE RISE OF THE POST-WAR PROPERTY MILLIONAIRES

When the Conservative Government was re-elected with a workable majority in 1951 legislation was enacted which first of all abolished the 100 per cent charge on increases in land value due to the prospect of development. In the 1953 Town and Country Planning Act taxable betterment was abolished and the justification given was not ideological but pragmatic; the collection of the charge was seen as impracticable. Building controls were abolished in 1954 and from that time the reconstruction process increased in intensity. The reconstruction boom was centred on City of London offices where unsatisfied demand prior to 1950 resulted in a ready-made number of tenants. Government demand for offices did not abate as the incoming Conservative Government largely left alone the social legislation of its predecessor and new growth industries based on servicing rather than manufacturing led to further increased demand. It has been estimated that by 1966 there was 140m sq. ft. of offices under construction or completed in London compared to 87m sq. ft. in 1939 (Marriott 1967).

Until 1958 bank lending was regulated by a government body, the Capital Issues Committee, and borrowers had to show that the reason for the loan was in the national interest. This, together with the advisory government curbs on lending, restricted the role of the bankers in property funding.

Funding of development schemes is essential for the developer and it was the insurance companies who largely financed developers at the beginning of the 1950s on fixed low interest mortgages and loans.

At this time it was possible to negotiate fixed price building contracts due to low inflation. The result was that most of the risks of building construction could be passed to the contractor and in a market of rising rental values the developer would benefit from any increases in rental value during the development period. It was as a result of this process that many of the post-war millionaires were created. The Conservative Government's economic policy was to regulate consumer demand by means of monetary policy, that is, manipulating interest rates rather than using fiscal policies which would impose taxes.

There remained underlying weaknesses in the British economy in spite of growth in the Gross Domestic Product (GDP) which averaged 2.8 per cent per annum between 1951 and 1973.

First, the government policy of allowing demand to increase led to balance of payments crises which were controlled by increasing interest rates. These stop/go policies meant that developers had to be particularly adept in their timing of development projects to catch the most profitable point in an economic cycle. Second, although Britain's GDP was growing, it was not growing as quickly as its European competitors. Third, Britain's share of world markets fell from 26 per cent in 1950 to an eventual 9 per cent in 1975 (Burden and Campbell 1987). It also became clear towards the end of the 1950–64 period that the reconstruction of British industry had not happened and that this problem would continue into the next decade.

From the point of view of the property investor, however, the early part of this period was one of rising office rents and profitable development. Accordingly, from 1959 onwards the institutions increasingly demanded equity shares in the developments which they funded or shares in the development companies which carried out the schemes. The increased interest of the institutions in sharing in the equity from development schemes preceded by a few years the 1962–3 recession which marked the end of the excessive tenant demand of the late 1950s. For a short period at the end of 1962 and the beginning of 1963 industrial production dropped sharply and unemployment rose accordingly. However, by this time many insurance companies had acquired a stake in a number of property companies and the legacy of this can be seen in present-day property company ownership. Apart from buying shares in property companies, institutions also become able to share in the equity from schemes by means of sale and leaseback deals which were particularly useful to developers during the credit squeezes which characterized the 1950–64 period.

Few projects during this period were a simple matter of buying a site, obtaining planning permission and selling the completed investment to an institution or retaining it by arranging a mortgage or leaseback.

Most major developments came about in a more complex way. The Euston Centre, for example, was developed by Stock Conversion after a lengthy period of site assembly. This site was acquired with great secrecy by a number of individual deals without either shareholders of Stock Conversion, the public, or the press being aware of it (Marriott 1967). Part of the expertise of the development process lies in site assembly and a major risk is that a developer may be held to ransom by the owner of the last piece of a site jigsaw. Secrecy is, therefore, in many instances vital to profitability.

Commercial developers profited from favourable economic conditions during most of the period and in the residential markets values rose steadily throughout the 1950s and continued during the 1960s. To some extent this reflects increases in real incomes during the period and social movements towards more private households rather than extended families. Greater prosperity resulted in increased public interest in life assurance and pensions and towards the mid-1960s many institutions were investing their members' money directly into property. Bankers also contributed to what was to become the boom which ended with the crash of 1974, by their keenness to lend money for speculative development.

1964–74: THE BOOM YEARS AND THE PROPERTY CRASH

One of the main features of this period is the constant increase of institutional funds into property investment, but continuing economic problems fell into mainly two categories. First, the modernisation of UK industry did not happen and capital was invested in other sectors including property. Second, perhaps as a result of this, Britain's share of world manufactured exports continued to decline. Economic growth continued during the 1964–74 period but the balance of payments problem continued. When Labour took office in 1964 there was a £400m deficit on current account and capital continued to flow out of the country. In 1967 a devaluation of the pound by 14 per cent, together with public spending cuts and tax increases, helped to engineer a budget surplus by 1969.

In spite of long and short-term economic problems for the property investor and developer, there were many opportunities during this period. An improved motorway network and rising living standards led to warehouse development on the urban fringes and town centre redevelopment being promoted by local authorities. It is during this period that many of the typical 1960s shopping centres were constructed of monolithic concrete construction, open to the elements, and with little to attract shoppers into the centre other than the necessity to shop. The Elephant and Castle shopping development in London and the Bull Ring in Birmingham are two such examples, but there are many more. Many of these investments are today either being refurbished or redeveloped.

The early part of this period until 1968 was characterized by increasing interest being shown in funding property investment by both the secondary banks and the financial institutions. When inflation began to increase in 1968 and share prices began to fall, interest in property investment hardly faltered. Property was seen as a secure long-term investment which would always grow in real terms, whereas the stock market was likely to be influenced to a greater degree by the weaknesses of the British economy. Institutional interest in property investment is shown in Table 4.1 which shows the percentage of insurance company and pension fund financial assets placed in property during the period 1966–75.

Table 4.1, particularly when viewed from the standpoint of the Pension Funds, shows the decline in the attractiveness of fixed mortgages and other loans compared to direct property investment and equity participation. It should be noted that with Corporation Tax appearing in 1965 it became more attractive for Pension Funds to invest into property by means of direct funding. In order to avoid double taxation, Property Companies from 1965 were subject to Corporation Tax which made their shares less attractive than direct property investment by the institutions. The options for a developer seeking finance were either to secure short and long-term funding from a Pension Fund or Insurance Company by means of a package deal, or fund the development short term by a loan from a bank before disposing of the investment when let. The willingness of the banks to lend money for property development during this period was a major contributory factor in the property boom which ended in 1974.

By 1970 when Labour left office inflation was 6 per cent per annum, a substantial rise which reflected continuing long-term economic problems. It was also expensive for developers to borrow money short term from the secondary banks. Interest would normally be charged at a margin above bank rate and throughout the later part of the period from 1971 to 1974 bank rate rose from 5 per cent to 13 per cent. Developers were content to borrow at high rates because rises in rental values based on historical evidence showed that even if predicted interest charges exceeded market

Table 4.1 Growth of institutional property involvement, 1966–75 (%)

	1966	1967	1968	1969	1970	1971	1972	1973	1974	1975
Insurance Cos financial assets in land property and ground rents	10	10	10	11	12	13	12	14	16	17
Insurance Cos financial assets in loans and mortgages	16	16	16	16	16	15	13	13	13	11
Pension Funds financial assets invested in land property & ground rents	10	10	10	13	14	12	11	19	21	33
Pension Funds financial assets invested in loans and mortgages	21	17	14	15	12	9	7	9	8	9

rents at the start of a development period, by the time the building was complete rental levels would have risen to allow an adequate surplus of rent above interest, thus making the development profitable. From the bank's viewpoint, so long as rental levels kept rising they could arrange apparently secure loans with property companies at high rates of interest. Both parties, bankers and developers, together with the institutions, were caught up with the property investment euphoria of the time and the risks inherent in a speculative boom were not fully appreciated.

Before considering further the causes and effects of the eventual crash of 1974 it is worthwhile reviewing the effect of government policy in this period. Economic policy between 1964 and 1970, as we have already seen, was concerned with balance of payments crises leading to devaluation and public spending cuts. The Labour Government during this period did not intervene in the capital markets and the provision of industrial and enterprise capital was left to the market forces. Market forces suggested that areas other than productive industry, notably property, provided a more profitable and secure avenue for investment funds. The Conservatives took office in 1970 with the balance of payments in surplus. A tight budgetary policy was followed at first but an expansionist policy from 1972 onwards was designed to stimulate growth in the economy. The boost was considered necessary due to continued rises in unemployment and a number of bankruptcies of major firms. Accordingly monetary policy was relaxed, income taxes were reduced and public expenditure plans expanded. Bank rate was reduced to 5 per cent in 1971 and new rates for bank lending increased flexibility in lending policy. A credit explosion followed which allowed developers to commit themselves to developments which were not viable without continued rent inflation. Other factors which made property investment attractive were the ban on new office development over 10,000 sq.ft. in central London ('the Brown Ban') without an office development permit, thus creating a severe undersupply of sites for development. Rent review periods eventually shortened to five and sometimes three years due to strong tenant demand. Government policy therefore combined with market conditions to fuel a speculative boom in property investment. In the banking sector it was not only the 'fringe' or secondary banks who were lending money to developers. Fraser (1984) has estimated that, in the period 1971–3, bank lending by secondary banks to property companies was less than one-third of the finance provided by the major banks.

Government policy was not only confined to economic issues during the 1964–74 period. The 1967 Land Commission Act represented the second attempt by a post-war Labour Government to control the supply of development land and collect a betterment levy from landowners who benefited by increased land values as a result of obtaining a planning consent. The Commission lasted for three years until it was abolished by the incoming Conservative Government which was elected in 1970. In each year of operation the commission had operated at a deficit which was over £1.5m for the year ending 31 March 1971, but the lack of political consensus over this issue meant that any organisation as radical as the Commission was unlikely to survive a change of government. Certainly the abolition of the Commission by the Conservative Government was welcomed by developers and landowners but it is likely that it only added more confidence to an already over-confident market.

1973–4: THE COLLAPSE OF THE PROPERTY MARKET

Much has been written about the economic problems which resulted in the stock market and property investment market collapse and it is generally accepted that this started in December 1973. Economic problems were compounded in 1972 by a worsening Labour situation, increasing wage inflation combined with government attempts at income controls, and restrictions on loans imposed by the Bank of England. Inflation steadily rose through 1972 into 1973 which led to increasing wage demands from the trade unions. World trade was growing fast at this time and price rises in important commodities resulted from supply shortages. The most significant economic event was certainly the rise in oil prices of 400 per cent in 1973–4 which led to balance of payments problems and additional costs for industry. In November 1973 Minimum Lending Rate increased to 13 per cent and the strong consumer spending which is an important factor in any boom could no longer be supported. The consumer boom had been built on the back of durable goods and retail prices had risen by 6 per cent in the year to 1970, 10 per cent in the year to 1971 and 6 per cent in the year to 1972 (*Lloyds Bank Review*, January 1973, no.107).

The result of high interest rates, the ending of the consumer boom, increasing commodity prices and rising inflation, was that few development schemes were contemplated and many of those in the course of construction were no longer viable. Furthermore, building costs at the time were rising at 25–30 per cent per annum. Developers who had borrowed money on the expectation of continuing rent increases were under pressure to repay loans on half finished buildings which were now unlikely to be let as companies expansion plans were curtailed by rising operational costs and interest rates. 1973 also marked the end of the bull market in equities which had lasted from January 1970.

Other measures taken by the Conservative Government such as the freeze on commercial rents in existing buildings from January 1972, together with radical land and betterment proposals by the Labour opposition, led to a reduction in confidence which worsened the prospects for property investors.

In December 1973 the Conservative Chancellor of the Exchequer, Anthony Barber, announced the imposition of a tax which would be paid on the first letting of commercial or industrial property. This tax known as Development Gains Tax, was calculated in a complicated manner but was intended, like betterment taxes before it, to impose a charge on the beneficiaries of the receipt of planning consent. If the developer had paid a price for the land which reflected the eventual planning consent for development no tax would be payable but where a speculative gain had been made the tax would bite. Part of the gain was also to be taxed under capital gains and therefore in the tax computation the capital gain element had to be separated from the development gain element. The imposition of these taxes caused uncertainty in the property market and did nothing to help the perilous position of many property investors and developers at the time. The general election of February 1974 was fought against a background of industrial unrest, economic uncertainty and a falling property and stock market. Few property deals received publicity and it was difficult to perceive a market in any sense of the word. The Labour Government which took office in 1974 almost immediately published a White Paper, 'Land', which described the Community Land Scheme and Development Land Tax provisions which would form the party's third post-war attempt to impose some control over the supply of development land and tax betterment gains.

Public sentiment in the mid-1970s was influenced by the perceived ugliness of modern buildings, and often their emptiness. There was a lack of empathy with the role of the property developer. Certain central London buildings, such as Centre Point, were cited in the press as examples of the wastefulness of much modern development and the redevelopment of many town centres was similarly not well received. The Labour Party's policy to attack property speculators was certainly popular with the public and statutory measures to restrain developers' activities as well as to tax apparently unearned income appeared to receive a large measure of public support.

The property market collapse led to a small number of public property companies going to the wall. Guardian Property failed in 1974 with Town and Commercial and Amalgamated Investment and Property both failing in 1974. Lipton and Stern both went into liquidation in 1974. Those public property companies which did not fail were the overwhelming majority of those quoted on the stock market. They consolidated their investment portfolios and waited for better times. Some property companies such as Slough Estates benefited greatly from owning investments in locations which would be profitable in virtually any economic circumstances and this type of low-geared company was well placed to avoid the worst effects of a recession. The Bank of England adopted a policy of supporting those secondary banks which would otherwise have failed and a 'lifeboat' was arranged whereby the cash withdrawn from the secondary banks by depositors was returned to them by the major banks where it had previously been deposited.

The immediate causes of the property market crash were therefore imprudent investment on the basis of consumer credit and optimistic investment commitments resulting from a belief that rent levels would rise at an increasing rate. Domestic credit rose from just over £2bn in 1971–2 to over £8bn in 1973–4 (*Lloyds Bank Review*, April 1977, no.124) and this underpinned the property boom. Long-term problems in the British economy dating from the 1950s can also be seen as significant contributing factors. These factors were low investment in industry, slow productivity growth in comparison with other European countries, and deflationary policies which supported the pound but impeded exports.

1974–9: RECOVERY AND THE REBUILDING OF CONFIDENCE

The Labour Government of 1974 took office at a time of economic trauma. The stock market continued to fall only until January 1975 but the prices of the quoted property companies continued to fall dramatically. Recovery was erratic and inflation in retail prices reached a peak of 24.9 per cent p.a. in 1975. From October 1976 to October 1977, however, Minimum Lending Rate fell from 15 per cent to 5 per cent, and as very little new development had been completed since the crash the opportunity existed for a revival of the property investment and development markets. The rent freeze was abolished from 1975 and it was clear that there was substantial tenant demand in certain areas of the economy. However, net annual investment by the Insurance Companies and Pension Funds into property showed an appreciable decrease in this period and in 1979 property amounted to 10.6 per cent of all Insurance Company acquisitions and 11.1 per cent in respect of Pension Funds. This compares with equivalent figures of 16.2 per cent and 15.5 per cent in 1975. It is ironical, however, that when property is analysed, not as a percentage of acquisitions, but as a percentage of a portfolio, a more discernible trend emerges. As a percentage of the portfolios of Insurance Companies and Pension Funds, property showed a decline from over 16 per cent in 1974 to just over 15 per cent in 1977, but the period from 1977 to 1979 showed an increase to over 18 per cent. In the period 1977 to 1979 property returns began to benefit from the lack of development activity resulting from the 1974 crash and the values of the existing stock benefited from the lack of new development on the market.

The policy of the Labour Government towards land reflected the previous attempts to control the supply of development land and to collect betterment consequent upon the receipt of planning consent. The 1975 Community Land Act had complicated provisions, but if it had stayed as a statute for long enough all land for development in Great Britain would have passed through public hands before development took place. In England and Scotland local authorities were charged with operating the scheme and in Wales a new organisation, The Land Authority for Wales, was set up to administer the Act and to collect betterment.

The Community Land scheme did not succeed in England mainly due to the lack of expertise of local authorities in carrying out the new role, and various concessions to landowners such as the right for a pension fund to develop its own land without leasing it back from a local authority. Also, economic problems, and particularly the need to reduce the public sector borrowing requirement, resulted in the scheme being underfunded in England and Scotland. The understandable reaction of landowners was a reluctance to bring land forward for development and wait for a change of government. By 1979 the Community Land account showed a deficit of £33m and many local authorities showed little interest in operating the legislation for either practical or political reasons. The Land Authority for Wales managed to run an organization which essentially speculated in development land on behalf of the state. A surplus of £800,000 was shown in 1978–9. The availability of compulsory purchase powers to force landowners to part with land was only used sparingly by this Authority as its approach was, and continues to be, pragmatic and land management lead. It is perhaps because of this approach that it was allowed to continue as a catalyst in the supply of development land in Wales by the Conservative Government which took office in 1979 and quickly abolished the Community Land Act.

1979–87: THE THATCHER GOVERNMENT AND THE SECOND POST-WAR BOOM

The government which was elected in 1979 adopted a policy of tight monetary constraint, promotion of privatization, reduction of public spending and constraints on the activities of trade unions. The control of inflation was seen as a major policy initiative, and in 1979 inflation was running at the high level of 19.69 per cent per annum for wages (Darlow 1983) and 17.2 per cent per annum for retail prices. North Sea Oil had begun to flow during the last month of the outgoing Labour Government and this helped the balance of payments. In the early years of the period up to 1983 company liquidations increased and industrial output fell by 11 per cent, far more than Britain's European competitors. Unemployment increased from 1.2m to 3.2m until 1983 whilst the public sector borrowing requirement declined from 5.4 per cent of GDP in 1978–9 to 3.4 per cent in 1982–3. By 1983 inflation had fallen to 5 per cent and the result of government policies was that, in some areas of the economy, productivity had increased: coal-mining is perhaps one apposite example. The UK manufacturing base had been undermined by the government's tight monetary policy and competition from world markets so that by 1983 the United Kingdom was showing a trade deficit on manufactured goods for the first time since the 1860s. There are, therefore, lingering doubts about the underlying healthiness of the British economy, particularly as production of North Sea Oil declines in the future. The stock market, until

October 1987, showed a steady long-term rise and this strong equity market has been underpinned by continuing low inflation for much of the period. From 1980 average output per hour and output per person in manufacturing industry has continued to rise whilst numbers employed have continued to fall. The strong bull market with low interest rates lead to companies, particularly in the financial and services sectors, being able to expand. Retailers showed confidence in growth in future retail sales, boosted by easy consumer credit.

Great Britain has also experienced significant growth in the 'high tech' industries based on the new technology and this demand, together with a new use classes order, has led to a substantial number of developments to cater for companies involved with information technology. The boom in retail spending has prompted those institutions with confidence in the market, notably life assurance funds, to invest heavily in the provision of modern shopping malls. Norwich Union's funding of the Bentalls Centre in Kingston upon Thames is one such example. Although the insurance companies have generally maintained their commitment to property investment throughout the period, however, the pension funds attracted by stock market opportunities have reduced the amount of property in their portfolios. Indeed, in 1987 Pension Funds were net disinvestors in property.

Economic conditions and the emergence of domestic and foreign banks as major property lenders led to substantial development taking place in the City of London where, following the 'big bang', dealing floors were increasingly demanded by tenants who also wished to occupy buildings which would deal with the new technology. Increasing prosperity, at least for those people in employment, has resulted in an increase in leisure parks and leisure allied to shopping. Out of town shopping, waterside housing and marina construction is a feature of the 1980s development market.

1987–8: THE OCTOBER 1987 STOCK MARKET CRASH AND AFTERMATH

The stock market at the time of writing is recovering from the fall of October 1987 and there are signs that the institutional investors are regarding property with fresh enthusiasm. Opportunities still exist for developers but at the time of writing interest rates are rising to make development opportunities appear less attractive. This factor, combined with declining growth in consumer spending, may mean that the property market is about to enter a cycle of consolidation after the large number of retail, high tech and office developments in recent years.

Not surprisingly, since 1979 the compensation/betterment problem has received scant regard from government. The Community Land Act was quickly repealed but The Land Authority for Wales has been reorganized under new legislation and performs effectively as a development catalyst in the principality. Urban Development Corporations, the largest of which is Teesside Development Corporation, have been set up to provide conditions in formerly depressed areas which will attract private investment. The emphasis remains on public initiative used to stimulate the private sector to create jobs. The ideological land and property issues which have exercised the minds of successive governments for many years are, since 1979, no longer on the political agenda and at present appear unlikely to reappear.

Chapter 5

Investors and portfolio returns

INTRODUCTION

The first question to be asked when considering the measurement of portfolio performance is 'measurement for whom?'. A property portfolio may be held for investment, speculation, for charitable purposes or for occupation. From the occupier's viewpoint the degree of satisfaction with building performance is often difficult to express in monetary terms, particularly for owner-occupiers. When a property portfolio is considered from the standpoint of the business occupier, it is not the return on the property investment which is the most important factor but the contribution of the property portfolio to the profitability of the business enterprise. From the multiplicity of individuals and organizations concerned with property performance, a classification can, however, be attempted. In this chapter we look at the calculation of return from the standpoint of the investor whose decision-making process is dominated by the need to achieve an adequate return. We look first at the background to investor's requirements, then at the measures used to calculate return.

THE INSTITUTIONAL INVESTOR

Pension funds

Pension funds exist to invest contributions from their members to produce sufficient cash flow to pay their members pensions upon retirement. The management of a pension fund is in the hands of the trustees of the fund and the power of the members over the activities of the trustees is determined by the terms of the trust deed. This will normally provide for employees of the organization or company associated with the fund to be appointed to the board of trustees with whom the investment policy for the fund rests. In deciding their investment policy the board of trustees are in an unusual position in the investment market. Most investors maximize their return and their investment policy is geared to this end.

With a public company higher returns will normally be reflected in increased dividends payable to the shareholders, a rise in the share price and greater capacity for the company to borrow further capital or promote a successful rights issue. There is no ceiling on investment performance. A pension fund cannot be perceived in this way as each fund is investing members' contributions and the necessary monetary value of these contributions at a later date can be accurately calculated. The calculation encompasses the ages of the present fund members, the probable future age structure of the firm or industry associated with the fund and the probable wage rates of retiring members in the future on which their pensions will be based. It is this essentially 'charitable' nature of pension fund investment that has resulted in the government allowing pension funds almost complete tax exempt status.

From the above analysis it might be expected that pension funds should take a radically different view of the investment markets than other investors. It might be expected that their investment policy would be governed not by the criteria of maximum return for acceptable risk but by the requirements to pay a certain level of pensions at a date in the future. Indeed, if the required return from pension fund investments in order to pay future pensions was below the level of return which could be obtained in the investment market, one might expect the fund's investment policy to be primarily concerned with risk minimization rather than return maximization.

In reality an examination of pension funds attitudes to investment return shows them to be chiefly concerned with maximizing returns in the short term. A fund's typical definition of the 'short term' may vary between one and three years. It is interesting to reflect why this should be.

First, the attitude of the pension fund investor towards performance seems to be influenced by the nature of the investment market rather than the eventual requirements of the fund's members. It would appear to be of little concern to boards' trustees if returns from investments outperform the requirements of the fund although this may lead to problems for management. The overwhelming proportion of pension fund investment is placed in equities and pension funds currently own some 40 per cent of all stock on the London stock market. A combination of low inflation and a prolonged bull market until October 1987 resulted in the funds concentrating on the equity markets, producing substantial surpluses over liabilities.

Property investment, which is seen as illiquid, difficult to value and expensive to manage by many funds, is often considered as a long-term investment in comparison with equities. Analysis of returns from property investment often concentrates on short periods and, not surprisingly, property has been seen in the past to perform badly in comparison with the competing investment media. Figures published by the *Financial Times*

(17 December 1986) show that in 1985 returns from property investments averaged 7.4 per cent, compared to 20.4 per cent from UK equities based on the *Financial Times All Share Index*. The attitude of the pension fund trustees when faced with such data seems to be that if high returns are available from highly liquid investments such as equities, why should they not claim them? The management reaction to investment surpluses, referred to earlier, has been in many cases to withdraw surplus funds to provide finance for company expansion or to fund a redundancy programme. There has historically been no reason for pension fund trustees to be concerned with surpluses produced by the fund although the situation changed after the March 1986 budget when the chancellor imposed a 5 per cent ceiling for pension fund surpluses. Fund trustees have a choice if surpluses exceed 5 per cent of the total fund value. Improved benefits can be offered to members, members contributions to the fund can be reduced, or excess capital can be withdrawn from the fund. This final choice attracts a tax penalty of 4 per cent. If the pension fund continues to produce a surplus above 5 per cent then the tax exemption on that part of the investment income would no longer apply.

Life insurance companies

Investment incentives for life insurance companies are broadly comparable with those of pension funds. Payment liabilities for the life funds can be accurately predicted by actuarial tables. The general funds cannot be regarded as investors in the same sense as the life funds as they relate to possible claims from policy-holders during a short period of time, usually not exceeding twelve months.

The life insurance companies have a long tradition of investing in property and in recent years the trend has been for them to invest a greater percentage of their assets in property than the pension funds. Why should this be seen to be continuing? Part of the answer lies in the management structure of the organizations. Insurance companies are generally well provided with in-house expertise in property investment. Many, such as Royal Life Assurance plc, take direct responsibility for decisions on property investment whereas the large pension funds often entrust investment decisions to outside managers who have little understanding of property but a great understanding of money markets. Second, where a pension fund is based on an old established industry, the future is harder to predict. The fund may become mature in the medium term if an industry is declining and this may mitigate against investments in property which is essentially long term. Also the new unit linked form of insurance policy has meant that the insurance companies are looking for property to perform in the short term rather than serving endowment policies by long-term income growth. In the context of property performance and investment returns, however, it is necessary for returns from equities, property and gilts to be capable of analysis and comparison.

Property companies

It is convenient to consider property companies in two categories; property investment companies and property development companies. Property investment companies acquire rent-producing buildings or development sites to augment their property portfolios. Property development companies acquire development sites or buildings for refurbishment, or redevelopment; they can let and sell the completed investment to a long-term investor. There are many differences between the two types of companies but the main one in terms of performance measurement is that property investment companies have a long-term interest in acquisition whereas property development companies exist to secure short-term monetary gains. Many development companies are subsidiaries under the overall umbrella of a large property investment company. For example, Brixton Estate plc is a property investment company whereas the subsidiary Brixton Development is a property development company. Many large firms of contractors have set up autonomous property investment and development companies either involved in long-term investment or developing, letting and selling. Examples are Taylor Woodrow and John Laing who were both major contractors before entering the property market.

From the point of view of a property investment company, a higher return on investment would be expected from a development than from the purchase of a ready-made investment property to take account of the risk of property development. In practice, the market for prime property investments has for many years been dominated by the institutions who have had the financial muscle and tax advantages to outbid most property companies. Low geared as the institutions are, they have a distinct advantage compared to the relatively-highly-geared property company. Today with innovative funding methods the larger property companies can often fund property developments from their own resources or sometimes by a successful rights issue. Smaller companies, however, rely on the institutional market and the banks to provide finance. The various ways in which this finance can be provided are considered in Chapter 11 but in funding property development, the institutions will be concerned with the returns from property in comparison with the other investment media. Although the property companies may not therefore be directly involved in investing in government or other stock, they are influenced by its performance in as much as it influences the institutions' attitude towards investment in property.

Other investors

Apart from the institutional investors, other individuals and organizations invest in property and this investment is indirect where the property provides some degree of personal utility. The freehold ownership of a dwelling house in the south–east of England has been a vehicle for many individuals to experience exceptionally high returns on investment. It is clear, however, that the necessity for most individuals to own a dwelling for occupation has resulted in most of those gains being unrealized. A number of property bonds have invested in the housing market in central London and have benefited by capital gains in the short term (up to three years). In some cases it has been possible for managers to invest in the futures market in central London residential property by agreeing to sell dwellings before the purchase is completed. Business occupiers also frequently invest in property at the same time as trading from it. Department stores may participate in profits from a development scheme as well as taking on the role of anchor tenant.

THE DATA REQUIRED

To evaluate the performance of a property investment the important factors are the valuation of the property and the income flow. In the case of a property investment, accumulation of data is a simple matter of historic income flows and valuations. Predicting the future when an investment or development site is about to be acquired is another matter indeed. The data available for property investments varies from that available for the competing investment media. Each property investment in a portfolio is unique, it may be valued infrequently and this valuation is rarely subjected to the test of an attempted sale. Conversely gilts and equities may be subject to substantiated capital value changes on each working day and each day their values may change. Furthermore, it is usually extremely difficult to predict rental income into the future in the case of a property investment, whereas with a government stock the yield is printed on the certificate and will not vary. The capital value of the stock will vary and this results in varying real returns over time. Shares quoted on the stock market also carry unpredictable patterns of income growth and the level of dividend provided to shareholders is a matter for management to decide. It cannot often be accurately predicted when shares are acquired. For those investors, such as the institutions, who invest in property, gilts and equities, some method of comparing returns is essential.

Historic performance is of great importance in enabling an investor to assess the competing investments in a portfolio. Of equal importance, however, is the use of performance measurement techniques to predict likely future returns in certain categories of investment. In this way, investments can be grouped together and overall returns calculated. For example, data relevant to stock market equities is provided by the *FT Industrial Ordinary Index*, the *FT Actuaries All Share Index* and the *FE SE 100 Index*. In the case of property investments the major firms of chartered surveyors publish indices relating to yields in respect of different types of property and compare these property investments with base rate and long-dated gilts on one graphical presentation.

METHODS OF MEASUREMENT

It is important first of all to appreciate the distinction between yield and return. Chapter 2 deals with various types of yield, all of which are used in the valuation of property investments. The measurement of a return seeks to measure the amount of capital or rental increase from an investment purchase (or valuation) over time and, as will be seen below, there are various ways of calculating this.

The techniques so far described to assess return are unsatisfactory in one form or another and can be criticized on the grounds of incompleteness or inaccuracy. What is required is a method which can accurately measure performance over time and which can be used for all types of investment media. Decisions reached by pension fund trustees, based on the respective performance measurement, must be accurate enough to allow management to reach informed decisions.

Pension fund managers employed as outside consultants will also find that their performance is closely monitored by Trustees and the method of measurement must allow for a fair assessment to be made of a manager's performance. A substantial amount of research has been undertaken on the subject of performance measurement mainly into two ways of measuring performance – money-weighted rates of return (MWRR) and time-weighted rates of return (TWRR). Initially a broad categorization can be attempted.

Money-weighted rate of return

The term 'money weighted' can be regarded as a generic description applied to any calculation where income and expenditure are discounted over time to arrive at either an internal rate of return or a net present value. The return arrived at is a return for the whole period which can, if necessary, be broken down into quarterly or even weekly periods.

Time-weighted rate return

Time-weighted rates of return are calculated every time that a cash flow occurs. Every time rent is received on a property or expenditure is undertaken, the return to the point in time is calculated, and is regarded as the return for that period. Subsequently, the returns may be chain-linked together to give a total time-weighted rate of return which may be compared with a money-weighted rate of return.

Some commentators seek to distinguish between MWRR and discounted cash flow (DCF) but it is more helpful to regard MWRR as a generic term where money is discounted and DCF as a more precise tool where flows of money are discounted to precisely reflect the timing of income and expenditure. An example will illustrate the technique which can be employed (see Example 5.1).

Example 5.1 Calculation of MWRR and DCF

A freehold property was purchased for £700,000 at the beginning of year one and at the end of year three was valued at £850,000. The property is let and in the first two years income of £50,000 per annum net is payable quarterly in advance. Rent payable in the third year increased to £60,000 per annum net. To calculate the return a table is constructed as follows:

Year	Rent per annum (£)	Capital value (£)
1	50,000	700,000
2	50,000	750,000
3	60,000	850,000

As rent is received quarterly in advance the DCF (regarded as a precise form of money-weighted return) will be drawn up which will show rent receipts being discounted per quarter. As capital value changes can only be substantiated annually, it would not be appropriate to discount cash flows for any shorter period of time than quarterly. With equities and gilts where capital value changes daily this would not be the case. The DCF will be as follows and the quarterly rate of return 'r' will be that which can be used in the following formula:

$$C = \frac{R1}{} + \frac{R2}{(1+r)} + \frac{R3}{(1+r)^2} + \frac{R4}{(1+r)^3} + \frac{Rn}{(1+r)^{n-1}} + \frac{V}{(1+r)^n}$$

where C = is the initial value of the investment
   r = rate of quarterly return
   R = rental income per quarter ($R1$ = 1st quarter; Rn = nth quarter)

V = final value of the investment property at the end of the measurement period

It will be appreciated that what is to be calculated is the value of r which will result in all the cash flows in the future, when discounted, being equal to the original outlay. In this way the true return from the investment can be calculated. Using the above figure the example will proceed as follows:

$$£700,000=12,500+ \frac{12,500}{(1+r)} + \frac{12,500}{(1+r)^2} + \frac{12,500}{(1+r)^3} + \frac{12,500}{(1+r)^4} + \frac{12,500}{(1+r)^5} + \frac{12,500}{(1+r)^6}$$

$$+ \frac{12,500}{(1+r)^7} + \frac{15,000}{(1+r)^8} + \frac{15,000}{(1+r)^9} + \frac{15,000}{(1+r)^{10}} + \frac{15,000}{(1+r)^{11}} + \frac{850,000}{(1+r)^{12}}$$

It is assumed that the final capital value figure of £850,000 is received at the end of the period and is thus discounted appropriately. With rent received quarterly in advance the final rental payment is discounted to the start of the last quarter.

If 0.034 is substituted for r in the above formula, it will be seen that the right-hand side of the equation approximates to the left. Calculations such as these are more easily performed by means of a computer, particularly where longer periods are required for measurement. The quarterly internal rate of return (IRR) is thus seen to be 3.4 per cent and the annual rate is therefore calculated as $(1.034)^4 - 1 = 0.1431$ which is 14.31 per cent per annum. The total money-weighted rate of return over the three-year period is $(1.1431)^3 - 1 = 0.494 = 49.4$ per cent.

As the above formula can only be satisfactorily worked with a computer, more approximate methods have been devised. One of which, suggested by some commentators uses the formula:

$$R = \frac{V1 - V0 + C}{V0}$$

where R = total return over three years
$V1$ = capital value at end of period
$V0$ = capital value at start of period
C = rental income in period

The calculation would be as follows:

$$R = \frac{850,000 - 700,000 + 160,000}{700,000} = 0.442$$

MWRR = 44.2 per cent over 3 years

Thus, with no element of discounting, a lower return results and this method of calculating return would not be preferred to the more precise method of discounting per quarter.

Example 5.2 Calculation of TWRR

It will be remembered that the time-weighted rate of return required a calculation to be performed each time that there is a cash flow. It was seen above that using the formula:

$$R = \frac{V1 - V0 + C}{V0}$$

for the whole of the time period results in an approximate MWRR, but if the formula is used per quarter, and the results for each quarter are linked together, the results would be a time-weighted rate of return as follows:

Year 1

1st quarter	$\dfrac{12,500}{700,000}$	= 0.0178 = 1.78%
2nd quarter	$\dfrac{12,500}{700,000}$	= 0.0178 = 1.78%
3rd quarter	$\dfrac{12,500}{700,000}$	= 0.0178 = 1.78%
4th quarter	$\dfrac{50,000 + 12500}{700,000}$	= 0.0893 = 8.93%

The total time-weighted return in the first year under consideration is therefore calculated to be:

$$(1.0178 \times 1.0178 \times 1.0178 \times 1.0893) - 1 = 0.1485 = 14.85\%$$

This figure compares with an average 14.31 per cent per annum using the DCF technique.

CRITIQUE AND APPLICATION

One of the major differences between money-weighted and time-weighted rates of return is in the treatment of changes in capital value. The DCF illustrated in Example 5.1 only takes into account capital values at the start and end of the measurement period, whereas using a time-weighted return, all changes in capital value can be reflected. Precise techniques do not accord with valuations which are often not tested by market forces, but it can be said that discounted cash flow techniques certainly value the present worth of a flow of income. Furthermore, the income valued has been actually received by the investor, whereas capital value changes in property investments are unrealized unless the property is sold.

There is no reason why returns from property should not be expressed in such a way as to make them comparable with gilts and equities and where capital value changes each day it is a simple matter to calculate daily return and subsequently link the return together to give an overall return. Frost and Hager (1986), writing for the Institute and the Faculty of Actuaries, suggest that assessments of pension fund performance are best made by the linked internal rate of return method, whereby money-weighted rates of return are calculated on a quarterly basis and subsequently linked together to give a time-weighted rate of return for the year. It is submitted that in the case of an individual property investment, the discounted cash flow technique which precisely measures the value of income flows over a period is the more appropriate measure of performance. This is particularly the case where a property investment is subject to refurbishment during the performance period. The rental income during the time of refurbishment will be reduced according to the timing of the expenditure.

During the summation, therefore, a subtraction representing expenditure will be discounted in the usual way. It will be appreciated that, for property performance to be precisely measured by DCF, every type of cost must be included in the calculation. Without these inclusions, the investment cannot be compared properly with other investment media. Management costs in particular can be underestimated and rental voids must be allowed for, particularly if the period of measurement stretches far into the future.

DCF techniques give a true picture of return but they have been criticized in recent years as it is felt that they give a distorted view of fund management performance. The management of pension funds is a highly competitive field with pension fund trustees taking an increasingly critical view of outside managers. If the performance of a fund is calculated by DCF alone, it is difficult to assess the success of the management. Inputs into a pension fund by future beneficiaries are not within the control of the pension fund manager and, if a manager is fortunate enough to receive money for investment when market returns are about to increase, the subsequent high return is not necessarily a result of his expertise. A simple example can illustrate this, and also the differences in calculating returns from a fund compared with calculating returns from an individual property investment. The usual method of calculating the money-weighted rate of return of a fund is by the use of the formula:

$$m_1 (1 + i)n + C_j (1 + i)j = m_2$$

where i = rate of return
m_1 = initial market value of the portfolio
m_2 = final market value of portfolio at time n
C_j = contribution of new monies at time j before the end of the period
n = number of periods
j = time at which injection of money takes place

This method of calculating MWRR for a fund benefits from its simplicity as it relates the growth that has resulted in an injection of cash to a final value of the fund. The formula cannot be used to analyse a property investment where rent represents earnings from the property, not an investment into it. However, using the above formula for a fund holding investments, an example can be prepared. It is assumed that two funds are subject to the same management policy and they have assets of £2,000 at the beginning of a year. These assets, due to market conditions, fall to £1,500 by the middle of the year. Returns improve during the second half of the year and both funds double their assets.

However, if it is assumed that fund number 1 receives a cash injection of £500 half-way through the year, the calculation of money-weighted return gives very different results as can be seen in Example 5.3.

Example 5.3

For fund number 1 with the cash injection the calculation is:
    £2,000 $(1+r)$ + 500 $(1+r)$ 0.5 = £4,000
    $r = 0.675 = 67.5\%$

For the fund number 2 without the cash injection, the calculation is:
    £2,000 $(1+r)$ = £3,000
    $r = 0.5 = 50\%$

On this evidence it would appear that the management of fund 1 has been more successful. However, if returns are calculated each time there is a cash flow, and subsequently chain-linked together to give a total time-weighted return, the results are as follows:

$$(1+r) = \frac{1,500}{2,000} \times \frac{4,000}{2,000} \quad r = 0.5 = 50\%$$

For the second fund the calculation is:

$$(1+r) = \frac{1,500}{2,000} \times \frac{3,000}{2,000} \quad r = 50\%$$

Using the time-weighting, the cash injection for fund number 1 does not distort the calculation if comparisons are to be made between fund managers.

Most pension funds receive injections of cash during the course of the year and these cannot normally be made subject to individual calculations to produce an overall TWRR. However, the principle of TWRR is that the timing of injections of cash should not influence judgements on a manager's performance.

In the case of property investment, decisions on such matters as refurbishment, lettings and marketing are in the hands of the property manager, and it can be argued that there is no reason why DCF should not form the basis of performance assessment both of the manager and the property. As has been seen above, however, it is quite possible to apply TWRR to property investments for comparison purposes so long as potential inaccuracies and uncertainties in the basic data are understood.

TARGET RATES OF RETURN

It is conventional to compare property with other investment media and indices in terms of internal rate of return. The most-often-quoted comparison is the gross redemption yield from government stock which is assumed to be a riskless investment. The gross redemption yield in respect of a government bond is calculated in exactly the same way as internal rates of return when applied to property. A rate of interest is used which discounts the redemption price of the bond and interim interest payments so that they exactly equal the current price of the bond. The market has conventionally applied a 2 per cent premium to property investment to take account of the risk involved in property when compared to government stock. It is true that interest payments on government stock are underwritten by the government, whereas rental payments depend upon the willingness and ability of a tenant to pay rent. However, some commentators, notably Fraser (1984, 1985 and 1986) have challenged the assumption that property should have a 2 per cent premium over gross redemption yield on government stock. It has been pointed out that, in terms of volatility, property investment compares well with government gilts which are subject to fluctuating values, and therefore returns, to a greater extent than property. Transaction costs are obviously higher for property investment but very few property investments are traded compared with gilts. However, in practice it is often the case to expect property investment to generate a greater yield than government stock, and estimates of an appropriate premium vary between 0.5 and 2 per cent. We debate this more fully in Chapters 2 and 6.

REAL RETURNS

A more useful comparison for return from any investment is to compare it with some form of index of inflation in the economy as a whole. A fund will invest in property, gilts or equities to make a real return and this is normally related to monetary values. The retail price index is a useful indicator of inflation and the real value of money. Rises in the retail price index can be compared in percentage terms with rates of return from property over similar periods. The formula which can be used for any investment to calculate real return is as follows:

$$x(1 + r) = \frac{yI_1}{I_2}$$

where RPI at start of period = I_1
RPI at end of period = I_2

x = value of investment at start of period
y = value of investment at end of period
r = real rate of return

The application of real returns to the appraisal and valuation of property assets has been the subject of much debate and the reader is directed to Baum and Crosby (1988) for a fuller consideration of real returns.

COMPARISON WITH STOCK MARKET INDICES

Return can also be compared with stock market indices which have been quoted earlier – the *FT Industrial Ordinary Index*, the *FT Actuaries All Share Index* and the *FT SE 100 Index*.

There are various ways of calculating these indices. The *FT Industrial Ordinary Index* is calculated by unweighted geometric mean and is a time-weighted rate of return. The formula for this calculation is as follows:

$$\text{Index} = i\,\frac{P_{1t}}{P_{10}} \times \frac{P_{2t}}{P_{20}} \times \ldots \times \frac{P_{it}}{P_{i0}}$$

where P_{10} is the price of share 1 at time O
P_{1t} is the price of share 1 at time t

The *FT Actuaries All Share Index* is calculated by a weighted arithmetic mean as is the *FT SE 100 Index*. The formula for calculating the arithmetic mean is as follows:

$$\frac{\Sigma N_o P_o}{\Sigma N_o P_o}$$

P_o = Price at time 0
P_t = Price at time t
N_o = No. of shares at time 0
N_t = No. of shares at time t

The formula for weighted arithmetic mean is as follows:

$$\frac{\Sigma N_t P_t}{\Sigma N_t P_t}$$

Indices are helpful for comparison purposes but they are not always consistent with methods of precisely calculating property investment returns where rent is received quarterly in advance. It is also possible with stock market equities or gilts to be precise about cash flows and values. With property, although a tenant might consent to pay rent quarterly in advance, the receipt of the rental payment may vary in reality for a number of reasons. Valuation of investment property without the test of market bids has also led in recent years to doubts being expressed about the accuracy of valuation. Greenwell *et al.* (1976), Trott (1980).

CONCLUSION

Property investment is always going to be an area where the entrepreneur with business acumen can produce investment performance by purchasing a property at the bottom of a business cycle and taking advantage of subsequent growth. Calculations of return are possible to make using historical data, but to be accurate the data has to be meticulously gathered and analysed. For gilts and equities the calculations are far simpler. It seems probable that the methods of calculation discussed will be increasingly used to compare the different types of investment, but it seems likely that discounted cash flow techniques will continue to be used for property investment valuations in the future.

Chapter 6

Risk and the individual investment

INTRODUCTION

In the previous chapter the concept of return was explained and the measures by which it can be quantified were outlined.

Any rational investor given a choice between investments will, all other things being equal, seek to maximize return, however defined. Frequently, however, return is not the only criterion, as investments have many differing qualities other than return.

We have already examined in Chapter 2 the advantages and disadvantages of various types of property in relation to these factors, and we have examined investors' different viewpoints on each. Some factors, such as the prospect of capital and income (rental) growth can be readily incorporated in the calculation of return by Discounted Cash Flow (DCF) – based techniques, but others such as liquidity and ease of management present more difficulties, and are normally dealt with by intuitive policy decisions.

Risk is a factor which is frequently treated subjectively, yet it has great influence on the performance of an individual investment and the overall return on a portfolio. The quantitative study of risk analysis of investments is of recent origins, and when applied to property is still in its infancy. Whilst compiling this book we contacted approximately sixty institutional investors, chosen as a selective sample. The responses showed that in practice property managers are not generally using quantitative measures, but that interest in the subject is growing. The level and type of response indicated that such interest is likely not only to be sustained, but to increase sufficiently that risk analysis will become a standard management technique. The reasons lying behind this are twofold: first, the competitiveness within investments media is such that it will be necessary to use all possible techniques to compare properties' characteristics with other investment media, and second, the increasing knowledge of statistical techniques and use of computers will render simple the type of analysis that, two decades ago, was impractical from a time and cost viewpoint.

RISK: A DEFINITION

Risk has been defined in many ways, but in essence, from a property investment standpoint, it may be defined as the level of probability that a required return, measured in terms of capital value and income, will be achieved. Over time the variance of actual return from expected return (the volatility) can be measured and used to help determine probability levels. Risk, then, is about the interaction of future returns, which can have a number of possible results, and the chances that any particular outcome will result.

The degree to which actual performance may exceed the expected performance is called the upside potential, whilst the amount by which it falls below expectation is known as the downside risk. It is with the latter concept that investors are most concerned, particularly when an investment is being funded by borrowed money. Upside potential is thus regarded as the 'added bonus' over and above the return targeted.

At this point a distinction should be drawn between risk and uncertainty. Risk has already been defined. It is concerned with variances and probabilities. The variations in return are usually calculated in terms of standard deviation, which itself is a measure of dispersion of returns around the mean. The term is explained more fully below; suffice it to say here, that the greater the standard deviation, the more widely the returns are spread, that is, the greater the risk and vice versa.

If something is uncertain, it means that no probabilities can be ascribed to the probable outcome. As such its assessment must remain qualitative rather than quantitative, although investors may feel fit to deal with such situations by the use of mini-max criteria, or by using a payback technique, both of which are explained below.

In this chapter and Chapter 7, we examine types of risk and its measurement in two contexts:

1 In relation to an individual investment.
2 In relation to a portfolio, as examined by Modern Portfolio Theory, and, more particularly, the Capital Asset Pricing Model (CAPM).

In essence, the reason to examine risk evaluation is to aid the decision-making process and, in particular, to help the investor answer the following questions:

(a) What is the expected rate of return or most likely outcome?
(b) What is the probability of making a loss (measured against a target return or cost of borrowing, or alternative investment return), or, alternatively, of exceeding the target?
(c) What is the variability or spread of returns in relation to the expected return?

It must be stressed that just because an investment shows high volatility of return, there is no reason for its automatic rejection. It could well be that given two investments, one has a high expected return with a large degree of volatility (for example, 20 per cent with a range of possible outcomes between 12 and 28 per cent), and another has a low volatility but low expected outcome (for example, 10 per cent plus or minus 2 per cent). Here the investment with the higher risk profile will be preferred.

TYPES OF RISK

The following are some of the types of risk which characterize property investments.

Income flow

With any investment other than government stock there is a risk of default: in the case of equities the size or very existence of dividends is not secure. With property the risk of default on rack-rented units will depend on the strength of the covenant, but in the case of reversionary property there is also a risk attached to the projected income flow, both in terms of possible voids, and in respect of the size of the reversionary income. With leaseholds there are additional concerns such as dilapidations claims. Many appraisals of property carried out now build in explicit expectations of rental growth, the amount depending on age and type of property and projected demand. Prime retail investments, which sell on capitalization yields of about 5 per cent, are conventionally regarded as low risk when compared with, say, an old industrial unit, selling at 10 per cent or higher.

This may be misleading. Assuming the same overall required return by the investor, a far greater level of rental growth expectation will have been built into the valuation of the prime retail unit than the old industrial one. As all future increases in income flow have risk attached, there must be a correspondingly higher probability that the expected rental growth will not be realized, that is, the risk involved in the former is arguably higher. Let us take an example. If an investor requiring an overall 15 per cent p.a. return purchases a property showing an initial yield of 5 per cent, then assuming five yearly rent reviews, he will require annual rental growth to occur at a rate of 10.86 per cent p.a., if he is to reach his target. However, if he purchases a unit at an initial yield of 11 per cent, the rental growth required falls to only 4.89 per cent p.a. Arguably the risk of not achieving the target return is greater with the low-yielding property.

Future outgoings

This risk is particularly relevant to direct property investment. Even in the case of a new unit let on full repairing and insuring (FRI) terms, there is a strong possibility that technological and fashion changes can affect a property sufficiently that premature obsolescence can set in, requiring large future expense by the freeholder, which was not reflected in the original appraisal. A good example of this is the office blocks in London Wall, City of London, constructed in the 1960s and now the subject of redevelopment. Investors now realize that if this can happen to what were regarded as prime investments, any property must be regarded as at risk from obsolescence. Accordingly, many companies are actively building in estimates of future refurbishment costs in initial investment appraisals.

Other expected outgoings include structural failures due to inherent defects, unforeseen legal costs, such as on disputed rent reviews, and items such as government legislation. A good example of the last was the Counter Inflation Act of 1973, which, during its life, prevented any rent reviews from being implemented.

Capital value

To a large degree the capital value is dependent on expected income flow, reflecting the level of likely outgoings. However, given no change in either of these, capital values can and do alter, due to a change in yields. This can be seen in its most dramatic form by the daily change of gilt prices. With property, too, yield pattern changes, though normally over a period of months, and often in a way seemingly unconnected with the gilts and equities market. The reason for property yield changes are complex and not yet fully understood, yet the risk of capital value realized varying from that predicted is one which can dramatically affect returns, as we saw in Chapter 5.

The reason why capital value predictions may prove inaccurate include general imperfections in market knowledge, incomparability of transactions and secrecy surrounding deals, together with the following factors:

(a) *Value error*: It is a commonly held belief that valuers, if asked to value the same property, will produce results within +/–5 per cent of each other. Even if this is so, and the report by Hager and Lord (1985) casts doubts on this, the level of difference in valuation can affect the return significantly, and clearly the choice of valuer might determine whether a property is deemed to have achieved its target return or not!

   The fact that property values are not tested on the market with the frequency that gilts or equities transactions take place also leads to uncertainty regarding capital value.

(b) *Market effect*: A valuation is normally carried out to open market value (OMV) as defined by the *Statement of Asset Valuation Practice* and *Guidance Notes* produced by the RICS (1990) but frequently the price that the investment actually realized is very different, due to the strength of the market at the moment of sale, or due to the presence of a special purchaser. The pressure of money on some institutions, and their need to reduce liquidity, may result in prices being paid which are well in excess of the theoretical valuation.

(c) *Legislative and fiscal impact*: Sometimes legislative and fiscal impacts can be predicted, but the risk remains that property performance can be significantly affected by government actions such as fiscal changes. Examples where a direct and almost immediate effect on property values was experienced following government action was the 'Brown Ban' of office development, 1964, which stopped all new development of offices in some areas, thus causing undersupply at a time of strong demand. The impact of the imposition of the Uniform Business Rate (UBR) in 1990 has also been significant in some areas.

Case law, too, can have an impact. An unexpected ruling in a dispute over, for example, a rent review can affect property performance. In the case of *Young* v. *Dalgety PLC* (1986) the interpretation of the rent review clause by the courts reduced the freeholders expected income flow by approximately £40,000 p.a.: clearly this has a large impact on return.

Included in legislative risk are planning considerations which can effect performance enormously.

(d) *Economic indications*: Changes in the economy may have an impact on the demand for either (i) property in general, as, for example, an economic slump, or, (ii) property of a particular type – such as the recent increase in demand for hi-tech investments, which were shunned by investors only a few years ago, or in a particular location, as evidenced by the factors such as opening of new motorways, and so on. Value changes within the same property type may be very location sensitive, so that whilst properties in one area may be experiencing strong rental growth, in other areas the picture is one of decline.

(e) *Obsolescence*: Whilst obsolescence is a factor implicit or sometimes explicit in a valuation, its impact may not be as predicted. Indeed the rate of change of both design and occupational requirements in offices over the last ten years has led to a degree of obsolescence totally unpredicted at the start of that period.

(f) *Inflation*: As property valuations include predictions of rental growth, either implicitly or explicitly, the effect of changes in the rate of inflation will clearly affect whether predicted patterns are achieved.

(g) *Legal risk*: Although it occurs in but few cases, a defective title can have a dramatic effect on property value and as such is a risk factor.

Comparative risk

In addition to the concern that he may have about the actual performance of his investment against its target, the investor will also be aware of his opportunity cost risk. By undertaking this investment he has (presumably) turned down other opportunities and he will be conscious of the returns he could have obtained elsewhere.

Timing risk

In Chapter 10 we examine the refurbishment and redevelopment process in detail, when we shall see just how critical it is to time a project correctly to obtain the optimum return. It will suffice here to point out that the question of timing has a bearing on risk: the best conceived scheme, carried out at the most appropriate time, will result in the least risk. It is when the developer is operating in an unsecured situation, for example, an out-of-town shopping centre, where rental values may be hard to predict and appropriate capitalization rate yet more difficult, that risks are very high. This risk factor will be reflected by investors when purchasing or funding such schemes. Another aspect of timing risk is the length of time that may be involved in selling property.

Holding period

Related to timing risk is the holding period. The longer the project life of an investment, in general, the greater the uncertainty attached to the likely income flows. If an investment is to be held for only twelve months, the prediction regarding income and disposal price is more likely to be accurate than if the holding period is longer. Hence the variance in actual return from expected is likely to increase commensurately with the holding period.

All these types of risk should concern the investor; the more he is able to quantify their levels, the more rational his investment choice decisions can be.

RISK AND THE INDIVIDUAL INVESTMENT

Although it appears that most property investors consider risk, they do so intuitively, or by simply demanding a higher return for a property whose future performance is considered difficult to predict. However, techniques are used by some organizations to help their decision process. Some techniques are crude, and not strictly risk evaluations, whilst others have a considerable degree of sophistication. As previously indicated, our research shows an increasing awareness of the value of attempting quantitative risk evaluation.

Some of the techniques which anyone wishing to pursue a study of risk should master are now considered.

Mini-max regret

As its name implies, this simple technique seeks to find the decision which will minimize any potential loss. It is frequently expressed in terms of a matrix, as follows:

Example 6.1   Mini-Max regret model

Investment options	Possible outcomes (probabilities unascribable)						
	A	B	C	D	E	Max. of row	Min. of row
1	20	5	7	9	40	40	5
2	5	0	7	20	52	52	0
3	−4	44	22	80	52	80	−4

Under mini-max regret, an investor would adopt option 1, as it is the only option for which a positive result will always occur, even though the potential maximum return is also least. Such an approach, whilst minimizing loss, does presuppose a very risk-averse attitude, and may result in lost opportunities.

Payback

The payback criterion is a very crude measure of return. Given two opportunities it evaluates the length of time taken to recoup the capital expenditure without any consideration for discounting, total return or volatility of return.

Example 6.2

	A	B
Capital cost	£5,000	£5,000
Return Year 1	£3,000	£2,000
Year 2	£2,000	£1,000
Year 3	£1,000	£20,000
Year 4	£1,000	£20,000

Using the payback criterion, investment *A* would be chosen in preference to investment *B*, as the capital is recouped in 2 years, rather than 3, regardless of the fact that the total return in *B* is much greater. The justification for use of payback as a decision tool can only be that in general the further one projects income flows, the more difficult it is to be certain that they will be achieved. It is, indeed, merely an expression of the saying 'A bird in the hand is worth two in the bush!'

Expected net present value (ENPV)

The ENPV (expected net present value) is not in the strict sense a risk evaluation technique. It is, however, an aid to decision-making, which takes cognizance of probability theory. It is, therefore, a technique which represents an improvement upon the usual price fixing mechanism for property investments. In general a capital value, or projected return, is normally calculated, making the assumption that each variable will have a fixed value. The expected NPV technique accepts that this is not the case and seeks to quantify the most likely outcome, taking into account the range of possible outcomes for each variable and the likelihood, or probability, of each outcome ocurring. It thus combines the basic elements of DCF and probability theory to produce a 'most likely outcome'.

Whilst the technique is well established in investment fields it is undertaken by few property managers, who tend to rely on spot estimates. Its use in developmental appraisal work is more widespread.

The actual technique is best explained by way of a hypothetical example.

Example 6.3

A fund has been offered a share in a retail development for a price of £1.75m. At the moment the scheme is not pre-let, but it is estimated that the most likely outcome (outcome 1) is as follows:

In Year 1 the fund will receive £60,000 in rents, in Year 2 £80,000 and in Year 3 the scheme will be fully let and the capital value of the funds equity share will be worth £2 million. Assuming that the fund is looking for a 7 per cent return on this investment, the NPV will be £7,942 as calculated below:

Outcome 1

Period	Cash flow	DF	DCF
Year 0	(£1.75m)	1.0000	(£1.75m)
Year 1	£60,000	0.9345	£56,070
Year 2	£80,000	0.8734	£69,872
Year 3	£2 million	0.8160	£1,632,000
			£7,942

Realistically these expectations may not be met. Let us now assume that the probability of achieving this is 40 per cent and, further, that the following outcomes are considered possible:

Outcome 2

Period	*Cash flow*		
Year 1	£50,000	Probability 20%	
Year 2	£70,000		
Year 3	£90,000		
Year 4	£2m	NPV at 7% discount rate:	–£42,895

Outcome 3

Period	*Cash flow*		
Year 1	£40,000	Probability 10%	
Year 2	£60,000		
Year 3	£80,000		
Year 4	£2m	NPV at 7% discount rate:	–£69,126

Outcome 4

Period	*Cash flow*		
Year 1	£70,000	Probability 20%	
Year 2	£90,000		
Year 3	£2m	NPV at 7% discount rate:	£26,021

Outcome 5

Period	*Cash flow*		
Year 1	£80,000	Probability 10%	
Year 2	£100,000		
Year 3	£2m	NPV at 7% discount rate:	£44,100

Total probability   100%

If the possible outcomes are now combined with the probability of each occurring, a weighted average NPV or 'expected NPV' is found:

Outcome	Probability	NPV × Prob.
−£69,126	0.10	−£6,913
−£42,895	0.20	−£8,579
£7,942	0.40	£3,177
£26,021	0.20	£5,204
£44,100	0.10	£4,410
Total probability	1.00	
	Expected NPV:	−£2,701

Thus it can be seen quite clearly that the moment 'point estimates' are relaxed and a *range* of values is considered, the expected outcome can alter dramatically; in this case a positive result at the funds target rate of return has become a negative one.

The example above is very simplistic and is open to criticism.

1 We have assumed that the variables are mutually exclusive. This may not be the case.
2 We have looked at one variable only, that is, the timing of the development and lettings. If the analysis is to be meaningful, then each variable in the project, from state of the economy to building costs and rental value, should be considered.
3 How are the probabilities assessed? In the absence of large amounts of comparable data these must be subjective so this, it could be argued, invalidates the claims of the analysis to be quantitative.
4 The calculation of the expected NPV is not truly a measure of risk, merely one step along the way; that is, it is concerned with predicting an unexpected return, rather than combining it with the measurement of the *variation* of the actual return from that expected.

Whilst all these criticisms are valid and defensible in our view, the technique is useful for the following reasons:

1 Although in complex situations the expected NPV is unsatisfactory, in many instances the property appraisal will depend to any significant degree on only one or two variables. It is in these simple situations that the ENPV, which can be worked out without the use of a computer, is helpful. Arguably, the ENPV technique should be incorporated into any property valuation.
2 Whilst it is true that the assessment of probabilities is sometimes subjective, the very process of considering their value encourages the appraiser to analyse critically the opportunity, and it is unlikely their use will result in a less accurate prediction than that reached by the use of a point estimate. The recent rapid growth of research

departments in many surveying firms would appear to reflect clients' increasing awareness in this area.

3   If point estimates only are used to arrive at an expected outcome, it is quite possible for two projects to be assigned the *same* value, whereas in reality the appraiser knows that the actual outcome of one is more likely to deviate from the estimate than the other. As an example of this, if two property investments were held for a funds portfolio, one a shop located in a good high street position and let to a good covenant, and the other an obsolete factory let to a dubious covenant and approaching the optimum time for redevelopment, both might be ascribed the same value in the portfolio, but if that valuation were tested on the market, the probability of the valuation proving market accurate for the later is less than for the former.

The use of the ENPV in our view can be regarded as a useful tool of management, though one that is subjective. It does not supply all the needs of the manager and suffers from one major flaw: it tells us nothing of the range or distribution of the possible values, and it is the distribution which, when combined with our projected estimate, indicates the level of risk. It would be tempting to conclude from ENPV analysis that if two investments had the same ENPV when discounted at identical rates, the investor should be indifferent in choice between them. However, consider the following two investments.

Example 6.4

A

(NPV) outcome	Probability	Prob. × NPV
−£200	0.2	−£40
£300	0.6	£180
£500	0.2	£100
	Expected NPV:	£240

B

(NPV) outcome	Probability	Prob. × NPV
£150	0.2	£30
£250	0.6	£150
£300	0.2	£60
	Expected NPV:	£240

Here the expected NPVs are identical yet with *A* the outcome has a range of 700 whilst *B* has one of only 150, with no negative result – clearly more attractive to the risk-averse investor.

Normal distribution theory

The use of normal distribution theory and the standard deviation to evaluate risk is perhaps the most widely-accepted measure. It builds on directly from the expected NPV theory whilst making use of further statistical analysis. If we look again at Example 6.4, it will be recalled that it is possible for two projects to have the same ENPV yet be very different.

Faced with a choice of these two investments, an investor should be indifferent between them based on ENPV, yet clearly *A* has a much higher risk, particularly on the downside – after all there is a 20 per cent chance that the project will show a loss. With project *B*, at worst the result is a positive 150. Thus most investors would chose *B* if they were at all risk averse, as the chances of an unfavourable outcome are minimized. However, the example we have chosen is unrealistic. It is not likely that the outcome will be one of a small limited number of possibilities; in reality it is to be expected that there will be a very large number of possible outcomes. If we plot the possible results of the projects graphically the best representation is by a probability curve (see Figures 6.1, 6.2).

In our example both investments have a normal distribution, that is, they are symmetrical around the 'most likely' point or expected value (μ). In reality this is not always the case and the distribution can be 'skewed' either positively or negatively. If dealing with distributions which are skewed it is important to assess upside potential and downside risk separately.

Where distributions are normal, statistical analysis is much simpler than where they are skewed. As the principles involved are the same, and many distributions do show a normal pattern, the assumption of a normal distribution will be made.

On examination of the curves it can be seen that where risk is higher, the curve is flat and wide in shape, and that where the risk, or volatility of return is lower, it is much narrower.

One of the characteristics of the normal distribution curve is that there is a measurable relationship between the area under the curve and the distribution of values around the mean point. This measure of relationship, known as the standard deviation (σ) holds true for *all* normal distributions. It can be shown that approximately 68 per cent of all values in a distribution fall within the area lying $\pm$ 1 σ of the mean (or average value); 95 per cent $\pm$ 2 and 99 per cent $\pm$ 3. This can be shown diagrammatically (see Figure 6.3).

The relevance of this is that, if the standard deviation (σ) is calculated,

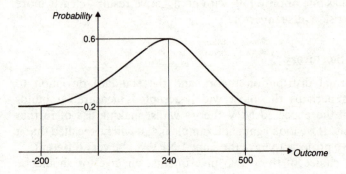

Figure 6.1 Diagram showing probability curve with normal distribution (Project A)

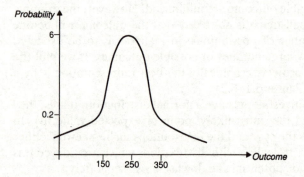

Figure 6.2 Diagram showing probability curve with normal distribution (Project B)

it gives a comparative measure of the risks of investments: the smaller the standard deviation the less is the variability of return and thus the lower the risk and vice versa.

The σ can be calculated by using the following formula:

$$\sigma = \sqrt{\sum_{i=1}^{i=n} P_i \, (x_i - \mu)^2}$$

where P is the probability of any outcome occurring and μ is the expected mean value for x.

Thus in our example the standard deviations are:

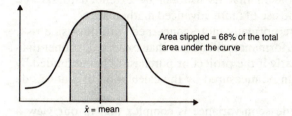

Area stippled = 68% of the total
area under the curve

$\bar{x}$ = mean

Figure 6.3   Diagram showing area contained within one standard deviation of the mean

(A)	Probability	$x - \mu$	$(x - \mu)^2$	$p(x - \mu)^2$
	0.2	−440	193,600	38,720
	0.6	60	3,600	2,160
	0.2	260	67,600	13,520
				54,400

Therefore the standard deviation $(\sigma) = 233.238$

(B)	Probability	$x - \mu$	$(x - \mu)^2$	$p(x - \mu)^2$
	0.2	−90	8,100	1,620
	0.6	10	100	60
	0.2	60	3,600	720
				2,400

Therefore the standard deviation $(\sigma) = 48.99$

We can see that the standard deviation of B is much less than A. Therefore B is preferred, as being less volatile and hence less risky.

Sometimes, having calculated the standard deviation, it is useful to calculate the coefficient of variation which is:

$$\frac{\sigma}{\text{ENPV}} \times 100\%$$

In the example A has a coefficient of variation of 97.2 per cent and B has a coefficient of variation of 20.4 per cent.

This particular calculation effectively translates results into standard units by expressing them as percentages. It is useful when comparing projects whose ENPVs are *not* equal. In this example B, having a lower coefficient, is again preferred.

The use of the standard deviation gives us a truly quantitative volatility measurement. It is flexible in that its use can be extended to skewed distribution, albeit with the use of more advanced mathematics.

In practice investors are normally more concerned with downside risk, that is, the chance that performance will be less than expected, sooner than upside potential, particularly if the project or purchase is being funded by borrowed money. This can be measured by the calculation of a downside semi-variance.

The use of the downside semi-variance is complex and in our view a stochastic decision tree (see below) may well be easier to handle and give equally satisfactory results.

Simulation

This technique, which is well established in accounting circles, has been used in recent years to assist in development appraisal. However, the concept is one which is capable of wider application, although at present its consideration in relation to property investment appraisal has only recently begun. In principle it is merely an extension of the techniques already described, as can be shown from the following example:

Example 6.5

An investor wishes to know how much he would be advised to pay for the following investment.

A shop currently let at £10,000 per annum with a review to open market value (OMV) due in two years' time. It is estimated that the current full rental value (FRV) of the premises today are £15,000, and it is considered likely that rental growth will be in the order of 5 per cent per annum for the next two years. An overall return of 12 per cent is required. In two years' time following the rent review the investment will be sold. The market capitalization rate likely to be achieved is 6 per cent.

In order to evaluate this a DCF would normally be prepared and, taking a target rate of 12 per cent, the resultant NPV is the maximum price he can afford if he is to achieve his required return. However, although our estimate of FRV is £15,000, this is only a spot figure and it would probably be more realistic to say that the FRV as at today was somewhere in the range £14,000–£16,000, as follows:

FRV £14,000: 20% chance
£15,000: 60% chance
£16,000: 20% chance

Even here our view is simplistic, as really the outcomes are not discrete but continuous. Likewise the rental growth is not certain; maybe we are confident that it will be within the range 2 to 12 per cent; 5 per cent is only the best estimate. The third determinant, the capitalization rate, is also likely to vary.

If we now assume that in practice there are not three but nine possible results for FRV today, each with differing probabilities, and a similar number of outcomes for both rental growth and yield, then there are 9 × 9 × 9 = 729 possible outcomes.

By manual manipulation it is clearly not possible to evaluate each of these and use of a computer becomes essential. To carry out a simulation it is necessary first to set out all the possibilities for each variable, together with their probabilities. Under the computer programme all these possible outcomes will then have random numbers assigned to them, the number being determined by the probability of that event happening. An appraisal is then carried out, using randomly-selected values. This process is then repeated over and over again to produce many different results or NPVs. When a great number of results has been obtained it usually happens that, when plotted on a frequency curve, the results will produce a distribution approximately normal in shape. From this distribution information can be obtained about the 'mean' or most likely result and the risk of achieving it can then be measured in terms of standard deviation.

The advantages of a simulation technique or 'Monte Carlo', as it is sometimes called, is that it is easily worked, given a suitable computer programme. It weighs up all the available information which may include risk of voids, refurbishment costs, and so on, and takes account of it each according to their respective probabilities. Thus the end result is statistically sound. It is an extremely useful tool for dealing with a range of variables, provided that the probability scores have been assigned to each variable with skill and care.

As a measure of risk it is extremely useful; it is flexible regarding both the information it can use as input, and the output, that is, it can calculate NPV on the internal rate of return (IRR) and the probability of any one outcome being achieved. However, as a method of comparing investments it may prove difficult to handle.

Sensitivity analysis

Although in property terms the use of sensitivity analysis is most commonly thought of in relation to assessment of the viability of development projects, its use as a quantitative measure of risk assessment for management purposes is increasing and indeed logical.

The concept is in essence simple. Sensitivity analysis seeks to answer the question: The performance of any investment is the product of many variable factors; if any factor changes, what effect will that have on the overall performance? Are there any factors which will have a greater effect than others?

An example is perhaps the easiest way to explain how the technique works: Whilst the figures are contrived, this is done for the sake of illustration only.

Example 6.6

An investor has the opportunity of purchasing a property for £20,000. He wishes to hold it for a two-year period and then sell it. It is currently let on a low rent of £1,000 and the landlord is responsible for outgoings estimated to cost £500. After the first year there is a reversion to full repairing terms and the rent, allowing for rental growth, is expected to be £2,000 p.a. net. A year after this he expects to sell for £25,000. His target rate of return is 10 per cent. He wishes to know whether the purchase is likely to be worthwhile.

First we calculate his NPV at the target rate:

Year	Monies out	Monies in	Net cash flow	DF at 10%	DCF
0	(£20,000)	–	(£20,000)	1.000	−£20,000
1	(£500)	£1,000	£500	0.909	£455
2	–	£2,000	£2,000	0.826	£1,652
3	–	£25,000	£25,000	0.751	£18,775
				NPV=	£882

On the basis of the projected cash flows the investment is worth undertaking. In order to analyse the sensitivity each variable must be considered in turn, holding all other variables unchanged, however unrealistic this may be. For each variable a calculation must be done to determine the amount of change necessary to render the proposal no longer worthwhile, that is, where NPV = 0.

In this example we shall asume that the purchase price and year one rent are fixed, but that all other factors, namely outgoings, reversionary rent, eventual sale price and target rate are variables.

Thus, taking each in turn:

1   *Outgoings year one*

Looking at the calculations will tell us that it is unlikely that the level of outgoings will affect the viability of the project. However to prove this:

Let outgoings = x

Substituting into our discount cash flow line and making the NPV = 0, we have $- £20,000 + [(£1,000 - x) \times 0.909] + £1,652 + £18,775 = 0$

From this $x = £1,470$

Thus outgoings may increase from the expected £500 to £1,470 before NPV is totally eroded. Expressing this in percentage terms:

The degree of change possible or sensitivity is

$$\frac{\text{absolute change}}{\text{best estimate}} \times 100 = \frac{970}{500} \times 100 = 194\%$$

Thus we can conclude that project is not sensitive to outgoings charge as it will take a massive change in that variable to affect viability.

2   *Rental value year two*

Applying the same technique but now letting the reversionary rent = x

$$-£20,000 + £455 + 0.826x + £18,775 = 0$$
$$x = £932$$

$$\text{Sensitivity} = \frac{1,068}{2,000} \times 100 = 53.4\%$$

3   *Capital value on sale*

$$-£20,000 + £455 + £1,652 + 0.751x = 0$$
$$x = £23,826$$

$$\text{Sensitivity} = \frac{1,174}{25,000} \times 100 = 4.7\%$$

4   *Discount factor*

It is not possible to find this by simple substitution as in previous cases. Here we must calculate the IRR (internal rate of return). This will be done using trial rates and interpolation. We already have a result at 10 per cent so only one more calculation is needed. Using a trial rate of 12 per cent the DCF becomes:

Year	Net cash flow	DF at 12%	DCF
0	−£20,000	1.000	−£20,000
1	£500	0.893	£447
2	£2,000	0.797	£1,594
3	£25,000	0.712	£17,800
			− £159

Therefore the IRR must lie between 10 and 12 per cent and is clearly nearer to 12 per cent.

Finding by interpolation and using the formula

$$\text{IRR} = \text{lower trial rate} + \left[\frac{\text{NPV lower rate}}{\text{NPV (lower rates + higher rates)}} \times \begin{array}{c} \text{difference in} \\ \text{trial rates} \end{array} \right] \%$$

$$= 10 + \left[\frac{882}{882 + 159} \times 2 \right] \%$$

$$= 11.69\%$$

Thus the sensitivity becomes:

$$\frac{1.69}{10.00} = 16.9\%$$

From this analysis it becomes clear that the viability is most sensitive to changes in the capital value upon sale, and to a lesser extent to the required discount factor.

The chief advantages of sensitivity analysis can be summarized as:

(a) It is simple to grasp as a concept and to calculate.
(b) It can be used in a wide range of situations including performance measurement and assessment of the reliability of valuations as well as its most usual property application, the projection of development returns.
(c) The use of the technique enables the manager to pinpoint those items which require additional care in calculation, and may point to research which must be carried out prior to the project going ahead. For example, using the illustration above there is clearly no point in the investor investigating outgoings costs in great detail as the impact of these is so small. What he should consider is the likelihood of being able to achieve the anticipated sale value, that is, is his capital yield estimation likely to be accurate, will the property be readily saleable?

On the other hand, the technique can be criticized as being very crude. To assume that one factor will alter in isolation to others is extremely unrealistic. In our example, if the rent on reversion was not £2,000 but £1,500 this would, of course, affect the sale value. Likewise, if long-term interest rates or economic conditions change, the investor's target return will alter as will general levels of capitalization rates. The second major criticism of the technique is that it does not give the investor truly comparative measure of risk – merely an idea of the volatility of each component part.

Stochastic decision trees

A decision tree, as the name implies, is a diagramatic representation of possible future outcomes, where, at various moments of time, differing events may happen, resulting in a wide network of eventual possibilities. Let us use a similar example to that taken for the Monte Carlo simulation.

Example 6.7

A property is let at £10,000 p.a. fixed for the next two years. Thereupon there is a rent review to full open market value. The FRV of the property as at today's values is estimated to be £15,000 p.a. However, as discussed earlier, it is not possible to be precise and being realistic it is thought that the range of possible values is £14,000 to £16,000. It is also thought likely that rental growth over the next two years will be in the order of 5 per cent p.a., but again, it might be ±4 per cent of this. In two years' time following the review the investment will be sold on an estimated 6 per cent basis. Income is assumed to be received annually in arrears.

Let us assume that an investor requires a return of 12 per cent, and that the asking price is £235,000. If the most likely values prevail he will achieve this return as demonstrated below (see also Figure 6.4).

Cash flow	DF at 12%	DCF
£10,000	0.8928	£8,928
£10,000	0.797	£7,970
*£275,622	0.797	£219,670
		£236,568
	less price	£235,000
	NPV =	£1,568

* £16,537 capitalized at 6%

What is the risk, however, that he will not achieve his return? If we assume that, although FRV falls within the range £14,000 to £16,000, three discrete figures of estimation can be adopted, and a similar assumption is made for rental growth, a decision tree may be devised as set out below. For the purposes of this example the eventual capitalization yield of 6 per cent is assumed not to be a variable. If he is to achieve his target return of 12 per cent an eventual sale price of at least £273,653 must be achieved, as:

Cash flow	DF at 10%	DCF
£10,000	0.8928	£8,928
£10,000	0.797	£7,970
£273,653	0.797	£218,102
		£235,000

Assuming that all lines of the tree have equal probability of occurrence then of nine possible outcomes, five will give him his required return, whilst four will not. Therefore the probability of achieving the target return is 55 per cent.

Whilst this may be a useful tool, it is clearly over simplistic, as:

1 At each step in the decision tree, or nodal point, the possible variables will not necessarily consist of a few discrete values, for example, rental value could be £14,100, £14,200, and so on. Yet to thus complicate the tree becomes very cumbersome. Had we taken £250 points and 1 per cent for rental growth, eighty-one eventual outcomes would have ensued.

2 It is unrealistic to assume that each individual value has an equal likelihood of occurrence. Thus the model should arguably be expanded to cater for varying probabilities. Once again, to do so becomes complex.

To overcome these difficulties Arnison and Barrett (1986), advocated the use of a stochastic decision tree, which combines the principles of simple decision trees with simulation techniques. With this technique at each node of the decision tree, a simulation exercise is carried out to

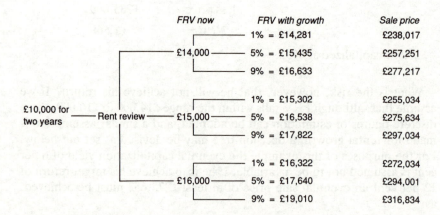

Figure 6.4 Decision tree model to show possible outcomes

find the most likely result. By combining the results at each nodal point many estimates of eventual outcome are produced. These can be plotted to form a normal distribution curve, from which can be calculated a most likely outcome and the standard deviation as a measure of the likelihood of such an outcome occurring.

As this method enables the outcomes to be plotted on a normal distribution curve, it is easy to identify the measure of downside risk. For example, our investor might decide that he will pay the asking price of £235,000 if there is at least a 75 per cent chance that his target rate will be achieved, that is, that the worth to him will be £235,000 or more.

If our analysis had shown, say, an expected value of £250,000 and a standard deviation of £30,000, then there must be a 68 per cent chance (approximately) that the value to him will lie between £220,000 and £280,000, that is, within ± 1 standard deviation of the mean.

This is illustrated in Figure 6.5 below.

If 68 per cent of values lie within ± 1 standard deviation, the remaining 32 per cent must lie outside. As the distribution is normal these values will lie equally above and below. Therefore the total *above* £220,000 is:

$$68\% + (32\% \times 0.5) = 84\%.$$

However, we want to find the chances that it is in excess of £235,000 (see Figure 6.6).

We call the distance between our required point (£235,000) and the expected value (£250,000) *z*. *z* can be found from the statistical formula:

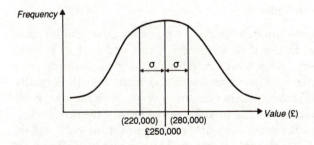

Figure 6.5 Diagram to show values contained within one standard deviation of the mean

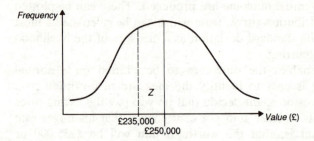

Figure 6.6 Diagram to show *z* value

$$z = \frac{x - \mu}{\text{standard deviation}} = \frac{235{,}000 - 250{,}000}{30{,}000} = -0.5$$

Using statistical tables we can look up the probability where the *z* value is 0.5:
From tables: probability of *z* value = 0.3085 approx.
Therefore the total probabilities that the value lies to the right of *z* = 0.5 (greater than the mean) +0.3085 =0.8085, that is, 80.85%.

It follows from this that to our investor the level of risk calculated is acceptable.

The use of such models has been advocated in general management decision theory for some years, but its application to property has only been considered during the last decade. In our view, until the need for risk analysis is more widely accepted by property professionals, and suitable computer software is widely available and understood, the use of this technique is likely to remain academic despite its clearly defensible stance.

The risk adjustment techniques

We make the assumption throughout this chapter that a rational investor will require additional return if he is to accept risk and that in general investors are risk averse. It follows, therefore, that if an investor is to be persuaded to purchase an investment which is risky, he will normally require an incentive in terms of higher return to do so, with the size of his incentive being dependent upon the volatility or riskiness of the investment. In other words, when calculating the worth of the project the NPV will be calculated using a higher target rate than that which would be adopted if a risk-free investment was being contemplated.

The amount by which the target rate is raised to take account of the riskiness of the project is known as the risk-adjusted discount factor (RADF). As a quantitative risk technique it is the most widely used.

Indeed, in relation to property, conventional wisdom states that an investor in property will require a minimum 2 per cent discount factor, or risk premium, over and above the prevailing rate on gilts, to reflect the risk and management difficulties associated with the property. We now need to examine how the size of the discount rate is chosen, and whether such an approach is justifiable. The concept may be explained by use of a simple diagram (see Figure 6.7).

Three questions arise:

1   What is to be regarded as the risk-free rate?
2   What is the slope of the line?
3   Where upon the line does the investment lie?

The risk-free rate is usually taken to be either the gross redemption yield prevailing on government gilts, or the short-term treasury bill rate, as such investments represent no uncertainty regarding the future returns. If you purchase £1,000 of undated gilt-edged stock paying £100 p.a. you will with certainty get 10 per cent return. However, a property investment with poor liquidity, high transfer cost, the possibility of tenant default and uncertain future income flows, is regarded as risky, and a development opportunity with uncertainty surrounding each element, riskier still. Thus a property manager might decide that a 2 or 3 per cent adjustment is appropriate for a fully-let prime property investment and 6 or 7 per cent or more for a development proposal.

The simplicity of such an approach is very attractive, particularly as the benchmark of return on gilts is so easily obtained and the theory has found much support among managers and property valuers. The use of 'gilts + 2 per cent' has been advocated as a target rate for appraisal of property investments by many valuers using 'equated yield' models.

Attractive as it may appear, however, the approach is open to criticism:

1   The choice of risk premium is entirely subjective.

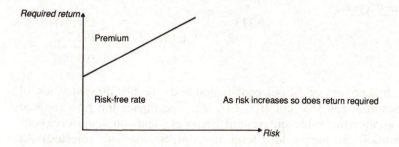

Figure 6.7 The risk/return pay-off

2   By increasing the discount factor greater weight is placed on earlier cash flows, with later ones being heavily discounted. Therefore, given two property investments let to similar covenants, one rack-rented and one reversionary, although both may involve the same types and amount of risk, the rack-rented property will be perceived to be more attractive. Thus the use of equated yields which are higher than traditional property yields tends to place less value on distant cash flows. In the case of reversionary investments this may be compensated by the estimation of future rental increases.

An example will show how two investments ranked equally at one discount rate will have different values if the discount rate is altered. The higher the discount rate chosen, the lower the comparative value of the investment whose return lies in the future sooner than the present.

Example 6.8

Shop A: Rack-rented at £6,500 p.a.
Shop B: Let at £2,750 p.a. for 5 years. It will then revert to full rental value estimated to be £8,000 p.a.

Assuming a capitalization rate or all risks yield of 7 per cent, both units would be ranked equally in value terms, as follows:

Shop A: Income £6,500 p.a.

capitalized at 7%	14.286	value	=	£92,859
		say		£93,000

Shop B: Income £2,750 p.a.

capitalized for 5 years at 7%	4.100			£11,275

Reversion to: £8,000

capitalized at 7%	14.286			
discounted 5 years at 7%	0.713		=	£81,487
		total value		£92,762
		say		£93,000

If a higher rate of 12 per cent is adopted, the net present value of A becomes £54,165, but B is £47,712. The higher the rate adopted the greater the value differential becomes. Thus on some occasions potentially profitable long-term investments may be rejected. As property is in essence a long-term investment this drawback can be regarded as serious.

3   The theory is based on the assumption of a known risk-free rate often assumed to be gross redemption yield on government gilts. However, as Fraser (1986*b*) has argued, it is erroneous to regard gilts as riskless. Although the future income from such investments is known, whereas that from property and equities is uncertain, the capital value of such stock is anything but certain unless the stock is held to redemption, as the value fluctuates from day to day. Therefore if return is measured in relation both to income and capital value change, which it normally is, the return on traded gilts looks anything but risk free. Indeed Fraser, on examining the returns from equities, gilts and property over the fifteen-year period 1970–85, found that the volatility of returns measured in terms of standard deviation was least in the property sector, greatest in equities. The same picture emerges if just the downside is considered. This is very important as it is the risk of *not* reaching target return which is of prime concern to investors. If this viewpoint is accepted then the use of gilts as providing a risk-free investment benchmark must be seriously questioned, and if that is so, to use it as the base rate which is then adjusted for risk is equally questionable. Indeed, if investors value low-risk investments highly then arguably the adjustment for property should be taken as a deduction from the gilt rate, not an addition to it.

We have already seen, however, that in practice many larger investors are shortening their time horizons for investments, thereby minimizing timing risk. Taking a shorter-term horizon, the comparative return from property, as measured against gilts and equities, may look very different. If taken over a two-year period of 1984–6 property showed poor comparative returns compared with equities yet in 1987–8, which saw a troubled equities market, property produced the highest returns.

4   If the gilts benchmark is discarded, there remains no obvious measure of a risk-free return, and if this cannot be calculated any method based upon a risk premium is meaningless.

None the less, the RADF is likely to remain a popular method of dealing with risk within the foreseeable future. Due to the deficiencies of this crude risk-adjustment factor, sophistications on the technique have recently been advocated, notably by Baum (1987). These variations take two forms – the certainty equivalent model, and the sliced income approach. Both are attractive in terms of being simple concepts, yet the underlying assumptions on which they are based have the same deficiencies of the basic RADF.

Certainty equivalent

Using this approach, the quantification of risk is put, not into the discount rate, but in the income flow. Thus, instead of looking at the most likely cash flows, arrived at by point estimate, the certain or near certain cash flows are used. Having arrived at cash flows attached to which is little or no risk, a risk-free discount factor may be used for capitalization. In Baum's examples an 84 per cent certainty criterion was adopted, although in theory any statistical level of confidence could be adopted. At this point it should be reiterated that for any normal distribution there is a 68 per cent chance that any one value lies within the range + 1 standard deviation of the mean. Therefore, as the remaining 32 per cent of values lie outside this range, equally divided above and below 84 per cent (68 per cent + 16 per cent) *must* lie *above* the value which is 1 standard deviation *below* the mean.

Example 6.9

A property investment has a current rental income of £10,000 p.a., with a reversion due in two years. The current FRV is estimated to be £15,000 p.a. with a standard deviation of £1,000, the rental growth is expected to be 5 per cent; standard deviation of this estimate is 1 per cent. A sale of the investment will take place following the review at a likely yield of 6 per cent, standard deviation of the yield 0.5 per cent.

Adopting an 84 per cent certainty equivalent, and a risk-free rate of, say, 10 per cent, the appraisal becomes:

Certainty equivalent of full rental value:
£15,000 less 1 σ = £14,000

Certainty equivalent of growth:
5% less 1 σ = 4%

Adopting these figures the FRV on reversion will be £14,000 × $(1.04)^2$ = *£15, 142*. This must now be capitalized. As we are concerned with downside risk a yield of 6 per cent *plus* 1 σ will be adopted, that is, 6.5 per cent. Therefore the likely sale price becomes £15,142 capitalized at 6.5 per cent = *£232,954*. The resultant cash flow is then discounted at the risk-free rate of 10 per cent and becomes:

Cash flow	DF at 10%	DCF
£10,000	0.909	£9,090
£10,000	0.826	£8,260
£232,954	0.826	£192,420
	Capital value =	£209,770

Alternatively the investment can be appraised using, for example, 95 per cent certainty equivalents (CE) as follows:

CE of full rental value: £15,000 − 2 σ = £13,000
CE of growth: 5% − 2 σ = 3%

Thus the likely rent on review at 95 per cent certainty level is *£13,792*. The capitalization rate is taken at 6% + 2σ = 7%.
   In this case the appraisal becomes:

Cash flow	DF at 10%	DCF
£10,000	0.909	£9,090
£10,000	0.826	£8,260
£197,024	0.826	£162,742
		£180,092

Although the approach is attractive, if standard deviations are large (as in this example) the degree of certainty adopted alters the figures dramatically and the model still suffers the problem of identifying an appropriate risk-free rate. If a rate such as that on treasury bills is adopted it fails to take account of the basic intrinsic differences in the nature of the investment under consideration. If, however, another bench mark is used, the problem remains which?
   The certainty equivalent model suffers from a further defect which makes the results misleading. If, for example, an 84 per cent CE is adopted, as Baum does in the *Journal of Valuation* (1987), the resultant cash flow which is appraised is not 84 per cent certain. In our case three variables are involved, each of which is only 84 per cent certain. As combined probabilities are subject to the multiplication rule we can say that the resulting cash flow is only 84% × 84% × 84%, that is, 59 per cent certain. Even at 95 per cent level nominal, with three variables, the certainty level drops to 85.7 per cent.

Sliced income approach

Essentially the sliced income approach is a combination of the certainty equivalent model, and the RADF. It has already been said that future income flows are uncertain; we cannot guarantee the result of a rent review, we cannot accurately predict rental growth or obsolescence. Such flows must therefore involve risk. However, payments currently receivable on contract under a lease may be regarded as relatively risk free. Thus Baum advocates that the income flows should be separated into those to which little or no uncertainty attaches, and which can be discounted at the risk-free rate, with the remainder or top slice being taken at the best estimates and discounted at a discount factor reflecting risk.

Using the same example as above, the income flow for two years is certain. At review we can be 99 per cent certain that the rent will be the best estimate − 3 standard deviation, that is, £15,000 − £3,000, that is, a minimum of £12,000. Likewise we are certain of rental growth of 2 per cent and a capitalization rate of 7.5 per cent.

The resultant certain cashflow is:

Year	Cash flow	DF at 10%	DCF
1	£10,000	0.909	£9,090
2	£10,000	0.826	£8,260
End of Year 2	£166,464*	0.826	£137,500
		Certain NPV =	£154,850

* £12,485 capitalized at 7.5% at the end of Year 2.

To this must be added the 'overage', that is, the difference between the most likely and the certain scenarios:

The most likely rent on review is £15,000 inflated at 5 per cent per annum growth = £16,537, and the most likely capital value is £16,537 capitalized at 6 per cent = £275,625. Thus the overage, is the most likely value (£275,625) less the certain value (£166,464) which equals £109,161. This can be appraised using a high rate of say 15 per cent:

Year	Overage	DF at RADR	DCF
1	–		
2	–		
End of Year 2	£109,161	0.756	£82,526

The overage is then added to the certain value to give £237,376, which compares with a figure of £209,770 produced by the certainty equivalent model.

The differences produced in this example are large as a result of the high standard deviation assumed. Whilst standard deviations will often be smaller it does highlight the problems of the method. In our view this approach, which depends not only on the calculation of a risk-free return, but also on an appropriate risk-adjustment factor, arrived at on purely subjective grounds, suffers the same theoretical difficulties as any other risk-adjusted discount rate approach. Despite this, the top slice approach, by seeking to identify with greater accuracy where risk attaches, does overcome some of the inadequacies of the certainty equivalent model, and may well be appropriate in the valuation of, for example, premises let on turnover leases.

Despite this, it would appear that risk-adjusted discount techniques are the only methods widely used by institutional investors, although other methods are being actively investigated.

SUMMARY

In this chapter we have sought to give a definition of risk and for the purpose of our examination of techniques to quantify it, we have defined it in terms of the variation of returns from those expected.

Property is often viewed in terms of its 'riskiness', yet there is not a general measure of agreement amongst those who appraise it and manage it as to how such risk should be evaluated. Indeed, a survey we carried out amongst a sample of institutional investors was indicative of the disparity of methods used to quantify risk, or, in many cases, the failure to analyse for risk at all.

Indications are, however, that with the advent of information technology and with an increased requirement by investors for their property assets to perform against targets, many more advisers and owners are seeking to quantify risk.

The study of risk in relation to property can be considered in two contexts; that of the individual investment and that of the overall portfolio. In this chapter we have outlined ways in which it can be considered in relation to individual property appraisal. In the next chapter we look at it in relation to the portfolio.

Chapter 7

Risk and the portfolio

INTRODUCTION

In the previous chapter the concept of risk was introduced and a definition given. We also examined ways in which it could be quantified in relation to individual investments. In this chapter we look at risk in relation to management of portfolio.

The study of risk in relation to a portfolio, portfolio theory as it is known, has its roots in common sense, but it has been developed and refined by theorists, mainly in America over the last thirty years, to the point where it is now widely accepted and its findings used in equity market investment. In order to fully understand the theory a good mathematical knowledge is essential. In this chapter, however, we shall be seeking only to explain the basic premises of the theory and then consider the possible relevance of such an approach to property management, and in particular outline the difficulties of such an approach. It must be pointed out that the application of portfolio theory to property is not general. Some analysts have sought to apply the theory to property, but the survey carried out by the authors confirms the view that its application is not currently widespread.

What then is portfolio theory? Why should the treatment of risk be different when you are considering not just one, but a combination of investments?

PORTFOLIO THEORY

In essence portfolio theory states that the risk relating to a portfolio of investments may be reduced through sensible diversification. This may seem a truism and indeed is easily grasped. What rational individual, if suddenly given a large capital sum, would invest it all in one project? Almost certainly he would seek to invest in several projects, or competing investments for (he would argue), by doing so, the risk of incurring loss would be reduced even if he might forgo the chance of the possibly high returns. From an analysis of any pension fund or other institutional portfolio it can be seen that in practice this is what happens, with diversification between sectors and between investments in each sector.

Diversification therefore is a principle that has easy acceptance, but to know in practice how far to diversify and into what is much more complex.

Consider the following example:

Example 7.1

An investor wishes to create a two-asset portfolio and there are three possible investments from which he can choose:

Investment *A* is low risk, whereas *B* and *C* are both very volatile – one is expected to do well in a time of recession, the other if the economy booms. For simplicity we shall also assume that 50 per cent of his funds will be put into each of the investments chosen, and that there is an equal probability of each state of the economy.

Expected Return

Investment	Boom	Static economy	Slump	Av. return	Standard deviation
A	12%	10%	8%	10%	1.63%
B	20%	10%	0%	10%	8.16%
C	0%	10%	20%	10%	8.16%

If he were to choose only one investment, given the premise that he is risk averse, he would choose investment *A*, as the volatility measured by the standard deviation is clearly the least. However, if he wishes to combine two, the returns become the average of the returns for each investment chosen.

Investment	Boom	Static economy	Slump	Av. return	Standard deviation
(A+B)/2	16%	10%	4%	10%	4.89
(A+C)/2	6%	10%	14%	10%	3.26
(B+C)/2	10%	10%	10%	10%	0

By any combination average return remains unchanged, but by combining B and C risk has been totally eliminated without any loss to average returns. To combine in this way is obviously the optimum solution. We must now ask (1) Why does this happen? (2) Will combining investments always reduce risk? (3)   Is it always possible to totally eliminate risk by diversification?

It is the answer to these three questions which portfolio theory seeks to quantify. Let us firstly answer the question in general terms, and then outline the theory. In our example the reason that the B and C combination provided the most acceptable solution was that the two investments reacted differently to outside influences, or in statistical language, they were negatively correlated. In conditions where one investment was expected to do well, the other was likely to perform badly and vice versa. If, on the other hand, two investments react in broadly similar ways to outside influence (that is, they show a high degree of positive correlation) then the benefits of diversification are minimal. Indeed, if the point is reached whereby they move in identical ways, then there may be no benefit to be obtained by diversifying.

Diversification will not always reduce risk – but it is true to say that where investment returns are likely to move other than in perfect correlation, then diversification can lead to some effective risk reduction. An example of two types of company whose return might be negatively correlated, would be a shoe manufacturer and a shoe repairer; in times of prosperity the shoe manufacturer would prosper, but in times of hardship the shoe repairer would do well.

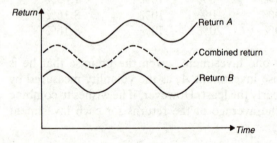

Figure 7.1 Perfect positive correlation of investments

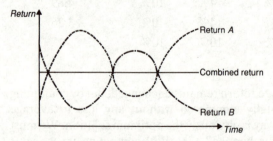

Figure 7.2 Perfect negative correlation of investments

In practice of course it is seldom possible to find investments whose returns are perfectly negatively correlated, as whatever the nature of the individual investment, nearly all will react to economic forces in similar ways. This is clearly demonstrated by observing the movements of share prices. During a period when the market is falling, shares in almost all companies will react in a similar fashion, albeit to a greater or lesser extent. Likewise with property investments – whilst one sector may for a while outperform others, performance in, say, the retail sector, is in general mirrored in other sectors too. A possible exception to this in recent years has been agriculture, whose yields have risen dramatically, whilst other sectors have remained largely static. However, location can well be a key factor; it is quite possible for performance in one area to boom, whilst in other areas it is depressed. A recent study by Jones Lang Wootton (1987) on risk and asset allocation, tracing office performance in differing locations, substantiates this. For practical purposes, however, it is normally regarded as impractical to create a totally risk-free portfolio.

It is clear that any investor should be seeking to maximize his return/risk ratio and thus, when a new asset is acquired, not only should the risk profile of the individual asset be considered, but also the effect upon the overall risk of the portfolio.

MODERN PORTFOLIO THEORY (MPT)

Whilst some understanding of the potential benefits of diversification have long been recognized, the development of a quantitative theory only dates back to the 1950s, when Harry Markowitz published an article and subsequently a book, on portfolio selection. His work has been developed and modified by many academics, largely in the United States. Whilst most of the theorists, and almost all practical work to date, have been concerned with its application to stock market investment, the potential application of modern portfolio theory to property is currently under scrutiny, and Jones Lang Wootton have devised a portfolio modelling approach based on the theories which are currently being tested on their managed portfolios. Whilst they are not alone in seeking to apply such models to property, 'there has been very little fundamental research in this country into the application and development of portfolio theory and asset pricing to property investment' (Brown 1988). Portfolio theory assumes that an investor is both rational and risk averse. As such he has the choice of almost any number of investment opportunities from which to construct his portfolio, as illustrated by Figure 7.3.

Each dot represents a possible combination of investments, whilst the line known as the efficient frontier is the line of best possible risk/return combinations. Clearly any portfolio lying beneath the line is not the maximum trade-off available.

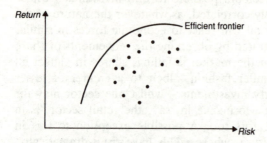

Figure 7.3 Investment opportunities

Having now established an efficient frontier it is necessary to decide just where along the line the investor will choose his portfolio: this must of course depend on his attitude to risk – does he wish to minimize his risk, albeit at the expense of return, or is he prepared for higher risk, in order to achieve maximum return? In property terms, traditionally, it is considered that pension funds must take a risk averse attitude, whilst some private investors may be able to accept higher risk profiles. This risk/return trade-off can be represented by utility or indifference curves (see Figure 7.4).

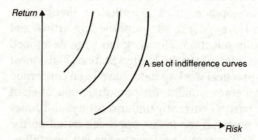

Figure 7.4 A set of risk indifference curves

Each curve represents a 'frontier' of the highest acceptable level of risk for a given return. Clearly the curve furthest to the left will, if available be the most acceptable. When indifference curves are superimposed on the efficient portfolio diagram, it can be seen that the optimal choice will be that at which the indifference curve just touches the efficient frontier (point A) (see Figure 7.5).

Although what has been outlined above looks simple, the plotting of the 'efficient frontier' is extremely complex. To plot it it is necessary not only to calculate future expected returns and variances, but the correlation between each pair of investments and it is this that Markowitz advocates. The measure adopted for this calculation is the covariance.

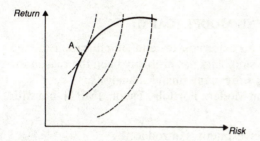

Figure 7.5 The optimal portfolio

To calculate the correlation between each pair it is necessary first to quantify the covariance by the formula:

$$\text{Cov}_{AB} = \sum_{1}^{n} [A_r - \bar{A}_r]\,[B_r - \bar{B}_r]\,P_r$$

where A_r = expected return from A
$\bar{A}_r$ = average expected return from A
B_r = expected return from B
$\bar{B}_r$ = average expected return from B
P_r = probability of each return being achieved

From this the correlation between investments may be obtained as the formula for correlation between two investments can be expressed as:

$$\text{Corr}_{AB} = \frac{\text{Cov}_{AB}}{\sigma_A\,\sigma_B}$$

It follows that once an investor's risk position is known, given any number of possible investment opportunities, all with different risk/return profiles, it is possible to evaluate which particular combination will be optimum for that investor.

From a practical point of view, however, there are not two but thousands of investment opportunities from which to construct a portfolio. Also the proportions in which each investment can be held are generally variable. The calculations therefore become extremely complex – even with computer aid.

Markowitz (1959) developed this model for efficient portfolio determination before calculators and computing were readily accessible and it is clear why portfolio theory remained of academic interest only for many years.

THE CAPITAL ASSET PRICING MODEL (CAPM)

This model was developed as an extension to, and simplification of, the Markowitz theory and its very simplicity has probably been the reason for its acceptance, with reservations, by many financial analysts.

The CAPM is developed from Modern Portfolio Theory (MPT), but with three major distinctions:

1   The concept of a risk-free investment is introduced.
2   A notional market portfolio is used.
3   An efficient market is assumed to exist.

In the original theory the efficient portfolio was comprised of investments all displaying some volatility of return as can be seen from Figure 7.3. However, it is always open to an investor to purchase an investment whose return is fixed, at least in money terms – such as government gilts. If these are included in the diagram a different picture emerges (see Figure 7.6).

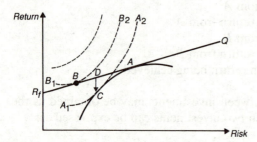

Figure 7.6 Investment choice

It will be recalled that previously our investor chose portfolio A, which just touches the 'efficient frontier' and lies on the indifference curve $A_1 A_2$. However, by *combining* this with investment in a low return risk-free investment (R_f), it is possible for the investor to improve his position to B, which lies on the indifference curve $B_1 B_2$. Line $B_1 B_2$ must of course be preferred to line $A_1 A_2$ as it lies to the left, that is, it has a higher risk/return pay-off.

This new straight line $R_f BQ$ is known as the Capital Market Line (CML). Taking the argument further, if the investor can borrow money at the risk-free rate (R_f) he can create a portfolio at any point along the

CML with any portfolio lying between $R_f Q$ being supported by borrowed funds.

This line is extremely important: no longer is the efficient portfolio choice defined by a curve but a straight line. By combining this portfolio of risky investments with risk-free securities, it is possible to increase return, without increasing risk. For example, a risk averse investor who would have chosen portfolio C under the Markowitz model can, by combining the two sets of portfolios, obtain portfolio D, which has a higher return for the same degree of risk. Clearly then the CML becomes the efficient frontier, and efficient portfolios are those comprising either risk-free investments (classically taken as short-term treasury bills), or, the optimal risky investments, taken as a fully diversified combination of equities, or a combination of both, the ultimate choice regarding the proportions held depending on the investors risk/return trade-off preference, and the investor's attitude to borrowing.

It will be recalled that risk for an individual investment has so far been defined as the volatility of an investments return, measured in terms of its standard deviation. For a portfolio, however, the risk depends upon the inter-reaction of the investments making up the portfolio, measured in terms of covariance. By diversification, risk may be reduced and in some cases eliminated. It can in fact be shown statistically that, although to reduce risk to a minimum, theoretically all possible investments should be held, in practice, to diversify from one investment to ten will reduce risk substantially; to include a further ten will reduce the risk by a much lesser amount, and so on until there reaches a point when further diversification will have no significant effect on the level of risk. This can be seen in Figure 7.7.

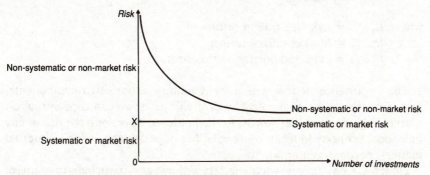

Figure 7.7 Risk reduction by diversification

The risk which can be diversified away relates to the individual characteristics of the investment, for example, whether a company's profit goes up due to good management or, down, due to losing a large contract, and so on, and are thought to be uncorrelated between investments. Such risk is called specific, non-systematic or non-market related risk. There does remain, however a certain degree of risk measured by OX in Figure 7.7 which cannot be diversified away. Such risk is called systematic or market risk, and it is caused by general economic conditions which tend to affect all investments.

This systemic or market risk, as applied to equity investments, is designated by CAPM as beta (β). Therefore β is a measure of market or systematic risk. Although all investments will be subject to such risk, some investments are more affected by general market movements than others. For example, a manufacturer of a standard food item, for example, bread, is less likely to be affected by general market trends than one manufacturing a luxury item. Where an investment is expected to react to systematic risk to a greater extent than the market portfolio, the β of that investment will be greater than one and conversely very stable investments will have a β of less than one.

How then is β for any individual investment calculated?

$$\beta = \frac{\text{Cov } (R_m R_i)}{\text{Variance}_m}$$

where R_m = the expected return from the market portfolio
R_i = expected return from an individual investment

and the expected return from any given portfolio is:

$$E(R_p) = R_f + \beta(R_m - R_f)$$

where R_f = risk-free rate of return
R_m = market rate of return
$E(R_p)$ = expected portfolio rate of return

The importance of this is that by dividing risk into two components, one of which can be eliminated by diversification, we can concentrate on market risk only. In other words, to the holder of a *portfolio* the risk of any individual property in terms of its volatility of performance due to internal matters, becomes unimportant.

Under CAPM theory what matters is how any particular investment behaves in relation to the hypothetical market portfolio. Once this is known, measured in terms of B, the effect of the inclusion of that investment within the portfolio can be measured. It can also be seen that CAPM avoids the need to carry out the vast number of calculations required under Markowitz's original theory, as no longer is covariance between each and every investment required, merely the covariance between the particular investment and the market. It is, however, entirely dependent on the basic simplifying assumption of an efficient market, and this may well not exist in the real world.

The CAPM can be expressed in a diagram (see Figure 7.8).

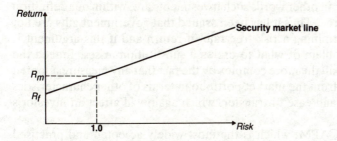

Figure 7.8 Capital Asset Pricing Model (CAPM)

USE OF CAPITAL ASSET PRICING MODEL (CAPM)

This is a brief outline of the theory which, as has been said, is widely used for the evaluation of equities. However, its application to the equities market is not without problems or criticisms, some of which can be summarized as follows:

(a) CAPM is based on very strict assumptions such as a perfectly efficient market, where it is assumed that existing assets start out being 'correctly' priced by having incorporated all available information. This view is open to much criticism, particularly if the reactions of the stock market in October 1987 are considered.

(b) The calculation of β is far from easy. It is normally done by market analysts offering risk measurement services on the basis of regression analysis of past performance of the company under consideration plotted against the market. Not only does this present difficulties in analysis, including choice of time period, but there must be doubt as to how accurate information on past performance will be in calculating future trends. Accordingly the actual calculation of β may be regarded as liable to error, and if it is, then the whole basis upon which CAPM is founded, flounders.

(c) In order to establish the expected return from a portfolio, not only must β be known, but also the risk-free and market rate of return. Given that the market portfolio is hypothetical not actual, the calculation of the market return is also a subjective measure. In practice the use of a market index based on a sample of shares is usually adopted as being the market portfolio.

The risk-free rate is also open to dispute as discussed in Chapter 6. Classically it has been taken as the return obtainable from short-term government bonds. However, although the income from such bonds is fixed and certain, capital values are very volatile, responding as they do to the slightest movement of investor expectation. Thus total return measured in terms of income and capital value change over a given time period is *not* fixed but volatile; in other words such investments are, within our definition of risk, not risk free. Thus it has been argued that government gilts are not suitable for determining a risk-free rate of return and if this argument is sustained the problem of what to use as a substitution arises. Indeed the situation is made all the more complex by the fact that any measure adopted is likely to differ from the market portfolio in terms of other characteristics such as liquidity and ease of transfer, which again will affect an investor's required return.

To conclude, CAPM, which is the most widely accepted and practised branch of MPT, does offer a theoretically simple and thus attractive quantitative measurement of portfolio risk. By dividing total risk into two, it dispenses with one by diversification and measures the other in terms of a relationship (β) between a given portfolio and the general market movements, such relationships being governed by the market and risk-free returns.

Its use by investors in the equity market to which its application is currently confined is now widespread. Once its limitations are realized and treated with the necessary caution it can be used as an aid to positive management, by enabling risk-return analysis to be carried out.

APPLICATION OF CAPM TO PROPERTY

An appreciation of MPT and CAPM is necessary for the property manager for two reasons:

1 Most large investors in property are owners of a mixed portfolio. As such it is essential to appreciate the decisions which prompt movements of investments, both within other sectors and between sectors.
2 The possible application of such theories to property is currently under consideration. For many years property investors have taken an instinctive approach to risk and have diversified in order to reduce or spread the risk. Indeed, the requirement by investors to have property portfolios such that no one property has dominated the portfolio has, in recent years, led to practical difficulties caused by the sheer value of some properties. For example, given a property with a value of £30m, if this is to form no more than, say, 10 per cent of a fund's property holding, then the only funds who could purchase such an investment would be those with property portfolios valued in excess of £300m. Given that the

typical fund will have at most only 20 per cent of its funds in property (and probably substantially less), this means that such an investment can only be held as part of a balanced and diversified portfolio, which exceeds a total worth of £1,500m. The result, of course, of such a policy is that the number of potential owners for such investments is very limited. The implication of this and one possible solution, namely unitization, is considered in Chapter 12.

The possibility of measuring portfolio risk for property is in its infancy, but the debate is increasing. The main difficulties, in addition to those affecting equities, are now considered:

1   There is a lack of a recognized market index from which to measure market return. There are several indices of property return, such as the Jones Lang Wootton Property Index (rental and capital), the Hillier Parker/Investor's Chronicle Rent Index, and the Richard Ellis Property Market Indicators, to name but three. However, these are all based on comparatively small samples. The Investment Property Databank attempts to pool these resources but 'They have met with limited success to date' (MacLeary and Nanthakumaran 1988).

   All of these indices are of necessity subjective as they are on the whole based upon valuations rather than market transactions. As the valuations are not, and indeed cannot be, reviewed with the frequency it is possible to achieve with equities, inevitably the figures will reflect past, rather than current, performance. Yet if a property index is not used, it is hard to see how any other reliable measure of market return could be calculated. However, imperfect though such indices are, as long as the imperfections are to a large extent consistent, it should be possible to derive a correlation between such market returns and properties of differing types, and once this is accepted, the basic concept of CAPM can be said to be relevant.

2   If CAPM is to be applied to property, it is a prerequisite that a standard method of appraisal should be adopted, yet as MacLeary and Nanthakumaran (1988) state, 'There is a continuing lack of agreement as to just how this should be done'. Discounted cash flow (DCF) techniques have been widely advocated but Baum and Crosby (1988) admit that they 'would wish to see the process of change accelerate'.

3   Brown (1988) argues that in practice all property indices are calculated in such a way that some specific (non-market) risk is left residually in the calculation. Hence the index return may not be the true return. If this is so, then the application of CAPM becomes meaningless.

The effect of risk reduction resulting from combining property investments of different types, for example, shops and offices and investment in other sectors, until recently has not been measured in any quantitative way.

Since the supremacy of the institutions as major landowners has become established, attention has been centred on measurement and maximization of return. As a corollory to this, risk has been considered and various ways of dealing with it have been developed, both for individual investments and most notably for combinations of investments. The latter depends for the most part on MPT and, in particular, the derived CAPM. Whilst the assumptions of this model, particularly in relation to the assessment of market and risk-free rates of return, creates both practical and theoretical problems, it is being pursued by both academics and practitioners. The acceptance of the model would seem to be far from universal, and many people would probably dismiss as impractical its extension of application to property.

However, it does in our view promote a region of thinking of importance to investment advisers, and as such is to be advocated. To quote MacLeary and Nanthakumaran (1988):

> It is generally recognised that the analysis of property investments should be more explicit and such analysis should include a formal treatment of risk. However, there is much concern over how this should be done given the nature of the asset and the market.

Whether the further research which will surely take place will provide evidence of practical application is not known, but it can at least be stated that a knowledge of portfolio theory cannot but help to improve the decision-making process of both advisers and investors alike.

To sum up the inherent difficulties of applying the CAPM to property:

The CAPM equation has three variables, namely the risk-free rate of return, the market return and the risk premium appropriate to that investment measured in terms of β.

We have seen from the above that there is no consensus regarding the calculation of either the risk-free rate or the market return. It will be recalled that it is calculated using the expected market return and the expected return from the individual investment. We have seen in earlier chapters that the calculation of individual return is fraught with difficulty. Thus, although the theory initially has its attractions, practical difficulties are encountered in respect of each of the component figures on which the theory is founded. Whether in the future satisfactory solutions to all these problems will be found we cannot say, but at least the issue is on the professional agenda.

CONCLUSION

In the past the question of risk in relation to property management was at best treated intuitively, and at worst ignored. The traditional view has been that property is generally low risk when compared to equities, but high risk in relation to government gilts. Hence in setting a required rate of return (equated yield) from property investments, investors have tended to accept a 2 per cent premium over gilts – this premium to reflect the increased risk and lack of liquidity when compared with gilts.

Chapter 8

Active management
(1) the commercial lease

INTRODUCTION

One of the features of property which distinguishes it from other investment media is its requirement to be managed.

Although all investments require at least some degree of management to ensure appropriate disposal and acquisition decisions, during the holding period the investor has generally little to do except receive the income. In the case of equity shares the shareholder does, of course, have voting rights, but in practice the investor is divorced from the day-to-day activities which determine the success or otherwise of the investment.

The same is not true of property; the fabric of the building must be maintained, decisions regarding improvements and redevelopments have to be taken in the case of investment properties lettings must be effected and monitored.

In this chapter and Chapter 9 we examine the process of managing commercial property both from the 'micro angle', looking at the minutae of commercial lettings, and from the 'macro angle', examining the ways in which the portfolio's performance may be maximized. The 'macro' look is undertaken in Chapter 9. In this chapter first, we attempt some definitions, and second, we outline some aspects of current commercial letting practice by looking at the main terms contained in commercial leases.

MANAGEMENT STYLES

Every property-owner must decide at an early stage of portfolio planning what management style is to be adopted as a norm: is it to be active or passive, 'hands-on' or 'hands-off'?

Passive management

As its name implies, passive management is a largely reactive style where the owner undertakes little or no positive planning to ensure maximum performance of his investments. Thus for an owner-occupied estate the occupational needs of the owner would be paramount with scant attention being given to the ability of the properties held to perform as investments. For investment portfolios a passive management style implies that the owner does not seek opportunities to maximize the performance of his investment.

Properties so held will tend to be let to good covenants, if possible on terms such that the occupier undertakes all responsibility for the maintenance, repair, redevelopment or refurbishment of the property. In short, it implies a delegation of authority from the owner to the occupier for matters other than disposal. Under passive management the owner involvement in the redevelopment process would normally be triggered by lease expiry, the tenant vacating or an approach by a third party.

The advantage of such a stance to the owner is that management involvement is minimized and, if the tenant is good, reliable and property 'aware', the property will doubtless be well maintained and improved as necessary and appropriate.

The disadvantage of adopting such a position is that very frequently an inappropriate estate is held and the individual properties may well not be producing their optimum returns.

Active management

In contrast to passive management, the owner seeking to actively manage will adopt a pro-active role, constantly seeking ways to improve the performance of the portfolio, both on an individual property and portfolio basis. This style of management will encompass both long-term strategy and short-term action; it is an attention to detail combined with a rigorous command of the overview. It is only by placing full weight on getting the details of any letting right and by fostering good landlord and tenant relationships that optimum performance will be achieved. Active management starts at the point of planning the portfolio, continues through the development process to the handling of day-to-day management matters and, in some cases, to eventual disposal. Where estates are held for investment purposes the terms of the lease will be a crucial matter; where it is an occupational estate, matters such as the handling of repairs and maintenance, and refurbishments will be paramount. With occupational estates the performance of the property as an investment as well as a unit of resource will also be an important consideration.

Hands-off/hands-on management

A different classification of management styles lies in the distinction
between 'hands-off' management and the 'hands-on' approach. In the
former any lettings arranged will seek to distance the property-owner from
actual day-to-day involvement with the property, whereas the advocate of
'hands-on' management will retain control over matters such as insurance,
repair and possibly maintenance and decoration.

It must be emphasized that the two classifications are not mutually
exclusive. It is possible for an owner to desire a 'hands-off' approach
to management whilst still pursuing a programme of active management.
Similarly, a property-owner whose estate is let mainly on short-term leases,
demanding detailed day-to-day management, may still fail to optimize the
use and performance of his portfolio by not taking sufficient interest in
strategic planning matters.

In summary, active management must in our view be the ambition of all
property investors, whilst the decision whether to adopt a 'hands-on' or
'hands-off' approach may depend on the type of property held and tenant
demand. For example, if a fairly weak letting market exists, then the tenants'
requirements and desires will dominate and it is likely that at least some
burden of repair liability will fall upon the landlord. If the market is strong
the landlord will be in a position to control the letting terms more rigidly.

Before looking at current practice, it is appropriate to consider briefly the
evolution of the modern commercial lease.

LEASING PATTERNS

A lease is in essence a commercial contract between two parties who are
free to strike whatever bargain they so wish, subject to certain overriding
statutory provisions, such as the Landlord and Tenant Acts 1927, 1954,
1969, and 1988 for commercial property and the Rent Acts (notably the
1977 Rent Act) and Housing Acts (notably the 1988 Housing Act) in respect
of residential lets. The effects of the legislation are in many instances far-
reaching and have a significant impact on the nature of investment patterns,
as we have seen in Chapter 3.

In this chapter we are concerned only with the terms of commercial
lettings, and even then only with some of the management aspects. To
have a full appreciation of the work undertaken by the manager involved
in arranging and advising upon commercial leases, involves a detailed
knowledge of the law of landlord and tenant, and readers are advised
to consult suitable law texts to gain a full coverage of the subject.

The modern commercial lease, described below, has evolved over a long
period as the needs and aspirations of both landlords and tenants has altered.
If we look back to the time prior to the industrial revolution, we will find
no leases that are comparable with those concluded today. Land ownership

was concentrated principally in only a few hands, the large landowning individuals, the Church, and charitable institutions. Lettings, which were largely agricultural or residential, tended to be short term in nature and the landowner would invariably retain responsibility for the repair and maintenance of the fabric of the buildings. The tenants had little, if any, security of tenure, and the system depended for its survival on a degree of goodwill between the parties and on the inability of the occupying tenants to dictate terms.

With the coming of the industrial revolution patterns of ownership, and indeed property structures and uses, changed.

Ground leases – pre-1945

In the mid-nineteenth century came the development of many residential estates, built by developers holding on ground leases of ninety-nine years. Although ground leases had been in use before it was at this time that their use became widespread. These agreements placed total responsibility for development, redevelopment and repair upon the ground lessees, and invariably were at a fixed ground rent. Indeed they can be seen as examples of both 'hands-off' and passive management on the part of the freeholders.

Ground leases – post-1945

The ground lease has, of course, become an established part of modern leasing practice, but it is only as recently as the 1950s that landowners were granting long leases at fixed rents without review. An example of this is St Giles Circus in central London which was a bomb-damaged site leased in the late 1950s to Oldham Estates for a period of 125 years at a fixed rent (see Marriott 1967). Today such leases would be considered totally inappropriate, and ground leases commonly incorporate rent reviews at ten-, or more commonly five-yearly intervals. Frequently, too, the term is 125 years, as many institutional investors are not prepared to regard ninety-nine year leases as suitable.

A ground lease, whether it contains reviews or not, represents possibly the ultimate example of the 'hands-off' management. Whilst it may be the only practical method of leasing for a landowner to adopt when his property requires capital injection which he cannot provide, there are always inherent disadvantages and difficulties with such agreements.

Probably the two most important revolve around the length of term and the mechanics for settling rent at review. With regard to the former, by committing the property out of his control for a period normally in excess of sixty years the freeholder has lost the ability to influence effectively the optimum management of the land for a very substantial period. Whilst a 'break clause' may be introduced to cover the eventuality of redevelopment becoming viable, such clauses are likely to be resisted by the ground lessee. The problem over rent review concerns the valuation difficulties that can be encountered in trying to establish the rental value of the site as if undeveloped. Inevitably assumptions have to be made regarding the type of assumed development and this has recently proved to be a fruitful area for litigation now that rent reviews have become commonplace in ground leases. Frequently, therefore, the reviewed rent will relate to the developed site and the rent will be fixed as a percentage of the full rental value of either the buildings erected on the site, or more probably upon the basis of a hypothetical development.

Occupational leases – pre-1945

Parallel to the development of ground leases has been the development of occupational leases. Prior to the post-war growth of institutional investment in property, the main investors were those with a long tradition of active involvement in property management; thus they were not necessarily averse to accepting liability for insuring and repairing. Offices were often buildings which had been constructed in the nineteenth century and let in suites with the landlord accepting full responsibility for all outgoings, apart possibly from internal decoration. Occupational leases were generally short. With the retail sector a stronger tradition of owner-occupation existed, but the lettings that did exist were either short terms at fully 'inclusive' rents, or long term but with the lessee accepting no more than an internal repair liability. Rent reviews were almost non-existent.

Residential and agricultural lettings up to the post-war period continued as before, on weekly or annual agreements, although residential ground leases of individual dwellings were commonplace.

The industrial sector was the exception to the general rule of landlord involvement, with a predominance of owner-occupation within the primary industries and full repairing leases widespread in the secondary sector.

Occupational leases – post-1945

The position since 1945 has changed dramatically, due largely to two factors. First, the emergence of the financial institutions as property investors, and second, inflation. More recently the impact of obsolescence has begun to affect investor attitudes.

Legislation too, as already mentioned, has been important in determining the terms of lettings. For example, the Leasehold Reform Act 1967 has given the right to most occupying residential long lessees to purchase the freehold of their houses at artificially restricted prices. This has had the effect of preventing the creation of any new long leases of dwelling houses. In the commercial field, the Landlord and Tenant Act 1954 gives to occupying tenants the right to take a new lease of up to fourteen years, albeit on almost open market letting terms, upon lease expiry.

The institutions, as landowners, generally had no historic background of property ownership and therefore lacked the expertise and indeed the desire to become involved in the day-to-day management of their investments. In short, although they have become large landowners, many are not committed to property *per se*, merely to property as an investment medium. This can be illustrated by the view that their investment norm for property is 'to be regarded as *zero* by fund managers unless they are otherwise convinced' (Brian Wootton, Hill Samuel Property Services Ltd, talking at a conference on property management in 1987). The pension funds in particular have sought to invest in properties let in such a way that their day-to-day management responsibility is minimized, a point of particular importance to those funds which cannot justify their own in-house team of property advisors. In short, the desire in general has been for a 'hands-off' approach as defined above.

The second factor that has brought about change, namely inflation, has influenced the shortening of lease terms from the commonly forty-two years which prevailed pre-war to the norm of twenty to twenty-five years current at the time of writing. More important than the change in term has been the emergence of rent review clauses. A previously fixed rent gave way in the late 1950s to a reviewable rent, with reviews every twenty-one or fourteen years then to seven-yearly reviews in the 1960s leading to the current norm of five-yearly. During the period of high inflation in the 1970s there was a brief flirtation with three-yearly reviews, but tenant resistance, combined with a period of fairly static values and protracted and expensive rent review dispute costs, soon led to the practice being abandoned for all but special circumstances.

The commercial lease pattern that has emerged, sometimes referred to as 'the institutional lease' (McIntosh and Sykes 1984) is outlined below, and it is this lease type which is discussed in some detail later in the chapter.

For properties other than commercial, namely residential and agricultural, the old short-term or annual tenancy agreements still prevail, although changing legislation in the housing sector has seen the introduction of different types of agreements. Heavy industrial properties continue to be dominated by owner-occupation, due to the specialist nature of the structures, which can render them unsuitable as investment vehicles.

Since 1980 there has been a growth in interest in leisure properties, as noted in Chapter 3, but there is little published information regarding the nature of these lettings and the ownership of such properties tends to be concentrated within specialist organizations.

The full repairing lease or 'institutional' lease.

The full repairing commercial lease, or 'institutional lease' as it has sometimes been called, is a concept rather than a reality. Every lease is a compromise, the result of negotiation between a landowner and a prospective tenant. When tenant demand for premises is strong the landlord will be able to dictate terms. When it is not the lease will more closely reflect the occupier's needs. Institutional investor requirements have been for properties let on full repairing terms and properties not so let will be either unacceptable to institutional purchasers or acceptable only on a higher yield basis. There is therefore considerable pressure upon letting agents to achieve a lease which effectively puts the onus of responsibility for all outgoings on the lessee.

The major hallmarks of such lettings are:

(a) A term of years, certain of twenty or twenty-five years.
(b) A lessee of recognized national standing. In the case of retail premises this is considered to be of particular importance.
(c) The lessee is responsible for all repairs, maintenance, and other outgoings; insurance is frequently arranged by the lessor but with the lessee paying the cost of the annual premiums.
(d) Some restrictions upon assignment, sublettings and the carrying out of tenant's improvements and alterations.
(e) In the case of multi-let buildings where a full repairing clause is not practicable a fully recoverable service charge.
(f) Rent reviews every five years, normally upwards only.

The practical implications of these clauses are examined below, but the general intention to note here is that such lettings are consistent with a 'hands-off' style of management. Whether this is coupled with a passive approach to management will depend upon the individual investor and is discussed in Chapter 9.

The full repairing and insuring lease (FRI lease) as outlined above has received almost unanimous acceptance by investors, and with strong demand for good commercial property it has proved acceptable to occupiers also. However, it is interesting to note that it is only in the UK that such a tenure pattern has become established, and in Chapter 12 we compare the standard UK FRI lease with practice in other countries. Even in this country there is comment as to the advisability or otherwise of total acceptance of this lease style (*Urban Property Management*, CALUS study paper 1970, also *The Maintenance of Commercial Property*, report of an RICS working party 1986).

THE FRI LEASE – ADVANTAGES AND DRAWBACKS

The advantages of the FRI lease are mainly connected to the certainty which it gives to both parties to the transaction. From the freeholder's viewpoint the income is known and predictable, not only up to the rent review, but beyond if an upwards only rent review clause is incorporated. Thus the downside risk is minimized. Any rise in rental values will be recouped by the landlord at review, any loss absorbed by the lessee. As many investors are now very conscious of performance measurement the ability to know what rent can be guaranteed in the future is important. This contrasts with the cases where the landlord retains liability for repairs and the income flows vary according to the annual cost of outgoings which fluctuate year by year.

The length of the term too is perceived to be an advantage for the lessor. It gives a long-term prospective to the investment, and from the lessee's viewpoint the term, when initially granted, is of sufficient duration to justify the carrying out of improvement works if appropriate and allow for amortization of the costs.

A further benefit, as mentioned above, is that this type of lease minimizes the landlords management costs and, in short, produces a readily saleable investment.

On the negative side the FRI lease can be seen to have drawbacks from both parties' viewpoints. First, although such leases may have freed the freeholder from the burden of day-to-day management, a glance at any Landlord and Tenant legal handbook will demonstrate amply that the repairing and other clauses are fraught with problems of legal interpretation. Questions such as the following arise:

How far does a 'full repairing' clause extend?
When does repair become renewal?
What is an improvement and what a fixture or fitting?
When is it reasonable for a landlord to refuse consent to assign?
What is the correct interpretation of a rent review clause?
What constitutes a 'reasonable rent'?

The answers to all these questions, which are only conclusive in respect of the particular lease to which they relate, are all problems which can easily yield higher financial returns to the lawyers than the landowner concerned!

If a matter of dispute arises in the interpretation of a lease the consequences can flow for the entire length of the lease. With short leases which have no review clause and those where the landlord retains responsibility for outgoings the potential areas for litigation are reduced.

Apart from these legalistic problems, other drawbacks to this form of tenure have become manifest in recent years. By locking themselves into leases of twenty-five years, freeholders have reduced their ability to respond flexibly to changing circumstances. To quote a hypothetical example:

In 1980 an institution granted a lease of a small office block on the edge of the business sector of a provincial town on an 'institutional' lease for a term of twenty-five years. At the time of the grant there were no planning proposals which affected the property, nor were any thought likely. In 1985 the local plan for the town was reviewed and a shortfall in shopping provision was identified. As a result of this, plans for a major shopping development encompassing the site of the office building were proposed two years later. As the lease at that time still had seventeen years to run, the price that the freeholder eventually achieved on the sale of their interest to the development consortium was considerably less than it would have been had the letting been for a shorter period or had at least contained a break clause.

Allied to the problem highlighted above is the problem of obsolescence. If a building is let on full repairing terms, whilst the tenants might comply with the letter of the agreement, by the end of the term the building may be obsolete in terms of design and in need of refurbishment or even redevelopment. If on the other hand the building had been subject to 'hands-on' management, it is frequently the case that the worst aspects of obsolescence could be avoided.

The last problem to highlight is that connected with the 'declining tenant'. This presents difficulties for both parties. When a property is initially let the landlord will seek to ensure that the lessee provides the best covenant achievable. Over the period of the lease, however, the lessee may wish to assign his interest, either through his changing occupational requirements or because the location of the property has changed in nature. Although most leases do provide for restrictions upon assignment, in practice the grounds upon which a landlord can refuse consent are limited so that by the end of the lease the lessee in occupation could be vastly inferior in quality to the original tenant. From the original lessee's viewpoint there is also an inherent danger. Under English Law a tenant remains liable for the covenants under the lease even following an assignment. Therefore a tenant who assigns his interest in a property could potentially find himself liable for an accrued claim arising years after his occupation of the premises has ended. With a short lease problems in relation to assignments are less likely to arise.

Despite the inherent problems associated with the institutional lease it remains the dominant lease type adopted for commercial property, although in the retail sector increasing use is being made both of turnover leases, where the rent, or part thereof, is allied to the audited accounts of the business, and of shorter leases as the cycles for redevelopment and refurbishment become ever shorter. In the Metrocentre in the north-east, for example, a combination of three different lease types are being used, depending on the nature of the trade, and the lessee.

It must be noted that the whole possibility of a FRI standard lease only exists where there is a strong tenant demand such that the landlord can dictate the terms. In cases where this is not so, the lessee's negotiating strength may well prevent the landlord achieving his objectives. This of itself has had a 'spin-off' effect in making prime properties, for which there is most tenant demand, the only ones that are let on terms acceptable to investing institutional buyers, so that over recent decades the yield differential between prime and secondary properties has increased.

It follows that there are implications for property performance. The prime unit for which the market is prepared to accept a lower yield will of necessity have to show greater rental growth than the secondary unit if it is to achieve the investor's required return.

As has been indicated, the current form of standard leasing pattern is under review by practitioners. Some investors, who a few years ago would have maintained an attitude of 'hands-off' management, are more prepared to consider taking a 'hands-on' stance in relation to their portfolios. However, despite this, many investors still wish to distance themselves from day-to-day involvement. Relevant to this is the recently-evolved policy of one of the major brewers to let a substantial number of their public houses on standard twenty-year full repairing commercial leases at open market rents, in replacement for short-term, non-assignable agreements with landlord repair liability.

Another change has also been taking place in management attitudes. No longer is a passive approach considered acceptable by property-owners, be they occupiers or investors. Instead, landowners are seeking ways in which performance may be measured and maximized. However, this desire for a pro-active approach does not appear to the writers to be coupled with a significant move towards 'hands-on' management, except with the newer forms of property such as business parks and shopping centres.

COMMERCIAL LEASE MANAGEMENT

The terms agreed for any new letting are fundamental to the performance of the investment and we now examine those aspects of a typical business lease which most affect the property's performance. Although all lease clauses will have some impact, to consider every one is outside the scope of this book and readers are advised to consult other standard landlord and tenant texts. Reference to case law in this section has been kept to a minimum as the law is constantly changing. The reader should, of course, ensure that he is aware of the most recent case law before making any major letting decisions. We have attempted to distil the main principles involved.

Tenant selection

Much has been written on the subject of tenant selection; indeed it has been argued by Thorncroft (1965) that 'The selection of tenants is the most important decision that a landlord takes'. As the value of property stems from the rent which it can command, the choice of tenant, who is the creator of the investment income, is obviously crucial. If a poor tenant is chosen, the owner may have to live with the decision for a considerable time.

The criteria for choice can be summarized as follows:

(a) The tenant must be appropriate to the building and the surrounding properties. This is particularly true in a shopping centre where the question of tenant mix must be considered. The freeholder will be attempting to achieve maximum attraction to shoppers and therefore the spread and quality of retailers is of utmost importance.

(b) The tenant must be investigated to ensure that he can pay the rent and fulfil the other covenants. If possible he should have a good track record or, failing that, produce good credentials. In this regard the value of any written reference often lies more in what it does *not* say than in what it does.

(c) The tenant must have sensible and satisfactory proposals for the use of the building. To say this, however, is not enough. In practice, the manager responsible for letting has a more difficult task to undertake: not only must he adjudge the prospective lessee on the basis of the available information, but he must use his skill and judgement in respect of the future likely performance of the lessee. When examining accounts it is important to ensure that the lessee is properly funded. This may involve some very difficult and perceptive questioning and a personal interview is always necessary, not only with the prospective lessee but also, in some cases, with his financial guarantor. In the case of a company, for example, research should be undertaken to establish that practices such as 'off-balance sheet' financing are not being used to distort the debt/equity ratios and give a misleading impression of the company's financial position.

When selecting a tenant for a prime property the choice may not be too critical – after all, if the tenant does default it should not prove difficult or slow to relet, and in practice the manager normally will have good applicants from whom to choose. It is in selecting a tenant for a secondary property that the judgement of the manager is really tested, when faced with a selection of poor prospective lessees. At this point it is essential to consider factors such as the proposed use of the premises – is it one for which there is likely to be a future steady demand or not? A secondary shop unit, whose only potential lessees are a bookshop and a ladies' fashion store, neither of whom are national retailers, is more likely to be the subject of default if let to the fashion retailer. No examination of the tenants' trading accounts will show up such factors; it requires a full appreciation of market forces, yet they are extremely relevant to the selection.

The term

Before any property is offered for let proposals for the term of the lease should have been prepared.

The length of term will depend upon the overall strategy for the property, and possibly the portfolio. Conventional wisdom dictates that, for good quality commercial property, without any immediate redevelopment prospects, a lessor will seek to grant a lease of typically twenty to twenty-five years, with regular five-yearly rent reviews. However, the significant shortening of the redevelopment/refurbishment cycle that has occurred in the last ten years, coupled with changing market conditions and greater international influences (see Chapter 12) has made some such decisions appear inappropriate at the very least. Admittedly, to put in a redevelopment/refurbishment break clause could arguably adversely affect the level of rent received, but such reduction in many cases would be more than offset if it enabled redevelopment to take place at the optimum time (see Chapter 10).

Tenants, too, frequently demand shorter leases, particularly if the company is one whose origins are in a country such as the USA where short leases prevail (see Chapter 12). The shorter lease gives them greater flexibility to move on when their business needs dictate without the aggravation of finding a suitable assignee. The length of the term should then be considered closely, and at a time when investment time horizons are short a degree of caution should be exercised before granting leases of substantial length.

Where it is a lease renewal rather than a new letting, the manager will always have regard to the possibility of a referral by the tenant to the courts under the provisions of the Landlord and Tenant Act 1954 (part 2). Under these provisions a lessee is usually entitled to a new lease at a market rent as defined in s.34. The s.34 rent will, *inter alia*, exclude the value of tenant's improvements provided that they were carried out:

by the tenant with the landlord's consent,
not under an obligation to the landlord,
at the tenant's own expense,
during the term now expiring, however long ago, or within the last 21 years, and
there has been no effective break in the tenancy.

If tenant's improvements are involved, judicious negotiation of lease term and rent review pattern should be undertaken so that the tenant's improvements revert to the landlord at the earliest possible date.

An example will illustrate this point:

A twenty-year lease is due to expire shortly and the parties are negotiating a new term. The maximum the court are empowered to grant under the statutory provisions is fourteen years, but the tenant would like a longer term. Improvements were carried out six years ago by the tenant and would fall to be disregarded in the calculation of a new rent by the courts under the provisions of s.34 of the Act.

If the landlord argues for a maximum of fourteen years, then not only will the improvements be disregarded at the current renewal, but also on a subsequent renewal, as they will by then still be less than twenty-one years old. However, if by agreement a fifteen-year or, indeed, a twenty-year lease is granted, subject to a 'model' rent review clause (see below), the landlord will realize the rental benefit in fifteen years' time, that is, as soon as the improvements are twenty-one years old.

At the time of writing the standard twenty- or twenty-five-year lease is prevalent, but there are indications that both landlords and tenants are adopting more flexible attitudes to lease length in the light of changing market demands.

The demise

Theoretically the demise should be a straightforward matter. However, mistakes do occur, and if possible the surveyor should inspect the property with the solicitor to avoid the stupidities that can occur. For example, the writers have experienced leases referring to outbuildings and gardens where neither exist, nor possibly could, or excluding part of the building such as the toilet accommodation. Similarly, the question of roof voids, for example, should be considered. If they always were, the case of *Hatfield* v. *Moss* (1988) would never have been heard by the courts.

Wherever possible the demise must be defined, not only in words, but also with accurate plans. When a lease encompasses the possibility of the tenant building extensions or other buildings on the site, the demise should be clearly stated to include the building currently erected together with any extensions and buildings subsequently built either by way of extension or replacement of those existing. If this is not done, there is a real possibility that at rent review such substitute buildings or extensions may be excluded from the definition of the demise.

In addition, it is essential that the demise is explicit regarding fixtures and their ownership so that disputes such as that which occurred in *Young* v. *Dalgety* (1986) are avoided. In that case the landlord and the tenant were in dispute as to whether certain fitting-out works including the installation of false ceilings, carried out by the tenant under an obligation to the landlord, constituted improvements or fixtures or fittings. The landlord argued that the works were improvements and thus fell to be rentalized, but the court held that they were tenant's fittings and thus not part of the fabric of the building.

If schedules are attached to the lease it should be ensured that they are clear and accurate. Buildings will inevitably change over the life of, say, a twenty-year lease, and it is important that schedules are still comprehensible at the end of the term. The use of plans, accurate and to scale, if possible, is advocated, together with the holding of photographic records, the importance of which cannot be overstated.

The problem of time obscuring the facts and intentions of the parties at the time of the grant are reduced in the case of relatively short leases.

Rent-free periods and fitting-out works

Very frequently an investor will wish to let a building in need of capital expenditure. In such cases he faces the choice of:

(a) Carrying out the work himself and letting at an enhanced rent.
(b) Granting a lease requiring the lessee to carry out a scheme of works to be approved by him and within a given timetable, usually in return for a rent-free period or on an initially reduced rent.
(c) Granting a licence or agreement for lease to the prospective lessee at a peppercorn rent in order that he might do the works with the subsequent grant of a lease on completion of the work.

There are many implications in this matter which the investor should consider before deciding which course of action to adopt. If the investor decides to pursue option (a) he will minimize any uncertainty at rent review regarding whether the works can be included in the calculations and he will maximize his rental returns. The drawbacks are that he has not only the initial capital outlay to fund but the necessity to plan and implement the work. Even then the eventual lessee may need to carry out further work to adapt the building fully to suit his operational needs. The tax position, and whether the landlord possesses the necessary expertise to handle the contract, should also be considered.

Option (b) is a course of action frequently adopted, as it releases the freeholder from the commitment to spend money, and by ensuring that the works are made a condition of the grant of the lease the rental benefit is received at the first rent review, thus bolstering performance, often very significantly. However, this route is not without its problems. Once the lease is granted it may in practice be difficult to monitor the speed with which the works are carried out and their standard of execution. Accordingly at review it may be found that the rental value has not been enhanced as much as originally envisaged. Also, if the demise was not very carefully worded and extensive works are carried out, much scope for argument may arise, as a plethora of legal cases indicates. Once more tax advice should be taken as to whether the works would be regarded as a premium in kind and taxable as such.

Option (c) should also be considered for its fiscal implications but it does have certain advantages over (b). It is much easier to persuade a prospective lessee to carry out a scheme of works acceptable in terms of both design and construction standard if the threat of failure to obtain a lease is present, than to try to enforce a covenant in a lease that has already been granted. In addition it does mean that the lease when granted will be of a property that can be accurately described and for which up-to-date plans exist.

Thus, in summary, the various options should be evaluated particularly in regard to financial and fiscal implications, ease of enforcement, management and effect on future rental performance.

Market rents and turnover rents

Most commercial leases are granted on the basis of an open market rent determined by market forces and being the maximum amount that a prospective lessee will be prepared to pay for the premises on the terms of the proposed lease. This will be established either by the letting agent or property manager using his skill and judgement as to rental levels in the locality, or by inviting rental offers informally or by tender. However, when this latter course is adopted caution must be exercised as the maximum offer may come from an applicant who will not be able to sustain the offered figure. In particular, with shopping centres, where it is essential to the success of the whole centre to have strong 'anchor' tenants, a more flexible approach may be required. There are many examples where investor owners have been prepared to grant leases of some shop units at concessionary rents to national retailers in order to enable the remaining units to be let more easily. There will subsequently be the opportunity to review once trading patterns have become established. A different method of assessing rents used for some shopping centres, notably those developed by Capital and Counties, is by reference to turnover. Turnover rents, commonly found in the United States, have become the subject of discussion among developers in the UK in the late 1980s but have so far not become widespread in use, although British Rail use them for most of their station trading operations.

Turnover rents in the UK are usually calculated on the basis of a 'base rent', commonly 80 per cent of full open market rental value, together with a percentage of the gross turnover shown in the audited accounts. The percentage adopted is determined by the type of trade and is often between 4 per cent (for food retailers who run a large volume, low profit business) to well in excess of 10 per cent for luxury clothes and jewellery where turnover is lower but profit margins are higher.

The chief arguments in favour of turnover rents are that:

(a) the rent more accurately reflects the tenant's ability to pay;
(b) it facilitates optimum tenant mix;
(c) it provides the landlord with a better understanding of the tenant's

business and encourages the landlord to take a pro-active role in the management of the unit; and

(d) it enables the landlord to benefit without time-lag from any capital injection he makes or any upturn in trade.

From the tenant's viewpoint the chief attraction is in risk reduction. Turnover leases are not without disadvantage. Ones which have been identified are:

(a) the possible problems at lease renewal occasioned by the operation of the Landlord and Tenant Act 1954, which makes no provision for any new lease other than one let on full open market rent;
(b) the additional administrative burdens are perceived to be disadvantageous by many landlords; and
(c) rental income fluctuates, and only 80 per cent of the full rental value is secure.

Whether the use of turnover leases will increase cannot be known but their use can be seen as a positive measure to reduce potential conflicts of interest between landlords and tenants and one which can help to foster good relations.

Lastly, on the question of drafting rent clauses, the dates for rent payment and provision for back payments should be spelled out. Normal practice is for rents to be payable quarterly in advance, which compares favourably with dividends, but in reality many tenants are habitually bad payers, thus involving the property manager with the task of pressing for the money each quarter. To avoid this, it is advocated that the lease should be drafted to provide for interest on all late payments of rent at a rate of, say, 4 per cent above base rate to discourage such practices. It is, of course, often the case that at rent review the implementation of the reviewed rent will be delayed due to a dispute over the new level of rent and it is important that there is a provision to collect interest on the back monies due, otherwise there is a positive incentive on the part of the tenant to delay agreeing revised terms. It is suggested that interest on such back payments should not be at a punitive rate or it could act as an incentive to the landlord to delay and that would be unduly hard on the tenant. Therefore it may be appropriate to have differing interest rates on outstanding rent, one punitive for default and the other not so, for disputed sums upon review.

Repair

The wording and implementation of repair clauses can give rise to problems. All too often the wording of the clause fails to define accurately who is responsible for what. If the clause is other than 'full repairing', extreme care must be taken to ensure that the liabilities are spelled out and, most importantly, that no part of the structure or grounds is overlooked, as the basic rule under English common law is that there is no implied covenant to repair by either party so far as commercial property is concerned. If the clause has not been satisfactorily drawn a liability gap may arise. The situation is somewhat different with residential property let on leases of less than seven years as, with these, covenants on the part of the landlord are implied (Landlord and Tenant Act 1985).

It follows that the first point to establish is that liability falls on someone. In practice, of course, many freeholders simply pass on the full burden of repair to the lessee, although even here defective draftmanship can lead to the case where certain elements are not covered. For example, if the lessee were responsible for repairing the demised building, but since the time of the grant the lessee has constructed further buildings on the site, it could be argued that the repairing liability did not extend to these additional structures. In this case the obligation would fall on neither party, although obviously it would be in the interests of both parties to reach some solution, but this could involve the landlord in unforeseen expenditure.

The landlord may further retain a 'hidden liability' due to the provisions of the Defective Premises Act 1972. Under the provisions of this Act it appears that where a landlord reserves the right to undertake repairs that the tenant has failed to do, and there is a breach of repair of which the landlord is aware, he will be liable for any injury or damage to persons arising out of such disrepair. As such powers to execute work are common in modern leases, the potential liability must be borne in mind and suitable provision made in the lease for the tenant to indemnify the landlord against such claims.

In the case of multi-let buildings, care must be taken to ensure that the owner will not incur liability under the Occupiers' Liability Act 1957.

Any repair must by definition involve some degree of renewal, but at what point does the obligation by a lessee to repair cease, as the work involved is in essence no longer a repair but a renewal? The point was considered by the Courts in the leading case of *Ravenseft Properties* v. *Davstone* (1979) when the replacing of defective cladding to a building, albeit a very expensive item and one which was not foreseen due to the age of the structure, was none the less regarded as repair, cladding after all being only a minor element in the total building. As a general guide, whether a work will be regarded as a repair or a renewal will be affected by the degree to which the main structure is being replaced, its cost in relation to the cost of the total structure and whether the building can be regarded as life expired. As buildings increasingly have shorter and shorter economic, sooner than physical, life expectancies some interesting points for the future are raised. To counter the problems, landlords have increasingly sought to place lessees under specific obligations to renew when necessary as well as repair. Even if such a clause is used, however, the lessee is under no obligation to do other than the minimum necessary to fulfil the covenant and there will not be a liability on him to replace a defective element with anything that could be regarded as an improvement on the original. Where the building which is so let is old or in poor condition, such a wide-ranging clause must be expected to adversely affect the rent negotiated.

The basic premise is that a lessee need not replace a worn-out life-expired building with a modern building of an improved specification. It is essential, therefore, that the freeholder regularly inspects the premises to ensure that repairs are carried out at the appropriate time before a total renewal is the only solution. The old adage of a 'stitch in time' is appropriate to the question of repairs, although in the interests of good relationships and management costs the service of notices under the Law of Property Act 1925 (s.146), and of interim schedules of dilapidations, should be treated with caution.

The question of inherent defect is likewise a difficult one. How far is an inherent defect a lack of repair? In the case of the *Post Office* v. *Aquarius Properties* (1986), an inherent defect, which led to an intermittent flooding of a cellar, was not regarded as being within the ambit of repair, and thus the lessees were not liable for the necessary tanking works to prevent further flooding.

Even though a clause may purport to be on full repairing terms, repair does not encompass total renewal and possibly does not include inherent defect, so the expression could be regarded as, to some extent, a misnomer. Whilst there is no way that a perfectly tight clause can be drawn, the drafting of such clauses, together with the treatment of inherent defects, should be closely considered. The use of schedules of condition may be appropriate although many landlords and tenants will not accept these as a matter of policy. If the landlord is adopting a 'hands-on' approach, and is prepared to accept liability for some repairs in return for a higher rent, some of the problems may be mitigated. The disadvantage of this to the landlord is that he has an uncertain income flow. An alternative is for the landlord to carry out the work and recoup the costs by way of a service charge and, indeed, with campus developments and complex multi-let structures this may be the only practicability. Many management problems are associated with service charges concerning both the level of charge and the basis of apportionment (see p.193 below).

As a final note on repairs, if the burden lies with the tenant, and the tenant is conscientious in carrying out his liabilities at the end of the term, the landlord may receive the building back in good repair but totally inappropriate for reletting due to obsolescence and changing market demands. If the burden remains with the landlord there is more scope to improve and modernize as repairs are undertaken, thus prolonging the economic life of the building and enhancing return.

At the time of writing most commercial leases are drafted so as to place liability to both put and keep the premises in repair firmly on the tenant, but recent court decisions have demonstrated that such clauses may not always satisfactorily protect the freeholder from all expenditure. From the lessee's viewpoint the full repairing clause has a further potential difficulty; in the event of an assignment the original lessee will remain liable under the legal doctrine of privity of contract. Therefore if the assignee leaves the premises in a poor condition at the end of the lease the original lessee could find that he faces a large claim for dilapidations.

Improvements and fixtures

Many leases contain a qualified prohibition on the lessee carrying out improvements, that is, they may only be carried out with the landlord's consent, such consent not to be unreasonably withheld (implied covenant under Landlord and Tenant Act 1927, s.19). But what is an improvement? Obviously it is not a repair, but likewise it is not a fixture or a fitting. There is no statutory definition and many leases are drafted without actually defining what is to be regarded as an improvement. Consequently, at rent review, problems may arise, such as in deciding whether works carried out by a tenant are improvements or merely fixtures or fittings. If they are improvements they will probably fall to be excluded from the rent. If on the other hand they are fixtures, they may constitute landlords' fixtures and be included, or tenants' fixtures and thus excluded. Indeed, if they are tenants' trade fixtures they will in addition be ignored upon statutory lease renewal as long as the tenant remains in occupation. *New Zealand Government Properties Ltd* v. *H.M. & S. Ltd* (1982) was an important case on this point as it overturned the previously-held view that at lease expiry tenants' fixtures automatically reverted to the landlord.

The question of where the distinction between improvements and fittings lies was discussed in the case of *Young* v. *Dalgety PLC* (1986) and the case demonstrates that too often the exact meaning of terms is not considered in sufficient depth and detail at lease grant.

It must be remembered that many so-called improvements do not enhance the rental value of the premises and are merely of value to the existing lessee. If this is the case care must be taken in drafting to ensure that at termination the lessee is obliged to reinstate the premises to their original condition so that the landlord's reversion is not damaged. This requirement should not depress the rental value during the term (*Pleasureama Properties Ltd* v. *Leisure Investments (West End) Ltd* (1985)).

On a practical note, whenever improvements are carried out by a lessee, it is essential that consents, plans and the date of completion, which in itself can be a contentious issue, are well documented to avoid problems in the future. In particular, the date of completion can have an impact at rent review or lease renewal as many rent review clauses and the provisions of s.34 of the Landlord and Tenant act 1954 exclude improvements completed not more than twenty-one years previously.

User clause

A variety of user clauses are found in commercial leases. A very restrictive clause may lead to a reduction in the rent achievable for a property in some, though not all, cases (*Plinth Properties* v. *Mott, Hay and Anderson* (1979)). On the other hand a widely-drawn clause decreases the freeholder's control over his property. If there is a total prohibition on any change of use the lessor can charge a fine or premium for consent for a change, but such clauses are rare, due in part at least to tenant resistance. They are unpopular with tenants as they affect the tenant's ability to sublet or assign his interest. It is in the wording of such clauses that the objectives of the owner should be borne very closely in mind.

Sometimes the user clause is worded so that the user must fall within a certain category or class of use as defined in the Use Classes Order. This practice is potentially dangerous because of the likelihood that the Use Classes Order will be changed at some time during the life of the lease. This last happened in 1987 when uses were realigned and some new classes, notably the Business Use (B1) Class, were created. This embraces uses that were previously defined as offices (old class II) and warehouses (old class X) together with hi-tech buildings which had previously not fallen in any Use Class. Thus a lease which had specified a class X use only, in order to prevent the lessee changing the use, *inter alia*, to offices, becomes difficult to interpret. Should it be taken to mean any use within B1, that being the successor to class X, or should it mean warehouse only? It is therefore good practice to draw user clauses in terms of actual, not planning uses.

In general the lessor is well advised to seek a middle line between open and restrictive clauses to ensure no detrimental affect on rent whilst retaining some degree of control. In part the former problem can be overcome by basing the rent review clause on a hypothetical user clause (*Land Law Company* v. *The Consumer's Association* (1980)). To attempt to do so is likely in the first instance to prove unacceptable to the prospective lessee, and second, if it is so agreed, it may create uncertainty at review.

Rent review clauses

The history of rent review clauses is long and vexed. The early clauses of the 1950s were simple in construction, many merely stating that the rent should be reviewed commonly every twenty-one years to a reasonable rent, or a market rent, and often with no express provisions for the service of notices or laid-down disputes procedure. These clauses have now developed into examples of very complex legal drafting. Five-yearly review clauses dominate commercial practice today, and most contain sophisticated machinery for timetabling of notices and for disputes. Throughout the history of rent reviews one overwhelming fact emerges, that they are easily the most litigious clauses found in leases and their complexity is a tribute to the failings of early draftsmen in their search for a clause with is watertight in providing the landlord with what he wants, namely a guarantee of obtaining the full rack rental value of the premises at the review date. The reason why disputes have occurred and been hard fought through the courts is simple – with escalating rental values the financial stakes have been high.

It is not within the scope or purpose of this book to go through the details of the case law of the subject, although every estates manager should be familiar with it. It is a constantly changing area and recourse to the latest legal decisions is the essential task of anyone negotiating rent reviews. However, from the plethora of legal opinions certain principles and guidelines do emerge:

1   Any lease when drafted must ensure that the clause is consistent with all the other main terms of the lease and the rent review clause must refer to the remaining reviews in the lease. Frequently the review will assume that the lease is for a minimum period of, say, ten years with one further review, even if this is not the reality of the situation. Where the device of referring to a hypothetical lease in the rent review clause is adopted difficulties have often arisen as in the cases of *National Westminster Bank PLC* v. *Arthur Young McLelland Moore & Co.* (1985) and *General Accident Fire and Life Assurance PLC* v. *Electronic Data Processing* (1986). For this reason it may be prudent to avoid the use of such clauses.

2   Rent review clauses come in many guises. To assume that two clauses which are very similar, but not identical, will be treated in the same way by the courts can be a rash assumption.

3   Where the review clause specifies time limits for service of notices, prima facie these will not be regarded as of the essence of the contract (*United Scientific Holdings Ltd* v. *Burnley Borough Council* (1978)). So many exceptions to this general rule have emerged that it may be unwise to assume that any particular form of wording is fully safe. It would appear that clauses where the time limits apply equally to both sides are least likely to cause the landlord failure in the event that the timetable for notices is not met. It does, however, pay to take great administrative care and obtain good legal advice before the service of such notices.

4   The rent review clause should never be considered in isolation; the user and improvement clauses in particular may have a substantial effect on the rent recoverable.

Partly in response to disputes concerning rent review clauses, the Law Society/Royal Institution of Chartered Surveyors issued in 1980 a model rent review clause and this was updated in the light of litigation in 1985 (reproduced in Appendix B). To date many leases predate these model clauses, but there is no doubt that if a standard form such as this were to be adopted by many of the institutions it could go some way to reducing the uncertainty in interpretation which currently exists.

Service charge provisions

Where buildings are multi-let, such as an office block, or constructed in complexes such as shopping centres and business parks, the question of service charges arises.

Service charges can be subdivided into charges for (a) provision of basic services such as cleaning, lighting, heating etc, and (b) repairs to common parts and, where applicable, to demised areas.

The first category of services are normally subject to an annual charge based upon an estimate of the costs to be incurred, with a balancing charge being made at the year-end if appropriate. The second category may be items of either a cyclical or non-recurring nature, and in an effort to spread costs evenly over a period of years many leases allow for a sinking fund, or contingency fund to be set up so that the monies can accumulate against the eventual major expenditure.

Whilst in theory these practices seem simple, reasonable, and a logical way of ensuring that the landlord will receive a fixed net income from the property, service charges are notorious for the conflicts that they can produce between the landlord and the tenant. For example, the parties may have different aspirations regarding the level of service applicable. Whether the apportionment of costs between lessees is fair and whether the charges are reasonable and represent value for money are also commonly matters of dispute.

From the lessor's viewpoint one of the major problems with service charges is the difficulty in actually drafting a clause which will remain appropriate throughout the term of the lease, particularly if this is for more than twenty years. During this time standards required may well change radically. This has been seen very clearly with shopping centres. In 1970 centres were largely uncovered and had only basic customer amenities. Such standards seem totally inappropriate to the impending 1990s. Thus over the period many centres have required substantial up-grading in order to defend trade. It can be, and is, argued by lessees that they should not pay via service charges for the capital cost of such upgrading and indeed once upgraded, should they be liable to pay for the increased services? From the lessor's point of view, if he cannot review the service charge provisions the scheme may not be viable. This illustrates the need to incorporate flexibility in service charges or the lessor could find himself facing a substantial shortfall in cost recovery.

Other clauses

In that it is the whole lease which will determine the quality of the investment, every clause of the lease is important, but above we have highlighted those which tend to have the most dramatic effect on investment performance. Other important clauses which should be investigated are those relating to assignment, where a total ban can reduce rental value on review and insurance, which goes to the heart of protecting the investment.

Statutory intervention

Apart from the operation of the lease the lessor should consider the effect of statute on the let investment. The most significant of the statutes affecting commercial premises is the Landlord and Tenant Act 1954 (part 2), which gives the occupying lessee the right to obtain a new lease for a maximum term of fourteen years at a market rent as defined in s.34 of the Act. A landlord can only defeat a tenant's claim for a new lease if he can prove one or more of the grounds for possession as set out in s.30 of the Act (as amended by the Law of Property Act 1969). A summary of these provisions

Table 8.1 Summary of Landlord and Tenant Act 1954 (s.30) provisions

---

(a) Breach of repairing obligation. The onus is on the landlord to show that this is a serious breach and one which the tenant either will not or cannot remedy.

(b) Persistent delay in payment of rent. Relevant here is the word delay. If a tenant has always been a 'bad payer' he cannot defend himself by merely ensuring that he is up to date by the day of the court hearing.

(c) Other serious breach of covenant inconsistent, in the court's view, with the grant of a new lease.

(d) The landlord is willing and able to provide suitable alternative accommodation on reasonable terms.

(e) Possession is required in the case of a subtenancy where a building is let in parts in order that a more advantageous letting of the building as a whole can be achieved.

(f) The landlord intends to demolish or reconstruct or carry out substantial works of construction and that he could not reasonably do so without possession of the premises. This ground has proved to be a fruitful ground for litigation and it is necessary for the landlord to prepare his case very carefully so that he can establish beyond reasonable doubt that he has the necessary consents and finance, that he intends to carry out the work – not sell the premises, and that possession is definitely needed.

(g) The landlord intends to occupy the premises himself, either residentially or for business purposes. In order to argue this ground the landlord must have owned the superior interest for at least five years. In the case of a company seeking possession under this ground it may be necessary to provide board minutes in support of the application to prove intent.

is set out in Table 8.1. Basically they fall into two types – those where the tenant has been in breach of covenant, and those where there are good estate management reasons for the landlord regaining possession.

Whilst the landlord and the tenant are free to negotiate whatever terms they wish for the new lease, in the event that agreement is not reached, the courts will decide provided that the parties have completed the necessary legal formalities to protect their respective positions. The parties will thus negotiate within the framework of a possible court determination. The implications of this are that it will be difficult for the landlord to alter substantially the terms of the preceding agreement other than the provisions for rent and rent review. This view was reinforced by the case of *O'May* v. *The City of London Real Property Company* (1982) in which the House of Lords refused to allow the landlord to insert a service charge clause requested by the lessors which would have effectively changed an internal repairing clause into a full repairing liability albeit that the lessee was being offered adequate financial recompense. In the case of *Charles Clements (London) Ltd* v. *Rank City Wall Ltd* (1978) the landlord's application to widen a user clause for reasons of financial gain was also rejected.

The reason for the courts' reluctance to alter terms is that the principle objective of the Act is to protect the occupying lessee in the running of his business. The reluctance by the court to update terms except in circumstances where it is considered 'fair and reasonable' so to do, may influence a landowner's decision regarding the scale of a planned refurbishment scheme. If the scheme requires possession the landlord will be able to achieve lettings on the refurbished unit on modern terms, whereas if a slightly lesser scheme is undertaken, he may have to accept leases which are legally obsolete at the date of grant, although in the latter case continuity of income may be achieved.

Other statutes affecting the policy and terms of lettings and the returns achieved include the Offices, Shops and Railway Premises Act 1963, the Occupier Liability Act 1957, the Health and Safety at Work Act 1974 and the Defective Premises Act 1972. Legal advice on these should be taken as to their implication on any letting.

In summary it can be said that to achieve the optimum performance the manager should:

1 Ensure the appropriateness of the tenant.
2 Let the building, or site, for a term consistent with the long-term estate policy, taking into due consideration factors such as the rapid changes in legal and design requirements.
3 Ensure that the clauses contained in the lease are consistent one with another, unambiguous and in the lessor's best interest.

CONCLUSION

In this chapter we have sought to introduce and explain the concepts of active and passive management and distinguish between 'hands-off' and 'hands-on' approaches to property management. We have explained this in the context of the evolution of the currently-accepted form of commercial lease, and we have briefly outlined its perceived advantages and disadvantages. We then examined some of the major terms of the commercial lease and outlined management considerations to be taken into account upon the grant of a new letting.

Although the twenty-five year full repairing lease is widely accepted, its demerits are becoming evident as the problems of obsolescence and litigation become more obvious. In our submission the time is right for property-owners to consider more carefully the appropriateness of such leases in each case. If a property is to perform to its maximum potential the owner must first ensure that the letting is appropriate to the circumstances, as it is this from which letting income is derived.

In the next chapter we examine ways in which a property-owner can adopt positive management techniques to ensure that optimum performance is indeed achieved.

Chapter 9

Active management
(2) performance

INTRODUCTION

In the previous chapter we examined the main consideration involved in the creation of a commercial letting, and the day-to-day management of such an investment. In this chapter we seek to put such investments into their wider portfolio context, or in other words, we take a 'macro look' at property management. It is never enough to simply adopt a reactive approach to management. The adviser must always be seeking to take a pro-active role to ensure that the ownership aims are fulfilled. Accordingly we will look at some of the actions open to the manager to ensure that the optimum portfolio is created and that the assets owned are performing to their maximum potential.

The role of any manager, in whatever sphere he operates, is to be an enabler, and through enabling, to achieve. He must ensure that the task, in this case the management of the portfolio, is undertaken economically and to the maximum advantage. The task of management itself has been defined by Brech (1975) as:

'A social process entailing responsibility for the effective and economic planning and regulation of the operations of an enterprise in fulfilment of given purposes or tasks, such responsibility involving:

(a) judgement and decision in determining plans and in using data to control performance and progress against plans;
(b) the guidance, integration, motivation and supervision of the personnel composing the enterprise and carrying out its operations'.

The job of the manager, therefore, involves planning, supervision and monitoring performance against targets. If these tasks are not undertaken the manager cannot be said to be actively managing.

The first priority of the portfolio manager when appointed, whether he is creating a new portfolio or taking over an existing one, will be to establish the long-term aims and objectives of the owner, and then within these constraints, to create a suitable portfolio. Decisions regarding the acquisition policy are crucial and should be established at an early stage as they will form the framework within which all shorter-term decisions are made. In the case of an existing portfolio, the acquisition policy will have to be formed in the light of existing assets and restructuring will have to take place over time. Once the policy has been set, measures can be taken to analyse existing assets with a view to establishing

(a) whether they are suitable for long-term retention,
(b) if so, whether they are performing optimally, and
(c) if not, whether they are suited to active management techniques, or whether a disposal is appropriate.

Accordingly, in this chapter we will first consider acquisition policy, then measures for performance identification, monitoring and improvement, and lastly disposal policy.

ACQUISITION POLICY

The acquisition policy of any investor should be a result of a reasoned examination of his investment criteria and of the market opportunities so that the resultant portfolio accurately reflects his needs and his risk/return profile. Thus the motivation for ownership is crucial, for example, is the purchaser only concerned with financial return or do other considerations such as status or occupational need come into play? The prospective time horizon of the investor, too, is very important as it will dictate attitudes towards redevelopment and reversionary properties.

Of course, this is the situation in a perfect world, where there is a ready supply of suitable investments. Such a world does not exist and inevitably a portfolio is a compromise between investor requirements and the availability of suitable property. If, as is often the case, major investors have similar requirements, the resultant high level of demands for certain types of property will cause yields to fall until logically a point is reached at which the investor's required return (or equated yield) will either not be achievable or carries a high level of risk of non-achievement.

Such would be the case if the property market was an efficient market. However it is not, and it is reasonable therefore for investors to seek to exploit these inefficiencies by analysing opportunities and acquiring those units which are underpriced. As progress has been made in recent years in establishing techniques for measuring actual and expected performance, so investors' ability to spot such underpriced investments has increased, and correspondingly there has been an increase in the level of property trading activities as some investors have indeed acted in this way.

For many investors, in theory at least, property is acquired as a long-term investment and to act as a balance in the portfolio against more volatile investments (equities) whilst providing good prospects for growth in both income and capital. The extent to which differing institutions adopt similar acquisition policies has been charted by Property Market Analysis. In their 1986–7 survey of fund managers they found that there was a high level of conformity amongst property requirements, both in terms of sectoral split and geographical location. At that time fund managers were indicating an 'ideal property portfolio' of 50 per cent shops, 30 per cent offices and 20 per cent industrials. This concensus is not surprising, given that many funds have similar liabilities. However, over time such requirements may alter with changes being linked, not only to a change in the nature of the fund's liabilities, but in the relative performance of each sector.

The decision regarding the ultimate objectives for the portfolio and the criteria for investment are ones for the property owner, be that a board of directors, the trustees of a pension fund or an individual. The property manager should, however, be closely involved with and consequently fully committed to those decisions.

A prerequisite to establishing the policy for property will be the setting of objectives for the entire portfolio and the establishment of the role that property is perceived to hold within that portfolio. Such perceptions vary dramatically from investor to investor. Whilst some may regard zero as the norm, for others there is a history of commitment to the principle of investment in property. Norwich Union, for example, hold approximately 25 per cent of their assets in property and (*Estates Gazette*, 8942, 11) they intend to retain that balance.

Before any property acquisition policy can be finalized, the following factors should be considered:

Minimum return

The first requirement must be to fix the minimum level of return that is acceptable. Much debate is taking place as to how property investments should be analysed and appraised for purchase using a target return, but there is no consensus as to the level of such a 'target', a problem accepted by Fraser (1988). This is not surprising as it must be a decision personal to each investor and determined by factors such as his tax position, risk/return preference, time horizon and level of borrowing.

Method of return measurement

Not only must the minimum return or target rate be set, but the way in which such return is measured must also be decided, together with the time interval between performance reviews. As we have seen in Chapter 5, the method employed may vary, and in Chapter 12 we outline the results of a survey of institutional investors asking, *inter alia*, what measures they adopt.

Risk

Another material consideration is the investor's attitude to risk and to its evaluation. If the attitude is one of risk minimization then the portfolio emphasis will be on full diversification and the avoidance of investments which have high individual risk profiles.

Finance availability

The total amount of monies available will have a substantial effect on the acquisition policy arrived at. As mentioned in earlier chapters, most investors seek to achieve diversification by investing across sectors. Hence the level of funds available may well dictate the type of property that can be contemplated, with only the largest investors being able to contemplate full ownership of substantial London office blocks or regional or subregional shopping centres. However, with the proliferation of funding arrangements it may be possible for investors to obtain partial interests in investments whose overall value would put them out of total ownership reach.

Portfolio shape

We have alluded above to the 'ideal shape' of a property portfolio, as revealed by market research. However, such an ideal does not exist: different investors will determine the split between sectors, size and location in accordance with their past experiences, their perception of future trends and in accordance with their expertise and inclination. Hence some may favour a bias towards offices (for example, Haslemere Estates and Norwich Union) whilst others concentrate on industrials (for example, Slough Estates). Despite this specialization, other investors are actively pursuing diversification policies. Amongst those seeking to diversify are the major brewers who, having become aware of their assets as investments, are diversifying into hotels, high street restaurants and golf courses, to name but three activities. With the advent of the single European market in 1992, some early signs are that UK investors are responding to the opportunities to alter their protfolio's shape to include mainland European properties.

Active management

A decision must be taken as to whether the investor is prepared to accept, or indeed has the ability to accept, properties which require active management. Over the last decade much interest has been awakened in the concept, but not all investors yet pursue such policies although, as mentioned briefly above, others have done so with considerable success.

Properties which are multi-let, or let on other than full repairing and insuring terms, do offer potentially higher income returns for those investors who are prepared to undertake a 'hands-on' approach, as such properties normally sell at yields slightly higher than those which are let on institutionally preferred terms. Additionally these properties, as well as providing higher initial yields, are often those which are suitable for active management techniques.

A recent survey carried out by Mew (1989) revealed a correlation between the size of the investor's available funds and management policy. The larger the fund the more likely the institution is to purchase property with a view to undertaking active management. One reason for this may be that the larger funds are more likely to have the professional expertise 'in house' to handle such work.

In-house or retained agents

Any large property investor, or institution, will have the choice whether to manage the portfolio 'in house' or put the work out to the management department of a firm of chartered surveyors.

Currently it is usual for smaller funds and individuals, where assets are up to around £15 million, not to employ in-house staff. Indeed, the assets involved are frequently held indirectly in the form of property unit trusts or shares in property companies.

Above this level the portfolio is likely to contain sufficient directly-held investments that substantial management is required, and therefore the decision must be made as to whether the property should be managed by an in-house team or external advisers.

There are advantages and disadvantages to both options:

The in-house team is fully committed to the effective management of the portfolio, it will understand the criteria and policy of the investor in a way that it is very hard for an outsider to do, and it can be made accountable by performance review and the operation of management bonus schemes. On the other hand, unless the portfolio is extremely large, the team, if it is to be comparable in cost with using outside agencies, will be small and thus the breadth of expertise that can be expected must be limited, and certain functions will still need to be undertaken externally. In addition, if the portfolio is geographically diverse, it may not be practical in logistical terms, for a central in-house team to manage adequately and positively. Asset valuation for the purposes of annual company accounts is one task that is normally required to be carried out by independent valuers (Royal Institution of Chartered Surveyors *Guidance Notes in the Valuation of Assets*). The use of outside agents overcomes this difficulty. Individual firms can be employed on an *ad hoc* basis for tasks requiring special expertise and managers can be appointed locally. On the face of it at least the use of the outside agent can often seem the most cost effective solution. The drawback, of course, is that the outside agent will only be accountable in so far as he must do a good and professional job in order to receive his fees; but this often does not call for the same attitude and involvement as can be required of the directly-appointed team member. Whilst many firms have excellent records, the incentive to use flair and innovative thought in the management of the estate can be lacking as inevitably the needs of various clients have to be balanced. In addition, without a suitable trained 'in-house' member, it is hard to monitor whether indeed the outside retained agent is doing the optimum job, or indeed receiving the correct instructions to enable him to do so. If a single expert is employed directly, then the problem of job progression and staff development can occur. It can be seen that the arguments for having an in-house team are strong.

It is often advisable, however, for such teams to use outside assistance to deal with specific areas of responsibility, such as implementing rent review negotiations, carrying out performance analysis or at times of abnormal workload.

In summary therefore, the requirements to manage a property investment cannot satisfactorily be avoided, and in our view the success of that investment is heavily dependent on the skills of the management team whose contribution should not be underestimated.

Tenure

Another important consideration is the investor attitude to tenure. Some investors have a virtually freehold only policy, yet leasehold investments, particularly if they have been priced using conventional valuation techniques, may produce extremely high internal rates of return, particularly for gross funds. This point has been realized by many fund managers and valuers and the competition for such leaseholds can often be such that the advantage is eroded. Nevertheless, many opportunities may exist. Whenever a leasehold acquisition is contemplated however, the end of term liability for dilapidations, and other onerous conditions on the lease, should be fully evaluated.

Where the building is being offered on a sale and leaseback arrangement, at a rent above the open market rent, considerable caution should be exercised as the performance at rent review may well be extremely poor.

In the previous chapter we have considered the various merits and demerits of effecting leases which impose full liability on the occupier. The decision regarding the type of property acquired should relate to the investor's attitude to 'hands-on management' and the suitability both in physical and demand terms of the property to certain types of letting agreements.

Location and tenant demand

Research should be undertaken to pinpoint areas where tenant demand is growing or likely to grow, due to demographic or other changes discussed earlier, and investments sought in these areas. Obviously where tenant demand is declining properties should not be purchased. In an era when short-term performance measurement is undertaken, consideration should be given to the cyclical nature of demand, both in location and sector demand.

Prime or secondary

It should not be forgotten that many properties not regarded as absolutely prime are let to substantial tenants and are in stable or improving locations. Thus a purchase of secondary property which will inevitably produce higher initial yield or income return may produce better performance over time. This has been proved to be the case in some recent years, with particularly good secondary shopping during the mid-1980's exceeding prime shops in terms of rental growth.

Comparability

It has already been seen that many investors are reluctant to diversify from the traditional sectors of retail, industrial and office. Although hi tech, retail warehouses and, to a lesser extent, out-of-town shopping schemes are now accepted as suitable for the placement of institutional funds, there has been a marked reluctance to move from the well-trodden path. One reason for this is that investors are conscious of the need to obtain satisfactory rent reviews, and this is more likely in cases where comparable evidence abounds. With new sectors the outcomes of a rent review will be much more reliant on the negotiating skills of the individuals involved, as the market is restricted. Fear of the unknown, and lack of confidence therefore, combine to produce a caution against investments for which there are few comparables.

It flows from this that as the market demand is restricted there may be opportunities to obtain higher returns, commensurate with the increased risk surrounding returns.

The portfolio effect

Above all else, the future likely returns of the proposed investment should be considered in relation to their effect upon the whole portfolio (see Chapter 7). It may well be that an individual acquisition, whilst appearing unattractive as a 'stand alone', will complement the make-up of the portfolio, and enable risk reduction through diversification to be obtained.

The time return horizon

Before any acquisition is undertaken it is essential that its estimated future returns are evaluated on a Discounted Cash Flow (DCF) basis over the investor's minimum proposed time horizon and adopting the investor's required minimum return. Any DCF must of necessity have a cut-off point when the investment is regarded as to be sold, or life expired. It is appropriate that this cut-off point is taken to concur with the investor's individual requirement. Traditionally the view taken of property is that performance should be considered over a long (15 to 20-year) period, though this is frequently often not the case, as we have already seen.

Occupational requirements

In the case of properties purchased for occupation, although all the above considerations are relevant, it is the needs of the occupier which are paramount. DCF calculations should still be undertaken but these will evaluate the total returns to the business, taking into account full costs in use, sooner than a conventional investment appraisal.

Portfolio composition

Whilst the above points relate to the factors to be considered when establishing acquisition criteria, a prerequisite is to establish the perceived role of property within the portfolio. Where the portfolio comprises a mix of media, the proportion to be devoted to property must be established. This may be a result of an 'in principle' decision, or it may relate to purely performance criteria. In reality the allocation between sectors of all funds will normally be reviewed on an annual basis.

As we have seen in earlier chapters, during the 1980s a strong shift in institutional investment patterns took place, with pension funds in particular reducing the allocation of new funds to property in favour of other media, notably gilts and overseas equities. The chief reason for this was, not so much an underperformance of property, but a prolonged period of high returns from equities. The increased opportunities for overseas investments may also have been a relevant factor.

Conclusion

The above outlines ways in which reasoned policies can be derived, and logical decisions made, regarding acquisition. In reality, as intimated earlier, investors do not always behave in such a fashion. In particular the intangible factors such as prestige and status will inevitably form part of the decision-making process.

PERFORMANCE IDENTIFICATION

Establishing the portfolio

Once an overall policy has been formed regarding the desired long-term structure of the portfolio, decisions can be made in respect of existing assets.

First a review of the assets owned must be undertaken, to establish the performance of each property, together with the reasons for any under-performance. Following on from this, decisions in respect of hold/sell and performance improvement can be undertaken.

Whilst many large organizations have very complete and sophisticated records of property ownership, it has been the case until very recently that many others had no complete records of ownership. A survey carried out by Simon Houlston and Partners in 1986 revealed that at that time there were many large companies who were ignorant of the exact extent of their estates.

Similar comments are contained in the Audit Commission report on local authority property holdings (1988a). Although it sounds almost inconceivable that such ignorance could be the case in the 1980s, it has to be seen in the context of mergers, take-overs and organizational restructures. If there has been a series of these events over a short space of time, the newly-formed or reconstructed organization will require time to establish a comprehensive property-holding terrier. The records that such a terrier should contain encompass the full physical and tenurial details of each unit. With the ready availability of suitable computer software, this task is now much simpler than it was only a decade ago. Only when this is complete can the review of asset performance start.

Even if the assets are accurately recorded, it is not always the case that proper investment objectives will have been set. A recent research report by Avis, Gibson and Watts (1989) has revealed that in a large number of organizations which own substantial property assets, those properties are managed from an occupational viewpoint with little attention being given to the setting of investment criteria or the monitoring of performance. It also reveals that many of the comments raised by the Audit Commission in relation to local authority property holdings apply equally to private sector corporate bodies.

Identifying poor performance

Only too often yesterday's star performer can become today's management problem and tomorrow's investment identified for disposal. The reasons why this may happen are many and varied, but it is always essential to establish what they are before taking any decision to either sell or inject capital monies.

Some of the reasons are set out below:

Legal obsolescence

Mention has already been made of the changes that are currently taking place in letting terms. In Chapter 12 we look at some of the common forms of letting agreements that occur in other countries as these may have an influence on the future workings of the UK property market.

In so far as the future is always uncertain, the risk of legal obsolescence occurring is an in-built hazard of any letting. Terms appropriate at the time of the grant may appear totally inappropriate at the date of termination. The risks of incurring legal obsolescence go up commensurate with the length of the lease granted, although it may be obviated to a certain extent by the introduction of a break clause. Normally, however, such clauses are only operational in the event of redevelopment or refurbishment requirements. With the rights of business tenants to take renewed leases under the Landlord and Tenant Act 1954 on terms which frequently mirror those found in the original lease term, there is a risk of 'built-in' obsolescence on such renewed lets. The desire to update lease terms may therefore be a significant consideration when taking decisions regarding the nature and scale of refurbishment works.

Physical obsolescence

Under this heading comes structural, functional and design obsolescence. Increasingly it is changes in the way buildings are used and tenants' design criteria rather than the physical wearing out of the structure which causes the rental value of the unit to fall in comparison with new buildings in an area. The design requirements of offices in particular has been fast moving. Twenty years ago buildings were designed generally with low floor to ceiling heights to reduce heating costs, and they had central heating but no air conditioning, except for prestigious London blocks. The rapid technological changes that have taken place since then have meant that tenants now desire raised floors and suspended ceilings to carry the wiring and cabling necessitated by information technology. The typical twenty-year old structure is often unable to be satisfactorily adapted. The hi tech building is an example of a building type which has only recently emerged, due to changing occupier needs. Emphasis is therefore now placed upon the ability of a building to adapt to changing occupational requirements.

Location factors

A location that at one time was considered prime can lose attraction due to external factors such as:

(a)   New Developments

A shopping centre development may often shift the pattern of pedestrian flows and hence values within a town centre, turning a previously prime position into a secondary one.

(b)   Road layout changes

Included in this are both the small-scale changes such as alteration to one-way systems, and imposition of parking restrictions, which can have very damaging effects upon retailers, to the ramifications resultant upon the opening of new motorways, as evidenced by the M25 which has brought escalating values in its wake.

Planning changes

An alteration to the structure or local plan may obviously affect the use and development potential of a property. Other global planning changes, such as the introduction of the new Use Classes Order 1987, can produce significant effects. Since the introduction of this Use Class Order it has been possible for many properties previously restricted to industrial use to be altered to office use without the need for planning consent, unless physical external alterations were needed, increasing rental and hence capital value.

Demographic changes

The reasons for demographic changes are in themselves many and complex, and rely on a mixture of planning, economics and social factors. Their effect on commercial property performance is an indirect one, but in the long term the areas where growth in population occurs will be those where demand for commercial property will experience growth too, although the level of growth will be combined with the social standing and economic prosperity of the population. Changes in population profile may produce change. The increasing age of the UK population will, for example, affect patterns of retail trading in the next decade.

Fashion changes

Although it is hard to define, let alone predict, fashions change, particularly in relation to aesthetics. The building which can retain its aesthetic appeal indefinitely has not been, and arguably never will be, designed. The 1960s preoccupation with modernization and concrete was replaced by a 'façadism' and a return to brick and stone elevation in the 1980s. However, buildings of poor intrinsic design and cheap construction tend to be those most at risk in this respect.

Legislative and government measures

Government measures can often produce a dramatic effect on property performance. This is best illustrated by an example.

The introduction of Enterprise Zones, with their freedom from rates and other fiscal advantages, changed the economics of development in many areas. One of the most striking examples of this is the development of the huge retail and leisure Metrocentre and Metroland in the Tyneside Enterprise Zone. Had it not been for the freedom from planning restraints, it is highly probable that this development would not have taken place and the site would have remained undeveloped.

A further example is the Merry Hill Centre in the West Midlands, developed as a shopping and leisure centre on the site of an old steel works. Because the site had Enterprise Zone status, the developers had no requirement to prove, by way of impact studies, that the development was appropriate in planning terms.

Fiscal measures

In that fiscal or tax measures are taken by government, they should theoretically be considered under the heading 'Legislative and governments measures' above. However, they are of such importance that they warrant a separate mention. Fiscal measures affect all investment media, but property, especially development property, is frequently singled out for special treatment. The last forty years have seen no fewer than four separate Acts passed, attempting to tax at least a portion, and sometimes the whole of, gain arising from the development of property. These taxes have been aimed principally at recouping from a landowner that value increase which arises from the grant of planning permission, sooner than the physical construction process. The four taxes involved, namely the Development Charge (1947–51), Betterment Levy (1967–71), Development Gains Tax (1973–6) and Development Land Tax (1976–84) were all, except Development Gains Tax, introduced by Labour governments, although DLT remained for some years under the Conservatives. They were all relatively short lived, administratively expensive and uneven in operation. None actually succeeded in fulfilling the function it was designed to undertake, that is, to give back to the community the wealth created by the granting of planning consent.

At the time of writing no such tax exists, but it is hard to imagine that there will not be similar measures in the future and the possibility should therefore be considered.

Capital Gains Tax and income tax considerations can affect property investments. The tax favoured position of pension funds and other 'gross investors' has been an important influence on the pattern of investment values. The imposition of VAT (Value Added Tax) on many property transactions is having a material effect on some portions of the property market.

Strength of covenant

At an initial letting of a property every effort should be made to choose a lessee with a satisfactory covenant, but over time the situation can change. With fluctuations in the other factors listed above, the prosperity of the lessee may alter, and with it his ability to pay the rent and fulfil other obligations. In addition, it is possible that the lessee may have assigned his interest and the assignee will be not such a good covenant. Whilst in most cases the landlord's consent to such assignment is required, the constraints put on the landlord by statute (Landlord and Tenant Act 1988) and case law are often such that a less than fully satisfactory assignee takes over. Although in common law the original lessee remains liable for the rent under the doctrine of Privity of Contract, in practical terms it may be very difficult to enforce against him. At the time of writing there are suggestions for legislation that would mean that upon assignment all liability of the assignor will cease.

Maintenance and running costs

Economics of costs in use also alter over time. For example, a heating system which a few years ago was the cheapest to run may suddenly look expensive, as happened to oil in the 1970s. Likewise, the ease of availability of materials, and their life cycles, can affect maintenance costs, and this in turn affects rental values. The approach undertaken to the management of maintenance, such as whether a planned or curative approach is adopted, will also affect the performance.

Management

The relationship between landlord and tenant in any letting is very important and with shopping centres, offices let in suites, or other multi-let buildings, it can be crucial. It is perhaps with shopping centres that the clearest indications of poor or strong management are manifested. If the management of a centre, by or on behalf of a freeholder, is poor, with little attention being paid not only to domestic matters such as cleaning, lighting and security, but also to tenant relationships and marketing, then the trade of the centre will suffer. This in turn can lead to frustration on the part of the retailers and the start of an antagonistic relationship between landlord and tenants as well as reduced profitability and hence reduced rental values.

This 'downward spiral' effect is evident in many centres where clearly the investor has lost confidence in the property.

It is interesting to note that there is an increasing awareness on the part of investors of the necessity to obtain high calibre personnel as shopping centre managers, and emphasis is now put upon the need to understand not only property maintenance and management matters, but also retailing and man management. This is in line with USA practice where the shopping centre manager frequently has a background in retailing.

Comparative performance

It may be that the property does not suffer significantly from any of the problems outlined above, yet its performance can be considered unsatisfactory by the investing owner. This may be because it is affected by an adverse cyclical trend, or it may be because its performance *comparative* to other investments appears poor due to an increase in other sector performance.

Summary

If the performance has been identified as inadequate for any reason other than the last, namely comparative performance, then it is appropriate to consider techniques for active management before making a decision to sell. If, however, the poor performance is comparative, then a view should be taken in the light of forecasting techniques, as to its future within the portfolio.

PERFORMANCE IMPROVEMENT

It is now widely accepted that active management of properties is essential to realize the highest returns. The recent institutional interest in trading of properties and the requirement for property to perform over a short-term time horizon are indicative of this growing awareness. Coupled to this has been the sophistication of performance measurement techniques which has improved the quality of analysis possible.

In this section we will enumerate ways in which investing owners can manipulate their assets in order to maximize performance, and hence create higher levels of rental and capital value.

Performance review

As a natural progression from the selection criteria outlined above, and in line with the methods outlined earlier in this book, the manager should regularly analyse the performance of each property and consider its contribution to the performance of the portfolio as a whole. If the performance is found to be satisfactory, no immediate action need be taken, although it would be prudent to consider whether such performance is likely to be sustained, bearing in mind the factors which can adversely affect property and particularly the factors underlying the performance achieved. For example, a shop is acquired at an advantageous price and shortly afterwards the rent is reviewed, with a rent achieved on review which could be regarded as exceptional. It is unlikely that the performance thus achieved can be sustained. Likewise, although a shopping centre may well be trading satisfactorily with good demand for units, the manager must be aware of the possible need for future capital expenditure, maybe of a defensive nature, to maintain the situation, even though no such spend is programmed.

It is likely that the review will reveal that some properties are not meeting criteria and for these properties action may be appropriate.

The intervals at which such performance review should be undertaken is debatable; the immediate response would be the more frequently the better. Against this, however, must be set:

(a) The costs of undertaking such a task, be it in house or externally, must be weighted against the resultant value increase.
(b) The availability of data. To determine performance, capital values will be required for all properties. Whilst specific events can change values overnight, for example, a change in the law or the implementation of a rent review, capital value changes of any interval of less than three or six months are likely to be difficult to determine with accuracy, and thus the exercise will be neither cost effective nor meaningful.
(c) Performance improvement measures usually take a minimum of six months to implement. To review more frequently loses purpose as a technique to assist management decisions.

Lease restructures

It has been pointed out earlier that legal obsolescence may result in poor performance. A property let on a long rent review cycle is regarded as 'inflation prone', and hence the capital value in relation to the rent passing is reduced. Even though the rent achieved upon the infrequent reviews may be above that which would be settled on a normal rent review pattern, a view seemingly supported by the courts (*National Westminster Bank* v. *Arthur Young McClelland* (1985)), the market will generally regard such properties as less attractive. In the case of multi-let buildings, outdated service charge provisions possibly resulting in a shortfall on cost recovery can also render an investment unattractive to institutional investors.

In any such case where it is considered that the terms of the letting are such that the value of the property is adversely affected, the possibility of lease restructure should be examined and discussed with lessees. In many cases the terms which are problematic to the landlord may also adversely affect the tenant. For example, a long rent review cycle may be unpopular with the tenant as well as the landlord, as upon review he may be required to pay a rent above the open market figure, a 'front-loaded rent', as it is known. This can have an adverse effect on the business cash flow. Accordingly the tenant might well be prepared to restructure the lease on to a shorter review cycle for a relatively small incentive.

Figure 9.1 illustrates that, assuming rents rise overtime, the parties are financially in the same position in absolute terms in both (a) and (b). The increasing rental value is depicted by the sloping dotted line FRV xx_1, and the rent paid is the solid line. The area under the solid line is the value of the income to the landlord and is equal in both cases. The value of the tenant's interest in (a) is the area hatched under the line xx_1, less the hatched area above xx_1, which represents the front-loaded element of the rent. The value of this equates to the sum of the two areas shown hatched in (b). Although financially there may be no difference, this is only true if the prediction of rental growth is accurate and if investors view both investments with equal favour, which we have already said they do not. Due to the effect of discounting, the break-even point will not lie at the five-year point, but to the left of it, as tenants will discount the value of their future profit rents. By moving from (a) to (b), both parties stand to gain: the tenant by losing front-loading and the landlord by reducing the downside risk of the investment and thereby increasing its attractiveness. It should be noted that such a negotiation is only likely to prove fruitful during a period where the lessee is suffering from front-loading, or where a review is imminent. During the period that the profit rent is increasing it is unlikely that the lessee would consider such a proposal.

An opportunity to restructure a lease may also occur if a lessee wishes to carry out alterations or improvements to the premises. The lease provisions will not allow the landlord to impose a lease restructure as a condition precedent upon consent being granted unless there is an absolute prohibition in the agreement to carrying out improvements, but it does provide scope for negotiation. In many cases, particularly where the unexpired term is relatively short, say less than twelve to fifteen years, the lessee may require a greater degree of security and will thus be interested in negotiating a surrender of the existing lease and the grant of a new one. This provides an ideal opportunity to restructure on optimum terms.

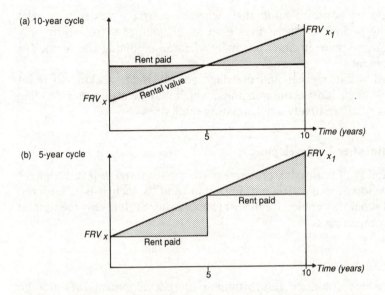

Figure 9.1 The effect of the rent review cycle on leasehold values

Mergers and marriages

These terms are frequently used interchangeably, though strictly speaking they refer to two different procedures:

Marriage value may be said to exist in any property which is let in such a way that if the lease, or leases as the case may be, were surrendered, the value of the freehold in possession would be more than the sum of the values of the freehold, subject to the lease or leases and the individual leasehold interests.

Merger value on the other hand relates to an increase in value that may arise when two separate legal holdings are put together, such as in the case of two small sites, each individually incapable of development but together forming a viable site.

The competent property manager should be alert at all times for such opportunities. To be so involves:

(a) Frequent revaluation of let buildings with marriage value in mind. It is most likely to occur where the leases are on obsolete terms and where the building is approaching time for redevelopment or refurbishment.
(b) Market research to ensure awareness of demand for the property.
(c) Consultation with local planning authorities in order to identify holdings where a merger might be possible.

(d) Being aware of the activities of landowners and occupiers in buildings adjoining the subject holding.

It should be borne in mind that, whereas marriage values may exist over a long period of time if they exist at all, merger is frequently only possible at one point in time, normally when an adjoining site is ripe for redevelopment.

Included within merger and marriage activity is the seeking to re-let buildings in their most economic units, which may involve either dividing large units or alternatively amalgamating small ones.

Refurbishment and redevelopment

The possibility of improving property performance through refurbishment and redevelopment is extremely important and as such it is considered worthy of separate detailed treatment (see Chapter 8). It is only mentioned here for completeness.

Improvements

In cases where complete refurbishment or redevelopment may not be possible or appropriate, performance can often be improved by carrying out judicious improvements. The scope for this will clearly depend upon the terms of the letting. In the case of a full repairing institutional type lease the freeholder may well find that he is powerless to impose the improvements upon the lessee, and that if the lessee wishes to carry out works, then unless it could be held to be unreasonable to do so, he must accede to that request. This will frequently mean that he will be unable to claim any rental benefit for upwards of twenty-one years, due to the operation of the rent review clauses and the Landlord and Tenant Act 1954. However, many improvements of only modest cost can yield a substantial return, sometimes in the order of 20 per cent or more. Accordingly, before agreeing to any request by a lessee to carry out improvements the manager should consider:

1   Are these genuine improvements which will enhance rental value and, if so, by how much?
2   If the rental return based on cost is such that it would increase the overall return of the investment, the landlord should consider carrying out the work himself and charging the lessee with an increased rent. The question of lease restructure should also be considered.
3   If the works are not ones which will enhance open market rental value, then any consent should be accompanied by a requirement on the lessee to reinstate the premises at the end of the term at his own expense, should the landlord so require.

In cases where the landlord retains control over part of the property, for example the landscaped grounds of a development of business units, or the malls and common parts of a shopping centre, small schemes of improvements such as upgrading toilets, introducing new lighting or planting schemes can enhance the investment's attractiveness to potential tenants and hence increase rental values. Such schemes, whilst not qualifying for the description of refurbishment, must form part of the philosophy of any owner interested in actively managing his portfolio.

Changes of use

The ability to change the use of a property to one of higher value will depend on (a) planning constraints, and (b) lease considerations.

An example of change of use, which combined with minor works can frequently lead to increases in value, is a change from residential to office use. Normally express planning permission will be required for such changes, but it should be noted that any change from one use to another lying within the same 'Use Class Order' created under the Town and Country Planning Acts is not regarded as development and does not require permission. Thus changes of use from, for example, a warehouse to an office, or from a public house to a restaurant or fast-food retail outlet, can be undertaken without specific planning consent, often resulting in increased value.

The freeholder's ability to take advantage of such measures will depend on the letting terms. If a building is let for industrial purposes, and both the user and rent review clauses are constructed in accordance with that use, it will be the end of the lease before benefit can be gained. Even so, the increased reversionary value will enhance the overall investment performance. The manager should, however, consider whether the levels of value are such that it is worth offering the lessee an incentive to surrender.

Changes of use will not always work to the advantage of the landowner. In London's Mayfair, shortly after the Second World War, at a time when offices were scarce following bombing action, and materials for large-scale rebuilding were not freely available, the City of Westminster granted temporary consents on many residential buildings for their use as offices until 1990. As the time approaches for these consents to expire, many freeholders are concerned about a likely large drop in value of these units, which will in turn lead to a shortage of office accommodation in an area which has become established as a popular office location.

Buying in leases

In the case of multi-let office properties or shopping centres, there is frequently a case for buying in a lease if it becomes available and re-letting it in order to establish a market rent, which can then be used as evidence at rent review time. This ploy has been successfully used in many instances, notably the Brent Cross Shopping Centre on the edge of London. Allied to this is the necessity to arrange lettings of multi-let buildings in such a way that the rent reviews do not coincide but follow on, so that a constant flow of comparable evidence is obtained.

Sale and leaseback

An occupying freeholder requiring money to finance a business activity or development may gain benefit by a sale and leaseback transaction. Under such arrangements the freeholder sells his interest to an investor and takes back a long lease which may or may not be on standard letting terms at a rack rent. Whilst such arrangements can be attractive to both parties, as it releases funds for the occupier to spend on his business and provides the investor with a property let to a strong covenant, care must be taken to protect the new freeholder's interest. If the lease so created is on 'special' terms, it may be unattractive to other potential investor purchasers. This possible lack of saleability should always be considered at the time of the deal.

Altering the demise

Over time the density of development allowed on any site may change. Frequently it may increase. If on examination it is found that a site is underutilized, it may be advantageous to negotiate with the lessee for part of the site to be surrendered and used for development. This is best timed to coincide with a rent review or a tenant's request to carry out improvements. Clearly the degree of underutilization may be such that a comprehensive redevelopment is indicated, but often this is not the case and judicious 'clawing back' of a small part of a demise may enable a fresh development to go ahead.

Fiscal planning

It is outside the scope of this book to comment in depth on fiscal planning and tax measures, which are complex and rapidly changing. It is a prerequisite for any tax planning that a thorough grasp of relevant tax law is acquired, that knowledge then being applied to various management strategies to produce the course of action which will minimize the incidence of tax, thereby maximizing returns.

In that many of the largest investors in property are gross funds, the concept of tax planning may be regarded as of little importance. This is not so, as even the gross funds will wish to be aware of the tax provisions that confront the other parties who may be bidding against them for the acquisition of a property.

At the current time, the levels of taxation on both capital and income are lower than they have been for many years; levels of income and corporation tax are steadily being reduced, the impact of capital gains tax has been reduced by indexation and there is no punitive tax on windfall gains arising through the prospects of development.

None the less, careful consideration of the implication of, for example, disposing of a property in one tax year as against another, should be considered. Likewise on letting, the decision whether to let at full rent or take a low rent and a premium can be significant. Other measures such as capital allowances under the income tax provisions are important considerations.

Owner-occupied estates

The majority of the measures listed above are relevant to both investment and owner-occupied estates, but there are other measures which may be regarded as being relevant mainly or exclusively to owner-occupied property. These include:

Notional rents

Many large companies owning properties primarily for their own occupation have no 'built-in system' for ensuring that as investments they are producing optimum returns. The properties are being used in effect as 'units of production', yet no production costs other than maintenance costs are attributed to the holdings. Thus, the business carried on in a freehold unit may appear to be giving more value to the company overall than that which is held on lease but this is not necessarily the case. In order to ensure that any landowner is making the best use of his resources it is necessary to analyse the performance in terms of opportunity cost. For example, a chain of retailers owning their properties freehold, may have no system for detecting the property which is ideally suited for redevelopment, and which could, if sold, produce funds sufficient to enable the purchase of two or three more units, thus enabling the company's net profit to be increased.

Similarly, in the public sector a local authority's landholding might include a day centre for the elderly housed in a Victorian building which is ripe for redevelopment as offices. Likewise a school could be sitting on a valuable residential site. In both these instances the use could probably be advantageously relocated, to a site less valuable but possibly equally suited to the authority's purpose.

To overcome this problem and to ensure the better and more efficient use of resources, some large landowners, in both the private and public sectors are introducing notional rents. Under such provisions, the notional ownership and control of all properties is vested in a central landholding division, which then rents out the properties to the individual user department, charging them a notional rent based either on a formula or open market value, bearing in mind alternate use value when applicable. In this way anomalous uses are highlighted and appropriate management decisions can be taken in the light of full information.

In the private sector the establishment of notional rents may not prove difficult, but public sector properties frequently include those for which there is no market demand. The difficulties thus incurred are currently the subject of research (joint research project Surrey County Council/Kingston Polytechnic) into the contractors' test method of valuation.

Planned maintenance

Planned maintenance programmes are appropriate to both owner-occupied and let estates, although in the latter only so far as the lessor retains control of the repair and maintenance of the building. The concept of planned maintenance is a simple one; by calculating the life of all building components from the major units such as roofing, to the minor ones such as light fittings, it is possible to plan when maintenance and renewal of components will be required. Hence accurate budgeting can be achieved, work can be undertaken at a time when it is least disruptive to the occupier and emergencies and consequential damage, if not totally eliminated, are reduced to a minimum.

Planned maintenance should, over time, prove to be cost effective, and indirectly it will improve a property's performance. An added advantage of such schemes is that where the costs are to be recouped by way of a service charge, the service charge estimates can be calculated with a fair degree of accuracy, thus reducing the scope for conflict and the need for balancing accounts at the end of the year. In addition, the work can be budgeted so that the costs are kept relatively even year by year.

However, planned maintenance is not always appropriate. In cases where repairing liabilities are divided between the landlord and the tenant it may not be possible, and in the case of short-life buildings, it may not be desirable. With the time cycles for refurbishment and redevelopment of many commercial buildings becoming ever shorter, and with improvements in technology and design producing low maintenance components, the scope for such plans may be limited. Despite this, any measure to reduce maintenance costs which may account for up to 30 per cent of the annual runnings of a building (Royal Institution of Chartered Surveyors 1986) must be a vital factor in determining what a tenant can afford to pay as rent and hence the capital value of the building.

Costs in use

Allied to the concept of planned maintenance is that of costs in use. To the occupier it is the overall cost of occupation which is of importance, rather than individual costs such as rent (real or notional), mortgage payment, rates, maintenance and running costs. It is this bottom line of total costs that will affect the viability of the business carried on in the property. Hence, to the investor the lower the building's running costs can be, the more the tenant can afford by way of rent, real or notional. As a building ages, inevitably the running costs will rise proportionately, and it is therefore beholden upon a property manager to consider the current and future likely costs in use of the building, both when initially appraising it for acquisition and when reviewing its performance. In the case of initial development or redevelopment, the question of cost in use should be built into the viability study.

Summary

In this section we have sought to set out some of the ways that a property portfolio manager can ensure that the assets under his control are performing to their maximum potential. This does not mean that the performance will always be satisfactory when viewed in comparison to that achieved by other investments. Demand for property is cyclical by nature and any investor must expect alternate periods of growth and stagnation. What he should be able to guard against is unduly poor performance caused by a lack of imaginative, committed and innovative management. By continued attention and monitoring it should be possible to achieve the optimum results.

Portfolios should by nature be dynamic. Even if the overall objective is investment in the long term, rather than trading of assets, there are occasions when investments should be sold, and in the next section the criteria for disposal policies are outlined.

DISINVESTMENT POLICY

Although there are many measures open to a property manager to actively improve performance, inevitably it will not always be possible to ensure that every property becomes an acceptably performing unit and a decision to disinvest must be seriously considered. If this is so, several points should be borne in mind:

1   The decision to disinvest must be a positive one, that is, the monies produced can be used to produce a better return elsewhere. It should not be, as so often happens, a negative decision taken because both owner and manager alike have lost confidence in the property and are

not prepared to first look at the possibility of improving it via active management.

2 The timing of the disposal can be critical both from the vendor's point of view and from the marketing aspect. Timing may well have fiscal implications; vendors should always ensure that disposals are so planned that maximum annual exemption and reliefs from capital taxes are obtained. A large disposal programme announced by a major company could well adversely affect the share performance, particularly if announced shortly prior to annual results. On an individual property level, it is often better to sell after a rent review has been achieved, unless there is a long time to go until review and thus the property could hold attraction to an investor seeking capital gain rather than income return.

From the marketing angle also, timing is vital; there is little point in disinvesting if the market for that type of property is on a cyclical low, unless there is absolutely no alternative. An example of this might be if the monies were required for reinvestment in a 'once only' opportunity to achieve a merger value. Timing can also be critical where sale and leaseback or other financial restructuring transactions are contemplated.

3 Before deciding to sell, the investor should consider whether the problem relates to that unit only, or whether it is a sector performance problem. If it is the latter, is the situation temporary only, or is it long lasting? In addition, if it is a sector problem, will it be necessary on the sale of this asset to reinvest within the sector, or can the funds be diverted to another sector or investment medium, without having a detrimental effect on the overall shape and risk profile of the portfolio?

4 The possibility of a major disposal programme creating a 'flooded market', should also be taken into account. Again, judicious timing can often prevent this happening.

5 Identification of areas where there is likely to be a performance problem in the future should be undertaken together with the disposal of units before the problem becomes established. To be ahead of the market is extremely difficult, yet by analysing transactions and calculating the rental growth implied in the yields realized, and by studying attained levels of rental growth, it may be possible to detect where underperformance is likely. An example will help:

You are aware that your clients seek an overall return (internal rate of return or equated yield) from prime shops' property of say 14 per cent. If a rack rented shop which is let on a standard lease with five yearly reviews and is similar to one held in your clients portfolio, has recently sold on a yield of

5 per cent based on the rack rent, then the purchaser in order to achieve the required return of 14 per cent would need to achieve annual rental growth in the order of 9.79 per cent. If you are further aware that rental growth has been in that order in the past but you anticipate that it will fall in the near future, due maybe to the imminent opening of a new shopping centre nearby, your clients could well be advised to sell now providing that suitable reinvestment opportunities exist.

It follows from this that a property manager should be aware of changes in rental growth pattern and changes in tenant demand, as well as levels of market value. Only if he is, can optimum disposal decisions be made.

SUMMARY

In this chapter we have sought to describe ways by which a property manager can ensure that the portfolio under his control is performing in accordance with the aims and objectives of the owner. In essence, it requires a sensible, reasoned approach to management in accordance with the basic principles of its practice.

The ways in which portfolios are shaped and created should flow from the investors' needs and this in turn should dictate the disinvestment policy. Above all, an acceptance of the need to actively manage the portfolio is a prerequisite to the satisfactory performance of the investment. For some years this art of direct property management appeared unfashionable, but with performance awareness now so widespread, to quote Wootton (1987), 'Before long there may well be competition between buildings and their managers as to the levels of management standards achieved'. This philosophy has long been adopted in other countries, notably the USA (see Chapter 12). We welcome its development in the UK.

Chapter 10

Redevelopment and refurbishment

THE APPRAISAL – PRINCIPLES

Property is held for investment or occupational purposes and the value of any property depends upon the degree of utility it offers to its occupier and other potential occupiers. Investment and occupation are therefore closely linked. When a property is first developed the specification and location will be the most appropriate to attract tenants or other users. Over time, however, the building may become less suitable for the occupier's business for a variety of reasons, including functional or building obsolescence. The quality of the location may also worsen as a result of infrastructure changes or modern buildings being constructed in the vicinity which more closely meet occupiers' requirements. At this time redevelopment or refurbishment becomes an attractive option. Valuation evidence shows why this should be, and regular appraisals using such evidence will indicate when a redevelopment scheme will be viable.

We have already seen that an investor in property will be particularly concerned with growth over time in rental and capital values. In considering the timing of a redevelopment scheme we must first of all consider the utility of the property to an end user. Conventional valuation techniques assume that a commercial property will retain an investment value into perpetuity, subject to a deduction for landlord's outgoings. However, it is a noticeable feature of the current property market that buildings constructed as late as the 1970s are now regarded as being suitable for extensive renovation or redevelopment.

Examples can be taken of office buildings on London Wall, built in the 1960s, which today cannot be economically adapted to suit the needs of the modern office user. Similarly, shopping centres built in the 1960s vogue of pre-cast concrete and without cover no longer meet the needs of the shopping public and, by definition, the retailer.

When a building is about to be constructed the proportion of site value to building value is readily illustrated by means of a residual valuation. Let us assume that a site is about to be acquired by a developer for the construction of 20,000 sq. ft gross of offices. Making reasonable assumptions in respect of rent, yield and building costs, the traditional residual valuation could be calculated as shown in Example 10.1. It should be understood that the calculation is simplistic and little more than a skeleton example to illustrate a technique. There are many omissions in the calculation which could invalidate the predicted site value and these are dealt with later in this chapter.

Example 10.1

Residual valuation	(£)	(£)
Rent: 17,000 sq. ft net @ £14 p.s.f.	238,000	
YP @ 5% in perpetuity	20	
Gross development value (GDV)	4,760,000	
Less disposal costs @ 4%	190,400	
Net realizable value		4,569,600

Expenditure	(£)	(£)
Construction: 20,000 sq. ft gross @ £65 p.s.f.	1,300,000	
Architect's + quantity surveyor's fee @ 12.5%	162,500	
Construction and fees total	1,462,500	

Interest payments	(£)
Construction	
0.5 × 1,462,500 @ 10% for 1 year	73,125
Developer's profit @ 20% of GDV	952,000

	(£)
Total cost	2,487,625
Gross site value	2,081,975
Present value 1 year @ 10%	0.909
Net site value	1,892,515
Say	1,890,000

Therefore, a developer considering the purchase of a cleared site with full planning consent for 20,000 sq.ft gross of offices will be able to purchase the site for £1,890,000 so long as he is correct in his assumptions that the building will let at £14 p.s.f. and can be constructed for £65 p.s.f. The assumption is also made that the property when let will sell immediately to an institution to show the investor an initial yield of 5 per cent. The developer will earn a profit of £952,000 and the site value as a proportion of investment value is 39.71 per cent.

The purpose of showing this calculation is to illustrate the relationship between investment value and site value. Typically, when a development project has been completed, site value will be approximately 20 per cent of investment value. In this example a cleared site was assumed and the value of the site is dependent upon the value of the building which will be constructed upon it which in turn is dependent upon the utility of the building to a prospective tenant.

THE TIMING OF DEVELOPMENT AND REDEVELOPMENT

The investor who purchases a newly-constructed fully let office building will purchase the investment to show a yield on cost of 5 per cent in Example 10.1. He will only do this if he can be confident that substantial rental and capital growth will occur during the life of the property (see Chapter 3). In most cases as buildings age they become less suited to tenants needs, for example office buildings may not have the capacity to incorporate the cable runs and duct space which is required by a tenant using new technology.

As tenant demand falls due to building obsolesence, so rental growth will decline and the investment yield that a property commands will rise. As this happens it is possible that the real value of the property will not rise consistently from year to year as is assumed by the initial valuation at 5 per cent, but capital values may only increase slightly, remain static or even fall. The investment value may not grow as fast as inflation during the latter part of a property's life and the investor may therefore experience losses in real terms. The proportion of site value within the total investment value of a property does not, however, reflect its current use but the potential value of a building which could be built and let on the site. Therefore, although the value of the building may fall slowly, the proportional value of the site upon which the building stands will tend to rise as the utility of the building declines. This can be illustrated by a simple diagram: (see Figure 10.1).

In figure 10.1 it is assumed that a property constructed and let at time 0 has a site value of $0X$ and an investment value of $0Z$. Over time the site value will rise as a proportion of total investment value until all the value of the property is in the site and not in the building which has lost all of its utility for a prospective tenant. This time is T_1. It is at this time that we would expect a redevelopment project to occur as the site value reflects the value of the potential building which could replace the obsolescent one on the site. Conventional valuation techniques assume that the period from zero to T_1 can be regarded as perpetuity and it has been generally accepted that the assumption relates to a period between seventy and one hundred years. Increased sophistication in the tenant market in modern times prompted by changes in the economy has drastically shortened this period. To illustrate this let us assume that early in the life of the property the tenant market experiences a dramatic change in demand so that a

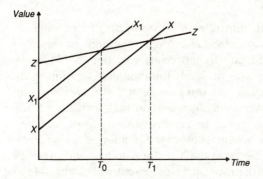

Figure 10.1 Timing of redevelopment

different type of building is required by firms seeking to occupy space. A good example would be the change in demand already referred to in the City of London to office buildings which are flexible, can cope with sophisticated computer equipment and are served by the latest form of air-conditioning. In this case the site value in our example will rise from X to X_1 and we would predict that redevelopment would occur at time T_0.

A similar phenomenon to the City of London market can be observed in the industrial/high-tech market. There are examples of warehouse buildings no more than ten years old being replaced by new 'high-tech' two-storey pavilions under the B_1 use of the new use clauses order. There is one reason for this, changing demand from the tenant market reflected in higher rents for property of B_1 use and a consequential rise in land value with the prospect of redevelopment.

The investor should be aware of changes in tenant demand which affect his property portfolio. Positive management of a property portfolio implies that redevelopment opportunities will be taken where the return on money expended justifies such a course. The investor does, however, have a choice. He can refurbish, and this refurbishment can range from cosmetic upgrading to major renovation, or he can demolish and redevelop. A third choice is also available; to sell the investment and reinvest elsewhere. Investors often take the third option when faced with an obsolent building and it has been estimated that, in 50 per cent (Hillier Parker 1986) of all shopping centre refurbishments, the property has been sold prior to refurbishment work commencing.

In general terms, therefore, a development scheme will take place when the value of the investment property is exceeded by the value of the site upon which it stands.

THE APPRAISAL IN DETAIL

The residual valuation used to illustrate the proportion of site value to investment value can now be examined. Residual valuations of this type attract criticism and it is not difficult to appreciate why this should be. A broad brush approach is taken with probably minimal investigation made into the figures used. The calculation cannot be regarded therefore as an accurate appraisal but it may serve as an indication that a viability study can proceed. A full viability study can be expensive in terms of fees, and a figure of 4 to 5 per cent of the eventual cost of the building is not unusual, particularly with complex schemes. Yet the investor who has made a policy decision to become involved with property development will not be able to carry out a full appraisal on each and every development opportunity which is put to him. Certain criteria will be adopted as principles. For example, investors may not consider development schemes outside of the south-east of England because rental growth is not predicted to be sufficiently attractive. Also an investor may restrict himself to retail or office schemes because that is where his expertise lies. An institution may only consider funding for a scheme where a pre-let has been agreed or an anchor tenant is likely to sign an agreement to lease. The residual valuation as proposed in Figure 10.1 can be regarded as part of a credibility study which will show in general terms if a site is worth considering further. If the residual shows that this is the case, and the landowner is asking a figure for the site which is achievable within the rents and yields used, the basic valuation can be worked up into a full appraisal.

The investigations which have to be made in order to produce the appraisal can be listed and criticism of the methods used in Example 10.1 can be made.

CRITIQUE OF THE OUTLINE APPRAISAL

Rent and Yield

Rent in the valuation is assessed at £14 p.s.f. It is conventional to use rents calculated on the basis that the building has been let at the time the valuation is prepared with any increase or decrease during the development period being ignored. The gross area of the building to be constructed has been reduced by 15 per cent to produce a net lettable area of 17,000 sq. ft. Both these assumptions on rent and area are fraught with uncertainty unless investigations are made.

The project may not be fundable without a pre-let and it is probable that a tenant on this basis will negotiate a concessionary rent. Without a detailed planning consent and architect's scheme design the net area of the building is also approximate and the requirements of the pre-let tenant exacerbates the uncertainty. The yield used to capitalize the rental income is usually that which the building would be valued at in the investment market if it was offered at the time of the valuation as a fully let investment. However, the valuation by capitalizing the rent, deducting cost and leaving the developer with a profit, assumes a forward sale arrangement. The yield agreed with the funder would certainly be higher as a consideration for entering into a forward sale, even with the presence of a pre-let tenant. Disposal costs re-emphasize the assumption that a forward sale is assumed. The costs in question represent the solicitor's and agent's costs involved in disposing of the investment to the institutional purchaser.

Construction Costs

Construction cost, assumed on a gross area, is taken at £65 p.s.f. Although a valuer can make his own assessment of cost using one of the published lists of data such as the Building Cost Information Service or Spons, the opinion of a quantity surveyor will normally be sought. The value of the information gained will only be as accurate as the certainty of the design. When only very tentative information is available the cost estimate will be inaccurate and will vary for a multiplicity of reasons when the architect has produced sketch designs. The constraints of a detailed planning permission, materials used, the requirements of the pre-let tenant, acceptable institutional specifications and general economic factors influencing the construction industry will all have an effect.

Increases and decreases in cost during the development period are ignored in the calculation and present-day costs are used in the same way as present-day rents. Sensitivity analysis of the valuation shows that changes in rent and yield have a greater effect on the residual figure than proportional increases in building cost, and probability analysis is used to predict the likelihood of changes during the development period. One method of probability or risk analysis used in development is the Monte Carlo simulation which is described in Chapter 6.

Architects' and quantity surveyors' fees

Architects' and Quantity Surveyors' fees are conventionally predicted as 12.5 per cent of the building cost. This figure can be a wildly inaccurate prediction, particularly in major projects, as it does not take account of time-based fees which are incurred at the start of the project. These fees are charged for all work which leads up to scheme design and, although they may be subsumed into subsequent percentage fees, the extraction of a brief for a client allied to the presentation of various options can be very expensive at the start of a project.

Although it is not usually stated in the valuation, the 12.5 per cent fee charge also assumes the presence of a structural engineer and a mechanical and services engineer. As an approximation, architects can be said to charge 5.75 per cent of construction cost for design and supervision services. Quantity surveyors can be assessed at 3.5 per cent of the value of the work and structural engineers 2.25 per cent of the value of the structural elements which he designs. Mechanical and services engineers can be assessed at 2 per cent of the total building cost for designing these elements of the building. As with any service, all of these fees are open to negotiation but there are also many other additional services which may be required of the design team which are not covered by the 12.5 per cent assumption.

Developer's profit

On the assumption that a forward sale has been arranged, it is assumed that to obtain funding the developer will need to show a level of profit of 20 per cent of the gross realizable value or in this case 36.28 per cent on cost. An institution forward funding a development of this nature is not in business to produce profits for the developer but will wish to see a reasonable return predicted at appraisal stage. If problems arise leading to extra cost during construction, the institution's yield is then protected by the level of developer's profit which will be reduced as other costs rise. In this calculation the value of the site is assumed to be the only unknown, but when the site is purchased it is the developer's profit which becomes the residual figure.

Interest payments

Short-term interest is assumed at 10 per cent in the valuation and is calculated on a yearly basis. The rate of short-term interest depends upon the arrangements agreed between funder and borrower. If a 'package deal' with an institution has been agreed, short- and long-term interest rates will both be negotiated at the same time and there may also be an incentive project management fee.

Interest charges will be compounded quarterly and not calculated on simple interest as in the example. It is important for the borrower to understand what this implies for his cash flows. If interest is quoted at 10 per cent per annum this will equate to 2.41 per cent per quarter compound and the money outstanding in each quarter will attract interest at this rate. The calculation is $\sqrt[4]{(1.10)} - 1 \times 100$ to convert an annually quoted rate of interest to a quarterly compound rate. The calculation of interest on construction cost is based on the assumption that interest will only be charged on the total amount borrowed for one half of the total period of the development. It is assumed that project expenditure takes place on a regular basis throughout the project with equal amounts being spent each month until completion. In fact the rate of project expenditure is irregular

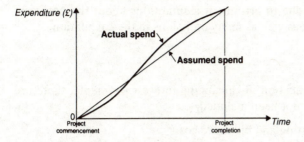

Figure 10.2 Construction expenditure

and a graphical representation will show the familiar 'S' curve, illustrated in Figure 10.2.

Taking interest for half of the period only is therefore a very approximate approach but one which is often adopted before the project design is developed and properly costed.

Time-scale

The residual valuation is not a discounted cash flow. Present-day rents and costs are used with interest payments assumed to be rolled up until the investment is sold. The valuation does, however, assume an unrealistic time-scale for the project which will lead to interest payments being underestimated. The residual valuation as written assumes the assumed time-scale shown in Figure 10.3.

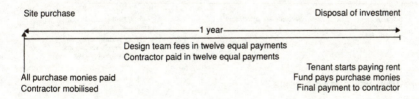

Figure 10.3 Assumed time-scale

The assumed time-scale is therefore far too simplistic to produce a realistic calculation and this is due to erroneous assumptions about the nature of contracting and leasing as well as many omissions in the calculation.

Omissions

Apart from oversimplification in calculating interest payments, there are many costs which have not been included:

(a) Agents' fees on letting and brochure costs
(b) Special consultant's fees
(c) Planning application fees
(d) Development consultant's fees
(e) Soil test and bore-hole survey costs
(f) Solicitor's fees in connection with lease if not borne by tenant
(g) Provision of landscaping
(h) A construction contingency
(i) Cost and time allowance for archaeological investigations

Calculation

A more realistic time-scale for the proposed development would be as follows and will allow for rolled up interest changes to be predicted more accurately (see Figure 10.4).

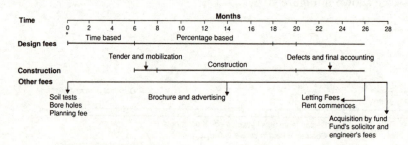

Figure 10.4 Revised time-scale

As a principle it is advisable for a developer to be aware at any time of the amount of uncertainty which lies behind generalized assumptions. Only when a project is complete is it possible to produce definitive calculations, but investigations must at any time be as thorough as the project information and client decisions will allow. Based on the revised time-scale, and with important omissions included, a revised residual valuation can now be produced (Example 10.2).

Example 10.2

Revised residual valuation	(£)	(£)
Rent: 17,000 sq.ft @ £14 p.s.f.	238,000	
YP @ 5.25% in perpetuity	19.05	
GDV	4,533,900	
Less disposal costs @ 4%	181,356	
Net realizable value		4,352,544

Expenditure	(£)
Construction: 20,000 sq.ft gross @ £68 p.s.f.	1,360,000
Architect + quantity surveyor + design + supervision fees @ 12.5%	170,000
Architects', etc. time-based fees say	40,000
Sub-total Construction + fees	1,570,000
Contingency @ 5%	78,500
Sub-total inc. contingency	1,648,500
Planning fee	3,500
Soil tests + bore-hole survey say	10,000
Agents fees on letting	23,800
Brochure costs + advertising	20,000
Sub-total all costs exc. interest	1,705,800

Interest payments (compounded annually)	(£)
Construction	
0.5 × 1,648,500 @ 10% for 1 year	82,425
Planning fee	
3,500 @ 10% for 28 months	817
Soil tests + bore hole survey	
10,000 @ 10% for 28 months	2,333
Brochure costs + advertising	
20,000 @ 10% for 14 months	2,333
Agent's fee	
23,800 @ 10% for 2 months	397
Sub-total interest payments	88,305
Developer's profit @ 20% of GDV	906,780

	(£)	
Total cost	2,700,885	
Gross site value	1,651,659	
PV 1 year @ 10%		0.909
Net site value		1,501,358
say,		1,500,000

Points to note regarding the revised residual valuation in Example 10.2 are as follows:

1   Simple interest has been used as the numbers are very small. For mathematical accuracy quarterly rests should have been used and interest compounded.
2   Omissions from the previous calculation have now been included and interest added from the time money is incurred until the development is sold to a fund.
3   Interest payments on construction are approximated and assumed to be payable for only half the period. For strict accuracy interest should be calculated quarterly based on the probable 'S' curve as predicted by the quantity surveyor. The whole of the construction cost less any client retention should be then charged to interest for the whole of the defects liability period until sale to the fund.
4   Fees are taken at 12.5 per cent but it is possible additional consultants such as a project manager may be required. It is perhaps safer to use 15–17 per cent for fees.

The valuation as recalculated is therefore unlikely to be precisely accurate in practice but it is more realistic than the previous example. The additional costs and interest payment together with a 'realistic' investment yield of 5.25 per cent (which is assumed to have been negotiated with an institution) have resulted in the predicted site value falling from £1,890,000 to £1,500,000. It is interesting to note that 44.4 per cent of this difference is due to the shading of the investment yield by one quarter of one per cent.

INCENTIVES FOR INVOLVEMENT

It is now necessary to examine the parties to development schemes and their varying reasons for becoming involved with development projects.

The institutions

We have already seen in Chapter 5 that the life funds and the pension funds have broadly comparable investment incentives. Both have long-term investment requirements but, in the case of the pension funds especially, have concentrated on short-term gains which have been widely available as a result of the stock market boom up to October 1987. Up to this time property investment was increasingly perceived as difficult to value, inflexible and expensive to manage in comparison with the other investment media. There is some evidence that the institutional investors are returning to property investment since October 1987 but at the time of writing it is too soon to predict whether this sentiment would survive a revival of the equities market.

The life assurance companies have displayed a far more enthusiastic attitude towards property investment than the pension funds during the past decade. The total UK assets of the insurance companies amounted to £22bn at the start of 1986 compared with £13bn in pension fund portfolios (Debenham, Tewson and Chinnock 1986). The life assurance companies have been consistently involved with major property developments, particularly in the retail sector. Norwich Union and the Prudential, for example, have both been increasingly involved with high profile retail schemes in town centre locations.

The institutions' definition of prime property is a narrow one and it is widely believed that the low yields achieved on many retail investments in recent years are a result of excess demand for town centre properties which are rarely available on the market, rather than careful analysis of predicted rental growth. Prime property simply defined is the 'best' available. In the case of retail schemes this implies a town centre location of maximum accessibility to the shopping public, tenant mix which will ensure strong pedestrian flow and a building specification which will result in an attractive ambience with ease of refurbishment at a later date. Lease terms will allow for the fullest possible control by the centre management and control over tenant mix by restrictions on assignment and subletting.

In undertaking a development scheme the institution will either be involved with a direct development, provide funding to a developer or be redeveloping or extending some of the properties in its portfolio. In becoming involved with property the institution will look for an appraisal which predicts a return consistent with the risk involved. We have dealt with this point thoroughly in Chapters 5 and 6. Institutions will be looking to become involved with developments where rental growth is about to take off after a period of stagnation. This wish to maximize short-term return coexists with the requirement to develop a scheme which will produce maximum rental growth over the long term and be consistently attractive to tenants.

In justifying involvement with a development property many institutions will regard the predicted initial yield as the most reliable indicator of viability. Overwhelmingly the institutions will use discounted cash flow, particularly the internal rate of return, as the preferred measure of investment performance. Yet it is questionable if these techniques are always used when the institutions are making a direct purchase of prime investment or development property. In investment terms the yield on prime shops between the first quarter of 1981 and the end of that year was recorded at just 3.5 per cent (Healey and Baker, 1988). To justify such a low yield the investor must assume that rental values will rise at close to 11 per cent per annum in perpetuity if the resulting internal rate of return is to match that available at the time from gilts. Evidence suggests that an acceptable initial yield for an institutional investor from a prime commercial development will be 2 per cent in excess of that which is regarded as the prime investment yield at the time.

It is important to draw the distinction between valuation and return when discussing an institution's involvement with a development scheme. A valuation can be regarded as a 'snapshot' in time and, depending on the precise instructions received by the valuer, will represent the market's opinion of the value of the property. A return may be defined in a number of ways, but the definition of return on capital employed is commonly used. When an institutional investor is involved with a development scheme he will try to maximize the return, but the eventual value of the development will be determined by market forces of supply and demand.

It seems anomalous therefore that investors should regard an acceptable return from a development scheme as 2 per cent above that used for an investment valuation. It is suggested that the correct way to regard return on capital employed in this sort of scheme is to calculate the probable return and then assess the likely rental growth to arrive at an IRR which can then be compared with that available for other types of investment.

Property development and investment companies

A property development company will become involved with a development scheme to receive a monetary profit in the short term. Typically, finance is borrowed from an institution and is rolled up with interest charged during the development period at quarterly rests. At the end of the development period the institution will purchase the developer's interest at an agreed yield, leaving the developer with a profit. There are a variety of funding methods which are explained in Chapter 11 but the fundamental point is that as the developer has only a short-term interest in a scheme his incentive will not necessarily match those of the lender. The relationship between the developer and the institution is evidenced by means of a financing agreement, in fact a contract, which is normally drawn up by the fund's solicitor. In common with most legal documents it is rarely concise but attempts to protect the institution's position by obliging the developer to seek approvals throughout the development period and to report on cost regularly.

Some funding institutions will prefer direct development schemes without using a developer to carry out the development. The presence of a developer is often preferred because the fund may not have the expertise or entrepreneurial flair to carry out the project. Furthermore, it is often the developer who will bring an opportunity to the notice of a fund in the first instance. By using a developer the fund can also reduce its risk of failure so long as there is enough profit in the scheme to accommodate the developer's profit. If the fund requires a minimum initial yield on first letting, incentives can be agreed with the developer if eventual rental levels exceed the minimum yield required.

Property investment companies are often closely linked with developers. Most of the largest investment companies have a development subsidiary through which developments can pass and be sold rather than be retained in a portfolio. Investment companies in one sense have similar incentives to an institution in that both invest rather than deal. However, whereas the institution is answerable to its beneficiaries through the trustees, the investment company is answerable to its shareholders through the board of directors. The institution will hold most of its investment by value in equities, whereas the property investment company derives its wealth entirely from its property portfolio. Share values remain of interest, of course, but only in that the share value of a public property investment company reflects market sentiment at the time. This may be due to a genuine opinion that the prospects for long-term growth are good, or a general rise in stock market values may be the cause. A rumoured take-over bid may also cause a share price to rise as the bidder actively seeks to purchase a controlling interest.

Property investment companies by their very nature do not have the flexibility of investment opportunities afforded to the institutions. Many property investment companies have traditionally specialized in one area of the market although it is noticeable that these distinct preferences are now being influenced by an approach which favours active management and a wider view of investment opportunities. Brixton Estate, for example, has always been known, with Slough Estates and Percy Bilton, as industrial property investors. Over 90 per cent of the portfolio of Slough Estates by area is invested in industrial and warehouse property (SEL Report and Accounts, 1987). This company is now investing or actively looking to invest in other areas of the market such as retail property and a similar phenomenon can be observed with Brixton Estate where opportunities have recently been sought outside the traditional area of the company's expertise.

Banks

As the pension funds have sought to reduce their investment in property in recent years, developers have turned increasingly to the banking sector for debt finance. Lending has been provided by the well-known High Street banks, merchant banks and overseas banks with offices in the United Kingdom. Debenham Tewson and Chinnock (SEL Report and Accounts 1987) have calculated that the greater proportion (60 per cent) of development finance is provided on a short-term basis with repayment required within five years. A smaller percentage of banks (40 per cent) are prepared for loans to extend beyond five years. The amount advanced is generally in the £5–20m range but syndication allows for a number of lenders to reduce the exposure to risk and offer larger loans. The banks' incentives in lending to the property development sector is the same as any other sort of bank lending. Security for the loan is required and a competitive rate of interest is available to attract borrowers. In most cases there will be a margin over LIBOR (London Inter Bank Offer Rate) but the size of this margin depends very much upon the nature of the borrower and the type of scheme. For smaller private developers the rate quoted is often 1.5–2 per cent above LIBOR.

It would appear that a number of factors have combined to result in the surge of bank lending in property development. Interest rates as evidenced by bank base rate fell steadily in the late 1980s from a peak of 14 per cent in the latter part of 1984. Combined with this trend has been strong tenant demand underpinning property values, particularly in city offices and the retail market. This has resulted in borrowers being able to introduce viable schemes to attract a lending package. A further factor has been the withdrawal from the property market of the pension funds, thereby making bank lending an increasingly important avenue for the borrower.

If the track record of bank lending is studied in recent years, there is a clear preference for central London offices with the Broadgate scheme by Rosehaugh representing a typical example. The Rosehaugh board have established a strong reputation in banking circles for being able to introduce attractive schemes to the lender. It is this factor which minimizes the bank's risk in lending which is crucial in this type of funding where the bank often has no long-term portfolio incentive. The current (late 1988) rise in interest rates caused by increasing trade deficits in the UK and USA will make bank lending less attractive as the cost of borrowing becomes more expensive. A trend has not yet emerged, but from the developer's viewpoint the return to the property investment market by some of the major funds is a welcome sign.

Local authorities

Local authorities are frequently involved in partnership schemes to develop town centre property where they are able to provide land in their ownership or use their CPO (Compulsory Purchase Order) powers to assemble a viable site. Recent examples abound and include the London Borough of Harrow and Laing Properties with Harrow Town Centre and Winchester City Council and Ladbroke City and Land with the Brooks retail development. Both these schemes resulted from partnership agreements negotiated by the council with developers and the council can often be regarded as the initiator of the scheme. The recent boom in retail investment based on buoyant retail sales has resulted in very many town centre retail schemes being local authority/developer/fund partnership. A typical arrangement is for the local authority to provide a town centre site either already in their ownership or acquired under a CPO or the threat of a CPO. A development brief is then prepared and developers are invited to make competitive bids for the site on the basis of a premium for long lease with or without the offer of equity participation for the local authority. Developers are also invited to submit designs for the proposed development so that the authority may then make a selection. The selection process illustrates the authority's incentives in becoming involved with the development scheme.

These incentives can be divided into four main areas: First, there may well be a planning reason for requiring town centre redevelopment, either because of non-conforming users or an antiquated road layout. Second, the authority may wish to maximize city centre rate income by promoting a new development. Third, the sums available for a premium deal in competitive conditions are considerable and this is also true of the authority's participation in the equity from the scheme by sharing the eventual rents. Lastly, civic pride must not be ignored. A local authority, an elected body, will normally be conscious of the wishes of the electorate and views may be sought by an exhibition of the various schemes under consideration. In reality, public consultation of this type is often a cosmetic exercise as other factors may outweigh public preferences. In the case of the Brooks development mentioned above, the public were invited to comment on three competitive designs for a town centre shopping scheme. The scheme least favoured by those who commented was eventually selected.

Major retailers

There are many examples in recent years of development schemes being promoted by department store owners. Retailing is a dynamic activity and recent developments in shop design to create an exciting shopping environment have resulted in many department stores being unable to provide a market-place suitable for modern shoppers' preferences. Also old-fashioned department stores will often occupy large sites which can be developed far more intensively. In these circumstances the retailer can come to an arrangement with a developer whereby the shell of a new department store is provided by the developer and the remainder of the site developed as a shopping centre with the department store as anchor tenant. The retailer in this way is able to fund his new store by exploiting the development potential of the site. There are many ways in which this type of development scheme can be organized and these are considered in Chapter 11.

Other participants

There are many other instigators of development schemes. In the public sector the Urban Development Corporations (UDCs) act as a catalyst to stimulate private sector investment in their designated area. Here the development incentive is to maximize the leverage available on any particular scheme so that it can be shown that as a result of public spending a greater amount of private development spending has resulted. The amount of leverage which is considered acceptable varies between each corporation and each scheme and the board of each corporation will normally make a judgement following an impact study which will predict the probable leverage and the benefits which will accrue in terms of jobs created. In carrying out their duties the UDCs are able to acquire land by compulsory purchase and provide grants to developers in terms of 'city grants'.

A unique organization, The Land Authority for Wales, is charged with the duty of acquiring land in the principality so that it may be developed by others. Compulsory purchase powers are available. The authority is therefore comparable to the UDCs in the way it acts as a catalyst to development. Both types of organization do not hold land for investment purposes but acquire it to assist development. The controlling interest will be passed to the private sector for development to take place.

The Scottish and Welsh development agencies are public authorities which act as developers in their own right and thus retain an investment portfolio. These organizations can be regarded as part of government's regional policy and the Welsh Development Agency and Scottish Development Agency will carry out development in areas where the return to the private sector would not be sufficient to allow development to take place.

Chapter 11

Funding and the development process

INTRODUCTION

Although it is possible for an owner-occupier to develop his own premises using finance from his own resources, most major property developments require a combination of the resources and expertise of a number of parties. In a town centre scheme, for example, three parties, fund, developer and local authority, will frequently act in a quasi partnership with each receiving some of the equity from the scheme. The relationships between these parties are given legal weight by a financing agreement between the fund and the developer and a ground lease between the local authority and the developer. The ground lease will be assigned to a fund at a later date or the fund itself may take on the role of the developer. During the development period, where a local authority is the freeholder, it is usual for the developer to occupy the site under a licence. In this chapter some typical arrangements between the major development protagonists are examined.

FUNDING

Methods of funding property development can be classified under one of two headings, equity funding or debt funding. In the former case the funder provides finance in return for a share in the profits, or the whole of the profits from the scheme to be created. In the latter case the funder has no share in the profits from the scheme but receives interest on the money lent. Substantial developers can also fund from their own resources and this is a form of equity funding. Smaller developers are usually in the position of having to seek funds from an institution or bank. Some developments are a mixture of both equity and debt finance where, for example, a developer will borrow money on a short-term basis to buy a site, build a property and let it. At the end of the development and letting period the capital and interest incurred will be repaid by refinancing on an equity basis perhaps by means of a sale of the investment or a leaseback deal. In this case debt finance is replaced by equity finance at a later date. The type of funding deal entered into is dependent upon the requirements and ingenuity of the parties. There are no standard methods, and in recent years property companies such as Rosehaugh have become renowned for arranging original and ingenious forms of funding.

TRADITIONAL FORMS OF PROPERTY FUNDING

Debenture

Property companies seeking finance for development can be in a strong position if they are property investors rather than dealers. Where a company has built up an investment portfolio it may be possible to raise debt capital by the issue of a debenture. Loans raised by this method are either recourse loans where the loan is guaranteed by the assets of the borrowing company, or non-recourse, which is a loan guaranteed by the value of a particular project or property investment. The borrower in this type of debt funding is free to use the loan for any purpose, and this element of flexibility is attractive compared to the restrictions imposed by the lender in respect of other types of funding.

Mortgage

A similar method of financing property development is by mortgage funding. Traditionally, a mortgage is raised on a proportion of the value of an investment property and with this loan the short-term borrowings which have been incurred to develop the building are repaid. In the 1950s and early 1960s when mortgage interest rates were very low this was an attractive form of funding from the borrower's point of view as it was probable that rental payments from the property would cover the initial mortgage repayment.

As rents grew the mortgagee would not benefit from the increasing value of the scheme but the mortgagor would benefit from an ever-increasing rental flow over and above the mortgage repayments. Many property developers grew rich during the mid-1960s by benefiting from this equity growth, particularly when regular rent reviews could be imposed on tenants. Loan and mortgages are similar because from the borrower's point of view he is committed to repaying capital and interest at regular intervals and he can assess the viability of his residual cash flow on this basis.

Leaseback

The realization by funders of the profits available from property development led to different financing arrangements which allowed a lender to participate in the equity from a scheme. A further reason for the emergence of this type of equity funding was that, as interest rates rose in the 1970s, so mortgage funding became less viable. As mortgage rates rose it became difficult for rental payments to cover the regular repayments of the loan and therefore the developer was placed into negative cash flow. Leaseback finance allowed developers to fund development and equity participation by lenders became common.

In a typical leaseback arrangement a developer will purchase a site carry out a development and let it with finance borrowed from an institution. When the building is let the developer will be in debt to the fund for his short-term finance. The developer then sells the building to the fund and simultaneously takes a long lease back from the fund. The rent the developer pays under this lease will be the return to the fund for their capital and rolled up interest debt. The developer's return will be the rent over and above that required by the fund as its return on capital and interest. There are many varieties of leaseback which have been used in the market. In the conventional form, as described above, the developer guarantees under his lease a return to the fund. As he retains a residual amount of rent this type of arrangement is called a 'top slice' leaseback as the developer takes the 'top slice' of income after paying his ground rent. As rent reviews are agreed with the occupational tenant in the future the rent under the ground lease may be increased in proportion. This is known as a 'geared' arrangement and it allows the fund to benefit from an ever-growing asset.

Capitalised 'top slice' leaseback

The conventional leaseback has major deficiencies from both the point of view of developer and fund however. The developer's slice of income is difficult to value and sell as it is a high risk arrangement with a substantial part of the rent received from the occupational tenant being paid to the fund. From the fund's viewpoint the full amount of rent and subsequent rental growth is not available. Furthermore, although the developer will normally carry out the management of the investment property, in being involved in a development scheme the fund is at risk. The scheme might reach the stage where increased costs or the lack of a tenant result in no rent being available over and above that required by the fund for its return. Even worse, the required return by the fund might not be available from the full rental value of the building compared to the costs of construction and short-term interest.

The disadvantages of the conventional top slice leaseback has resulted in its replacement by other types of funding where the long-term lender benefits from all the rent and rental growth in the building and the developer has no further involvement with the scheme after it is let. He takes a fee which is built into the development costs drawn down as borrowings from the fund during the development period. By this method the developer takes a once and for all payment in terms of a lump sum fee instead of a flow of income when the building is let. This arrangement is sometimes referred to as a capitalized top slice leaseback, but in fact it is often the case that title to the land will not pass through the developer's hands at all. His profit from the scheme will be a fee normally calculated by a capitalization rate being applied to the amount of rent remaining after the fund's minimum yield is met.

It must be emphasized that this type of funding arrangement is frequently negotiated as a package deal with the fund providing short- and long-term finance. The rates of short-term finance and the fund's minimum long-term yield are both to be negotiated, as is the timing of the payments referred to in the funding agreement. Simple numerical examples can be used to illustrate some conventional forms of development funding. A simplistic example (Example 10.1) is used in Chapter 10 to illustrate the relationship between site and building value. Although this calculation was made more realistic and criticized, the figures will be used to illustrate the funding techniques described above. The calculation showed that site value was £1,890,000 and it can be assumed that this figure was paid for the freehold of the site.

EXAMPLES OF DEVELOPMENT FUNDING

Forward sale

In a typical forward sale arrangement the developer will build a scheme and an institution will purchase the development when it is built and let. The funding arrangement will be entered into when the developer has identified a possible site purchase, and a short-term rate of interest will be negotiated together with the fund's required yield at which it will purchase the development when it is let. In Example 10.1 the developer has negotiated a short-term interest rate of 10 per cent and the fund will purchase the investment to show themselves a yield of 5 per cent. The developer will make a profit of £952,000 when the purchase is made by the fund, so long as he is correct in his development assumptions.

Top slice leaseback

With a conventional top slice leaseback the fund and the developer will share in the rent produced by the scheme with the fund lending the developer all of his short-term finance. This money will enable the developer to purchase the site, carry out the development, let it, sell it to the fund and take a long lease back. As the fund will not be receiving all of the rent from the scheme, nor all the rental growth in the future, the yield that will be required is assumed to be 1 per cent higher than that negotiated for the forward sale.

Example 11.1

	£
Site purchase including short-term interest on purchase price	2,081,975
Total development cost including short-term interest	1,726,025 (construction cost + fees + disposal costs)
Total capital and rolled up interest owed by developer to fund at end of development period	3,808,000*
Initial yield required by fund, say 6%	228,480
Total rent received by developer from occupational tenant	238,000
Developer's profit rent or 'top slice'	9,520

* This figure is the total cost of the scheme excluding developer's profit as the developer's profit is in this case received as an income flow.

Capitalized top slice leaseback

There are many variations to the simplistic form of capitalized leaseback. Frequently the institution will guarantee the developer a project management fee with the promise of an additional fee if the scheme lets at a higher rent than that predicted at the time of signing the funding agreement. The usual arrangement is for the guaranteed fee to form part of the short-term cost and it attracts interest which is rolled up from the time the fee is paid until the time that the development is taken over by the fund. Using the same example as previously, let us assume that a deal is struck on the following basis:

(a) The developer is guaranteed a fee of £200,000.

(b) In addition to the guaranteed fee the developer will be paid:

    (i) Fifty per cent of the amount by which net rents exceed 6 per cent but shall not exceed 7 per cent of the fund's short-term lendings including rolled up interest. This sum is referred to as T.

    (ii) Sixty per cent of the amount by which net rents exceed 7 per cent of the fund's short-term lendings. This sum is referred to as $T1$.

(c) To calculate the developer's incentive payment T and $T1$ as defined above are summated and capitalized by a YP of 16.66.

Let us assume that the building eventually lets at £290,000 per annum rather than the £238,000 predicted at the start of the development period. Example 11.2 shows the calculation, although it is assumed for the sake of simplicity that all costs remain as Example 11.1. In practice some, such as disposal costs, would rise.

Example 11.2

	£
Total capital and interest owed by developer to fund at the end of the development period	3,808,000
Add guaranteed fee (assume paid half way through development period)	200,000
Interest on guaranteed fee 200,000 @ 10% for 6mths (2.4% per quarter)	9,715
Total fee and interest	209,715
Total expenditure by fund excluding incentive payments	4,017,715

Calculation of first incentive payment to developer	£
Minimum yield to fund @ 6% × 4,017,715	241,063
Maximum yield for 1st tranche of 'extra' income @ 7% × 4,017,715	281,240
1st tranche income (281,240 less 241,063)	40,177
take 50%	20,088
YP @ 6%	16.66
1st incentive payment to developer	334,666

Calculation of second incentive payment to developer	£
Total expenditure by fund excluding incentive payments	4,017,715
Take % on 1st tranche @ 7%	281,240
Rent from occupational tenant	290,000
2nd tranche income	8,760
Take 50%	4,380
YP @ 6%	16.66
2nd incentive payment to developer	72,971

Summary	£
Total expenditure by fund excluding incentive payments	4,017,715

1st incentive payment	334,666
2nd incentive payment	72,971
Total expenditure by fund	4,425,352
Rent from occupational tenant	290,000
Yield to fund	6.55%
Total payment to developer	607,637

In Example 11.2 the details of the incentive payments are all subject to negotiation between developer and fund. As a principle, however, it is commonplace for the funding agreement to give to the developer incentive payments for letting a building at the highest possible initial rent. As will be seen this means that the funding agreement will contain rights to the fund to approve lettings. In the case of a shopping centre special arrangements will be required for lettings to anchor tenants where rental income can hardly be said to be maximized compared to conventional lettings of standard shop units. When the incentives of the long-term investor are considered it may be thought that encouraging the maximization of initial income may be inappropriate. The long-term investor will be mainly concerned with rental growth and the quality of the tenant. A higher rental income will increase the return but it may result in disadvantages in terms of tenant management and investment quality.

Leaseback arrangements became popular in the 1960s and early 1970s but have tended to be replaced by bank funding in recent years for the larger schemes. Many insurance companies which invest in property development will agree an incentive and guaranteed fee with a developer in the form of the above example and in seeking funding developers can choose from widely varying sources with different types of equity or debt financing.

From the calculation above it will be appreciated that from the developer's viewpoint the greater the guaranteed fee the smaller will be the eventual incentive payment as the former is regarded as part of the total development cost.

Mortgage funding

When interest rates are low, mortgage funding becomes a possibility, either on a straight repayment of capital and interest, or in some form of 'balloon' mortgage where interest only is paid on the loan until redemption when capital is repaid. A typical arrangement can be examined.

If Example 11.3 is used the total development cost is £3,808,000 including short-term interest. It is assumed that the developer has borrowed the finance to carry out the scheme from banking sources, and when the scheme is complete and let he will arrange long-term finance by means of a mortgage with the building as security. The mortgage rate over the course of the loan will vary, but initially it can be assumed to be 10 per cent. The developer's position is as follows:

Example 11.3

	£
Investment value of property	4,760,000
Loan required (developers profit excluded)	3,808,000
Loan as % of building value	80%
Yearly sum to repay capital and interest on loan for 25 years @ 10%	
$\dfrac{3,808,000}{100} \times 0.9181 \times 12$	419,535
Rent from property	238,000

From Example 11.3 a number of points are clear. First, the loan required is 80 per cent of the investment value of the property. It is doubtful whether the lender would regard this as sufficiently secure for a loan of this type. Second, the rental payments do not initially cover the loan repayments. Indeed, even if interest only is charged the repayments would still be £380,800 per annum (calculated on an annual basis) which would still result in the developer having to finance the deficit in the first part of the building's life. The mortgage funding arrangement could be made to work if the rate of interest was at very low level or if the scheme was let at very high rental values. If there is substantial rental growth during the development period and the scheme is let speculatively the resulting cash flows could make the scheme viable with conventional mortgage funding but other arrangements will allow the developer to avoid the deficit cash flow of this type of mortgage.

Alternative methods of development funding

Alternative methods of development funding have emerged during recent years especially related to bank finance.

We have already seen that a conventional mortgage is not viable unless interest rates are at a very low level. If the developer is unable to fund his scheme by means of an end purchaser agreement, the alternative selected is often bank finance. Techniques which have been commonplace in the world of corporate finance have been transferred to development schemes very successfully.

The simplest method for a developer to use bank funding is to simply agree a loan either at a fixed rate or within a 'collar' of interest rates. This means that over the course of the loan interest rates will only move within narrow specified limits. A fixed rate loan is likely to be at a high rate of interest for the obvious reason that the lender is at risk if general interest rates move during the course of the loan. Developer's can use bank loans of this type as short-term facilities to carry out the development, but they are rarely viable on a long-term basis for the same reason as the long-term mortgage is not viable.

Varying techniques have been adopted to allow the developer to borrow, with interest rates being controlled to some extent. By paying a lump sum to the lender at the outset the developer can negotiate a 'cap' on the rate of interest throughout the term so that interest rates will not rise beyond an agreed level. Similarly, if a developer negotiates a loan with rates which float freely at a premium over LIBOR (London Inter Bank Offer Rate) he may also be able to negotiate a transfer to a fixed rate of interest late in the loan period if interest rates fall. This is known in finance jargon as a drop lock. Using established banking techniques, developers may switch from variable to fixed interest rates by exchanging or trading a loan commitment. Known as 'swaps', this technique can also be used to the developer's advantage by allowing access to markets which were not available at the time of agreeing a loan. All of these techniques allow a developer to manipulate the interest rate on his loan and thereby increase the profitability of a scheme.

Where a major project is proposed the loan required may be too large for any one lender to contemplate. Securitized loans have been negotiated which serve to spread loan guarantees over a wider base than concentrating on one lender. A security can be regarded as a guarantee against default of a loan repayment and by negotiating such guarantees developers have been able to arrange further loans to carry out development schemes. For securitization to be successful a promissory note has first to be negotiated and against this finance to undertake a development scheme can be obtained from a bank. The companies subscribing to the promissory note do not receive interest nor do they actually provide development finance. The usual arrangement would be for the companies to receive shares in the company carrying out the scheme (the developer) when the development has been completed.

It is, of course, open to the developer at this time to refinance the scheme using a conventional mortgage or debenture and discharge the companies providing collateral. This would only be viable if an adequate cash flow was available from the scheme in terms of rent to cover capital and interest payments to the new lender.

PARTNERSHIP SCHEMES

Development projects which involve a local authority providing the site and the developer carrying out a project are commonly referred to as partnership schemes, although in reality these are based upon a development contract between the parties. They are partnerships in the sense that the developer and the authority will agree to share the equity in the scheme in terms of rent. On occasions the developer may be a fund or an insurance company or a developer may be involved during the development period with finance provided by an institution. Typically, the development will be a central site owned for many years by the authority and perhaps acquired by the use of compulsory purchase powers.

The local authority can be seen as the initiator of this type of scheme and their first step is usually to invite interested developers to register their interest against a development brief produced by the authority or their consultants.

Development briefs can be concise documents but often provide detailed guidance on the type of scheme which is favoured. The authority upon receiving approaches from developers may select a limited number, six seems to be most popular, to tender for the site against the development brief. Developer's bids will be on the basis of a premium for the ground lease offered by the authority together with a site layout and design sufficient for the schemes to be compared. The successful developer is then invited to agree heads of terms and subsequently signs a development agreement and ground lease. The development agreement is a complex document as it is intended to be comprehensive. As a result there may be some delay between the time that heads of terms are agreed and the document is signed.

The terms which will be normally found in the development agreement will relate to the following summary of those matters usually included:

1   General objectives and responsibilities.
2   Proposal on pre-lettings; report at time of agreement.
3   Provision of new capital.
4   Definition of the parties mentioned in the agreement.
5   Definition of net income.
6   Treatment of premiums.
7   Head lease provision.
8   Local authority's responsibilities (compulsory purchase, road closures, provision of access, and so on).
9   Developer's responsibilities. This will be lengthy and typically will cover the following:
    (a)   Appointment of main contractor to be approved by local authority.
    (b)   Contribute an agreed percentage of new capital at defined times.
    (c)   Insure buildings.
    (d)   Report on management of completed scheme.
    (e)   Instruct solicitors on occupational leases.
    (f)   Carry out market research.

(g)   Prepare a programme and update for authority.
(h)   Appoint consultants, and so on to be approved by the authority.
(i)   Negotiate with statutory undertakers.
(j)   Agree a letting campaign with the authority and agree optimum terms.
(k)   Direct preparations of post-completion documents (operation manuals, record drawings, and so on).

In short, the development agreement will be drawn up in such a way that the local authority receives from the developer information for its approval on all aspects of the scheme. It is understandable that a local authority would wish to restrain the activities of the developer in this way and it is equally understandable that the developer would agree to share the rents with the authority and to pay a premium for the ground lease but would not wish to seek approval to other aspects of the development.

Local authorities are frequently forced into a situation where the developer is allowed to delete many of the rights of the authority to control the development and the reason for this is in the time-scales involved and position of the authority as an elected body. Between the time that a bid from a developer is accepted in principle and a formal agreement is signed the details of the scheme will be decided upon. Elected bodies often find themselves being committed to carrying out a scheme to a time-scale which has been well publicized and may tie in with other infrastructure developments in the town centre. Having agreed in principle to proceed with a developer, the authority is reluctant by its very nature to renegotiate with another party which may delay a project for a considerable time. It is during the time between acceptance of a bid and the signing of a development agreement that a shrewd, in some instances unscrupulous, developer can seek to renegotiate heads of terms so that the authority's powers are eroded and rights of approval reduced.

The financial aspects of a typical local authority/developer partnership will provide for the developer to pay a premium for a long lease with rent paid to the authority as a percentage of the occupational rents. The lease will usually be for ninety-nine years with an option to renew for another twenty or thirty years to avoid incidence of stamp duty. In analysing bids from developers the authority will be very much influenced by the financial terms offered, although a prudent council will also wish to deal with a competent developer with proven expertise in the type of development which is planned. If the developer has a separate agreement with an institution he will normally assign his leasehold interest to his institutional funder on completion of the development, particularly in the case of town centre shopping schemes, where the quality of the occupational covenants is sufficient to attract an institution.

Some local-authority-promoted schemes are not regarded as sufficiently attractive by institutions for them to become involved as the eventual managing landlord. Institutional money is, however, necessary for the scheme to be built. Some councils have found a solution to this problem in making themselves the tenant of the institution, thereby providing an acceptable covenant. The way in which this can be arranged is for an authority to retain the freehold of a site and grant a long lease to a fund which provides short-term finance for a development to be carried out. When the development is complete the authority will take a leaseback from the fund and will pay the fund rent as a return on the capital and rolled up interest provided as short-term finance. The fund will therefore have an acceptable covenant and provide finance to an otherwise unfundable development. Schemes which can be considered suitable for this type of funding arrangement include the provision of small workshops in areas of low private investment, and a number of these types of deals have been negotiated in south-east London. There is always, however, a reluctance by institutions to invest in schemes where they cannot retain a very strong influence over the management of the investment. It is exceptional for a fund to become involved with a local authority managed investment. In the case of a town centre retail scheme the institution will wish to actively manage all aspects of the property and this will include multi-storey car parks serving the development. Property investors as a result of experience with local authorities do not, it appears, consider them reliable enough or fastidious in their management of property and prefer to assume these responsibilities directly. Examples will show the type of financial arrangements which can be agreed between local authority, institution and developer. For the purposes of the example it can be assumed that the scheme is a town centre retail development with costings and residential rental income as follows:

	£
Predicted rental income	1.5m
Predicted investment value	25m
Predicted development cost, including all fees and rolled up interest but excluding land cost	12m

Example 11.4

A developer obtains short-term development finance from an institution together with a commitment to long-term funding when the development is complete. The developer's profit will be a capitalized slice of the income from the scheme calculated on the following basis:

	£
Total development cost as above	12,000,000
Minimum yield required by fund @ 7%	840,000

Residual income	660,000
Take 50% for local authority ground rent	330,000
Developer receives remainder of residual income from fund capitalized @ 10%	
50% residual income	330,000
YP @ 10% perpetuity	10
Payment to developer	3,300,000
	(27.5% of total development cost)

The final position of the parties is as follows:

1   The developer takes a fee of £3,300,000 as a project management fee and departs.
2   The fund takes a long lease from the local authority and pays £330,000 per annum initially in ground rent. The amount of ground rent is reviewed at the same intervals as the occupational tenants and the share of total rent stays the same between fund and authority at subsequent occupational reviews.
3   The fund's initial yield from the scheme is as follows:

	£
Rental share (1.5m less 330,000)	1,170,000
Development cost including rolled up interest	12,000,000
Developer's fee	3,300,000
Total costs	15,300,000
Initial yield to fund	7.64%

In creating the investment, therefore, the authority has received an initial ground rent of £330,000 and an institution has acquired a long leasehold in a prime retail scheme at a yield of 7.64 per cent. They are not admittedly receiving all of the rent or rental growth in future.

What is the local authority to think about such a proposal by a developer and fund, as shown in Example 11.4? Certainly the figures as written suggest that the authority is not receiving the amount of ground rent that it should for the site which, on the basis of a very approximate residual valuation, should be worth £9.5m freehold. The authority is therefore receiving a return of 3.47 per cent on the value of their input to the scheme without including staff costs involved with any possible compulsory purchase orders. One might expect the authority to receive at least a substantial premium in addition to the ground rent offered in these circumstances and to retain rights of control over important aspects of the scheme.

PARTNERSHIP SCHEMES WITH MAJOR RETAILERS

There are a number of examples in the south-east of England of development companies and major retailers becoming involved in town centre shopping developments. The retailer, who owns the freehold of the site, will receive a shell of a new store and some profits from the scheme whilst the developer will acquire a shopping centre with a guaranteed anchor tenant. There are many ways in which this type of scheme can be negotiated but two are worth examining as they have each recently formed the basis of partnership schemes.

Sale with later capital payment to retailer

The first type of arrangement presumes a large measure of uncertainty about probable rental levels for standard shop units. Because of this the value of the development site cannot be agreed between the developer and the department store owner who is the freeholder of the site. Negotiations result in an agreement that the department store owner will sell the freehold of his site to the developer and will receive three benefits in consideration. First, he will receive a monetary sum which is considered to be some way below the true value of the site by both parties. Second, the developer will agree to construct a new department store on the site to a shell standard. Third, the retailer will receive an additional payment upon the final letting of all the shop units, including the department store. The final payment will be calculated on the total rent roll from the new centre including the department store rent capitalized at an agreed yield. From this figure is deducted all the costs of the development including the amount paid to the retailer for the site with rolled up interest added at quarterly rests.

The resulting residual amount will be paid to the retailer as additional profit from the scheme upon completion. Using assumed costs and rents, Example 11.5 shows the calculation.

Example 11.5

Assumptions	£	
Rent agreed as pre-let for shell of new department store	1,500,000	per annum
Total development cost of scheme including rolled up interest and all fees	34,000,000	
Amount paid for land including rolled up interest	6,000,000	
Total initial rents from scheme including 1.5m paid by retailer	3,000,000	

The retailer's final overage is calculated on the following basis:

	£
Total rents from scheme	3,000,000
Agreed yield of 6.5% perpetuity	15.38
Capital value	46,140,000
Total development cost including rolled up interest and all fees	34,000,000
Land including rolled up interest	6,000,000
Total	40,000,000
Final overage payment	6,140,000

Lease and leaseback by retailer

An alternative arrangement to that described in the section above has been used where a department store freeholder owner will dispose of his holding on a ground lease to a developer and subsequently take a long lease back on the shell of a new department store which the developer will build. The ground rent payable to the freeholder will be agreed as a proportion of the passing rents from the scheme and will be reviewed at the same time as the occupational tenancies. Both freeholder and head lessee receive the same proportion of the rent at review as they did at first letting.

As in the previous arrangement, the basis of this type of development is a site which is not used to its optimum intensity. This allows a new department store and shopping centre to be constructed on a site which previously would only accommodate an old-fashioned department store. Certainly the freeholder in this case is in a stronger position in receiving a proportion of rent from the scheme rather than an eventual capital sum. The incentives of retailer and developer will coincide on this point as both will want a well-let centre with maximized pedestrian flows and the highest possible rent. However, certain potential problems remain. There is the interface between the contractor for the shell of the new department store and the contractor responsible for the fit-out of the store who will be employed by the retailer. Also a policy must be agreed to deal with changes to the scheme required either by developer or retailer which may have 'knock on' effects to the detriment of either party.

THE MANAGEMENT OF THE DEVELOPMENT PROCESS

A depth of management expertise is required for any property development. We have examined the incentives of the major protagonists and these incentives have to be addressed in terms of planning and co-ordinating a project. There are three main areas of management which have to be encompassed to a greater or lesser extent by all the parties involved with a development project. These are:

(a) The co-ordination of each individual and organization associated with the project.
(b) Comprehensive forward planning which allows a degree of flexibility as project information becomes more definitive.
(c) The motivation of the project participants to create a resourceful and effective project team.

In a typical development project it is the property development company which is responsible for organizing most of the project work. Finance will be obtained from an institution or bank and a finance agreement signed. In these circumstances the developer is often referred to as the project manager but in reality, within the developer's organization, individuals will be selected to carry out this role or a consultant project manager will be appointed. The funder, although not directly involved with running the project, will require management input in identifying the constraints, rights of approval and the time-scale in the finance agreement. In considering the management role it is convenient to refer to the stages of a development project and relate these to the management task undertaken by the participants. The stages can be listed as follows:

(a) credibility
(b) viability
(c) funding agreement
(d) design and construction planning
(e) tender, contract and construction
(f) commissioning/letting and sale/refinancing

Credibility

As a principle a competent project manager will not allow his client to commit himself to any expenditure without clear advice about the options available and the consequences of the commitment. Some projects will never proceed to viability and will not be regarded as credible from the start. A credibility study is carried out without detailed investigation of any aspect of the project but with a substantial cost and time contingency included in the financial appraisal. At this time all aspects of the project may be unclear. Costs will be included in broad brush figures, rents will not be subject to a detailed investigation of the tenant market and the availability of financing may be doubtful.

Developers may be involved with very many credibility studies as development opportunities are introduced to them and it is when a project appears to have a likelihood of viability that costs start to be incurred.

Viability

Viability studies require investigation of all aspects of a project if they are to be regarded as at all meaningful. The negotiation of a funding agreement can be regarded as a natural continuation of the viability exercise. A viability study can be expensive in terms of time-based fees as advice will be required from an architect, quantity surveyor and structural/mechanical engineers. Site surveys will have to be undertaken and a marketing investigation will identify potential tenants or a pre-let tenant. The end point of a viability study is often the arrangement of finance and the purchase of a site or an option to purchase. The project manager acting for developer or fund will make his client aware that options are being reduced as uncertainty is reduced. Financial commitment will always be preceded by a report to the client analysing the available options and recommending a course of action.

The management task does not involve any technical input but efficient co-ordination requires that the studies undertaken on behalf of the client will be of a thorough and realistic nature. In the financial appraisal the project manager will wish to see figures produced which are appropriate to his client's incentives. It may be that the client wishes to know the probable initial yield or profit from a scheme at first letting. However, it may be that an institutional investor will require a discounted cash flow with an internal rate of return related to rental growth patterns. The rates of growth used in the calculation cannot be guaranteed but a probability analysis can be produced to show the likelihood of obtaining at least the required IRR (Internal Rate of Return).

The time-scales assumed for the project and the participants involved with the project will be listed with their fee implications made explicit in the appraisal. Architects may work through a project appraisal on the understanding that they will only receive a fee if the project proceeds but with major projects this is not often the case as the work involved is so great.

At the end of the viability stage the client will have firm prediction, based on thorough investigation, of how the scheme will fulfil his development requirements.

A developer will wish to see an adequate level of profit in the short term; an institution will wish to see a return of perhaps 2 per cent over the Gross Redemption Yield (GRY) from gilts and a finance agreement which allows control to be exercised over the developer. A major retailer involved with a scheme as anchor tenant will wish to exercise some control over the letting of the centre and will require safeguards to be built into his letting agreement to deal with changes to the agreed specification. It is important from the point of view of any client that the project manager ensures that clear information is available before financial commitment. He must also make his client aware of the degree to which project uncertainty

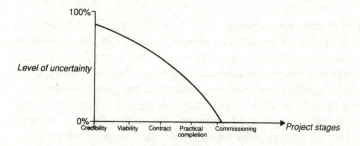

Figure 11.1 Stages of a Project and levels of uncertainty

is reduced as a project proceeds and the consequences this has in terms of options (see Figure 11.1).

The funding agreement

The funding agreement which is negotiated between developer and funder will be the subject of careful analysis by the project manager. Most institutional investors will use a standard form of agreement which has been produced by their solicitors. It is not enough, however, for clauses to be written down and made part of a contract. Each obligation placed on the developer has a management implication and the question has always to be asked, what will happen if the developer fails to abide by this clause? It may be, for example, in practical terms that it is not possible to enforce a clause which requires all changes to a scheme to be approved by the lender before implementation. The developer may argue that a decision had to be made immediately to avoid extra costs and delay. What is the funder to do in these circumstances? If he seeks legal redress for the developer's actions this can hardly be in his best interests. Such a course of action will destroy any atmosphere or co-operation and partnership between the parties and lead to even greater delay. If he ignores the developer's action the scheme may not be to the required standard for long-term investment.

The clauses in a funding agreement have to be considered as part of a management strategy and it cannot be assumed that the signing of a contract between developer and funder will ensure that either party will be able to take action to protect its position in practical terms. Funding agreements are long and complex documents, but all contain rights and obligations under the following general headings:

Calculation of payment

This will refer to the calculation of the developer's profit usually as a guaranteed project management fee with a multiplier applied to rents over the level of the fund's minimum acceptable yield.

Specification and design

This will ideally be agreed between funder and developer before the contract is signed. Any changes will require further approval (see below).

Responsibility to build

The agreement will place an obligation on the developer to complete the scheme within a certain time period. The responsibility for organizing the construction contract will be placed on the developer with the design team and other consultants providing a duty to care and collateral warranties to the fund.

Obtain planning and other statutory consents

The agreement will ensure that the developer is responsible for obtaining planning consent and other statutory consents for the scheme agreed.

Completion

Completion of a scheme is usually regarded as the time when the architect signs the certificate of practical completion. The funding agreement will make this approval subject to the separate approval of the fund's own consultant who may be a structural engineer or building surveyor.

Once again this is intended to provide the fund with protection from building defects as the architect is, of course, the developer's consultant. In practice there is intense pressure at this time on the fund's consultant to approve the architect's certificate and strong evidence of defects has to be available for the fund to refuse to accept the scheme. The usual reason why completion should not be accepted by the fund is that certain minor but important items, such as the landscaping, have not been completed.

Retention and defects

In the same way as a developer will hold a retention on a building contract until the end of the defects liability period, so a fund will hold back some short-term money from the developer until all defects are remedied and the scheme has been properly completed.

Rights of approval and inspection

The funder will wish to have rights to inspect the development during the course of construction and will employ its own consultant for this task.

Lettings

The funder will specify criteria for an acceptable tenant and the developer will normally seek the funder's approval to all lettings. The form of the lease and a shopfitting guide (in retail developments) will have been agreed between developer and funder.

Advances and payments, provision for interest

Interest payments will normally be calculated at an agreed rate with quarterly rests. The developer will draw short-term money down from the fund as required, but the fund will wish to ensure that these borrowings are required under the building contract. There have been many examples where developers have drawn down money from a fund and placed it on short-term deposit before paying the contractor, thereby making an investment profit with the funder's money.

Other items

There will be reference in the finance agreement to the consequences of default and arbitration should the parties fail to agree on certain items where approval is necessary under the agreement.

The signing of a finance agreement commits a funder to provide finance for a development scheme upon the terms agreed and puts obligations and responsibilities upon the developer. The agreement will be signed when a viability study shows that the scheme meets the participants' development incentives. Where the funding agreement itself does not provide the practical protection for the funder, management strategy must be considered.

Design and construction planning

The needs of any development participant can normally be defined in terms of time, cost and performance targets. We have seen how there may be some conflict between the requirements of the project participants. It is important, therefore, that the forecasts made at the time of the viability study are realistic and later variations can be contained within acceptable limits.

A project manager acting for a long-term investor will appraise the project time-scale proposed in a viability study. A logical sequence of activities will be drawn up as a network analysis and the use of a computer programme will predict the timing of the project completion and activities

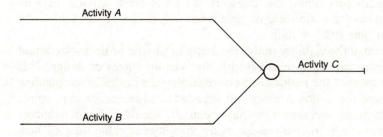

Figure 11.2 Part of Projects network

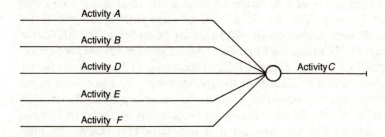

Figure 11.3 Part of Projects network

which form the critical path of the project. Costs and resources will be loaded into the programme so that a cash flow prediction can be made. It is appropriate at the viability stage to have a substantial float in the network programme to take account of client changes or those items which are accepted as unclear at that stage. It may be, for example, that although an anchor tenant has agreed heads of terms he has not signed an agreement to lease. A contingency will be inserted into the cost plan to take account of this and a float used in the network to take account of additional time required. The planning strategy should result in the parties to a project accepting a target master programme derived from network analysis with provision for scheme changes to be incorporated into the time and cost plan.

Martin Barnes (1983) has identified areas of risk in a network plan which could be eliminated by careful planning. As a principle the number of separate activities feeding into the sort of critical activity should be reduced to minimize the risk of delay. To take an example – in Figure 11.2 two activities must be completed (*A* and *B*) before activity *C* can start. If both *A* and *B* have an 80 per cent chance of finishing on time, *C* has a 64 per cent chance of starting on time. In Figure 11.3 five activities, A, B, D, E and F have to be completed before C can start. If each of these activities have an 80 per cent chance of finishing on time C has only a 32.8 per cent chance of starting on time ($0.8^5 \times 100$).

At the end of the viability study all participants to the project will commit themselves to expenditure involved in the various stages of design. It is likely that most of the major decisions regarding the design of the building envelope and the letting strategy will already have been taken in principle and targets for project return will have been set. The design team members will already have been involved during the viability stage, but they will now be formally appointed. It is sometimes the case that developers will appoint the design team by an exchange of letters referring to the standard form of consultant appointment. However, the task of the team will be not only to design the scheme in accordance with the client's brief but also to report regularly on progress and programme their work so that time and cost targets can be met. The standard form of engagement are the Royal Institute of British Architects (RIBA) *Standard Conditions for Architects*, the Association of Consulting Engineers (ACE) *Standard Form for Services and Structural Engineers*, and the RICS *Conditions of Engagement for the Quantity Surveyor*. The clauses in the model forms are sometimes vague in connection with cost and time control and some important matters are not referred to at all. To ensure that the project can be controlled by the client through his project manager it is necessary that the model form should be supplemented by additional clauses which impose further duties and obligation on the team. The following items usually form part of the addendum to the standard form:

(a) The architect shall seek the written approval of the client before proceeding to the next stage of his work.
(b) Each consultant agrees to co-ordinate his work with that of the other design consultants.
(c) Each consultant agrees to carry out his work in accordance with the project procedures drawn up by the client's project manager and approved by the client.
(d) Each consultant will programme his own work and the architect will co-ordinate these programmes into a design team programme.
(e) Each consultant will report monthly on progress against time, programme and cost targets.
(f) Any time-based fees will be approved in writing by the project manager before work is undertaken.
(g) Each consultant shall carry professional indemnity insurance to a level agreed in writing with the client.

The aims of these additional conditions of engagement are to control the progress of the project and they attempt to eliminate common causes of extra costs. Typical of these, particularly where the project is complex, is lack of co-ordination of the building work with the structure and the Mechanical and Electrical services. Also it has been a common occurrence for time-based fees to become uncontrollable on a complex project. The reference to procedures is important as the architect must be provided with a method of extracting a brief from the client and receiving firm approvals. Clients, particularly with owner-occupiers as anchor tenants, are rarely represented by one person only and approval procedures will identify the proper responsibility. Regular cost reports from the quantity surveyor will be required as the design develops and the scheme becomes more certain.

Tender, contract and construction

There are a number of contract strategies which can be used on a project and the one selected will depend on the client's development incentives. If a scheme is fully designed with full bills of quantities and a minimal number of prime costs or provisional sums, the conventional route is to seek a lump sum tender under the Joint Contracts Tribunal (JCT) 80 form of contract. The contractor in these circumstances will tender against a complete design which should give the client cost certainty during the course of the contract. If a lump sum tender is sought and the design is unfinished, however, there are dangers that the contractor will be able to claim for additional cost and extensions of time under the JCT 80 form of contract.

Other forms of contract have become popular in recent years, particularly management contracting which can be regarded as the employment of a construction consultant to organize the building contract. The management contractor will agree a fee for his services with the client, and although he will carry out a minimal amount of work himself, he will subcontract the project in convenient packages. He will do this as design progresses and will be consulted in terms of buildability by the design team. It has been said that this method of building procurement has many advantages in terms of flexibility and speed, but if the client wishes to have the greatest certainty regarding cost the method most often adopted is to fully design the scheme and for it to be costed on full bills of quantities. If the client changes his mind about the design at a later date, however, there is no flexibility in this arrangement and extra cost and delay is likely to be the result.

When the client has committed himself to a contractor, the progress of the work is supervised by the supervising officer who is usually the architect. Variations which arise during the course of the contract may require changes to the scheme and the architect will instruct the contractor to do this by means of an architect's instruction. On a major scheme there is usually some divergence between the value of the work which the contractor claims he has completed and the value of the work certified as complete by the employer's quantity surveyor.

Similarly, the cost effect of architect's instructions is often the subject of disagreements. The client's project manager is restricted by carrying out his role without having any responsibility under the form of contract, but he should ensure that any architect's instruction which will relate to a variation is classified, so that the client is aware of why it has occurred and why cost has risen. Any variation is due to one or more of the following:

(a) Firm costing of a prime cost sum.
(b) Firm costing of a provisional sum.
(c) Contingency spend for an unforeseeable variation.
(d) Change of design not instigated by the client.
(e) Client variation.
(f) Payment to statutory undertaker or variation resulting from statutory undertaker's requirements.

Most of the variations listed above are self-explanatory, but typical of the type of variation under (d) above is that caused by lack of co-ordination within the design team, so that the design has to be changed during the course of the contract. Close monitoring of the progress of the design during the design phase is therefore seen to be a very important service to the client.

Commissioning/letting and sale/refinancing

The architect's final certificate will signify the completion of the construction phase, although the defects liability period, for which a retention is provided, will involve the contractor in repairing minor defects to the building. The commissioning phase will involve a tenant taking occupation of the building and a rent-free period is often negotiated to allow him to bring in stock or arrange for his office fittings in business premises. In retail developments tenants will be provided with a shopfitting guide which specifies the type of work which is acceptable to the lessor. Shop units are normally let as shell units and the design of the tenant's signboard will be controlled by the lessor to ensure that it co-ordinates with the design of the centre. With major multiple retailers this sometimes causes friction.

On the completion of the development the long-term funder will often take on a controlling interest as freeholder, but before the scheme is transferred to the fund all minor defects and areas uncompleted such as car park surfacing, will have to be finalized. Tenants will be provided with information manuals which will explain their responsibilities and identify, in a retail scheme, the landlord's representative on site. In setting the time-scale for a retail development, the opening ceremony is seen as a very important occasion for the success of the scheme, and the developer will wish to ensure that the majority of tenants at least are fully trading by that date.

Chapter 12

International influence and current trends

INTRODUCTION

Property investment patterns are changing with a rapidity totally inconceivable one or two decades ago. For the manager of any investment estate the success or otherwise of his policies will be dependent to a high degree on his ability to spot and take opportunities to improve the performance of the portfolio under his control. To obtain the highest rewards the manager must identify trends ahead of the market, enabling him to reallocate assets if necessary.

We do not propose in this book to indulge in 'crystal ball gazing': that is not the role of an introductory text. However, it is relevant to outline a few of the indicators of change.

INDICATORS OF CHANGE

The transatlantic factor

There is nothing particularly new in this phenomenon. The influence on British culture of the American way of life is well documented and evident in every high street. How far does this influence extend to property? Certainly the last decade has seen the development of shopping/leisure complexes (for example, Metrocentre and Metroland) and leisure parks (for example, Alton Towers) which owe much in terms of design and concept to American developers. The 'festival market-place' first brought to international notice by the Baltimore Harbor development has been imitated in part by the Ocean village development in Southampton and plans exist for a festival scheme in Manchester.

It is not only in the fields of retail and leisure design that an influence has been felt: in the area of finance, foreign investors, notably the Japanese and Americans, but more recently the Europeans, have been very active. The level of investment activity of overseas investors has risen significantly since the deregulation of the stock exchange in 1986 which heralded a much freer investment market. The impending single European market has doubtless also been a catalyst.

Another aspect of the 'transatlantic affect' concerns the ways in which property is owned and leased which bears little resemblance to the UK institutional lease.

Foreign investment

The significant American influence on UK life-styles is probably greater than that emanating from any other country. However, in the direct workings of the investment market they are certainly not the only players exerting influence. In Chapter 4 we have examinined the role of the British institutions in respect of the property market which for many years they have dominated. In the late 1980s the position underwent considerable change with the market being heavily affected by bank lending, notably foreign banks. In the first half of 1989 Edward Erdman in their *Investment Commentary* (1989) estimated that foreign institutions had injected £1 billion into UK property thus equalling the level of UK institutional investment. Of the foreign investors interested in placing funds in the UK, the Japanese have been at the forefront, followed more recently by the Swedes.

The reasons for such increases in foreign investment in UK property are complex. Undoubtedly the freeing of the financial markets in 1986 was a significant factor, and foreign investors have perceived the London office market in particular to have good and stable long-term prospects. It is in that sector that funds have tended to be concentrated. Another attraction must be the maturity of the UK property investment market when compared with their home markets.

The flow of funds has not, however, been one way. Many British institutions have been active in both Europe and America for some years and we will refer to this again below.

With the advent of 1992 and the creation of the single European market, many commentators are anticipating that the level of international property investment will increase as it is seen to be a way of establishing a fully diversified portfolio. Whilst there will almost certainly be possible gains achievable by such diversification, a note of caution must be made. The attractiveness of any foreign holdings will depend not only on the 'domestic' performance of the asset but on exchange rates as well. In their commentary Erdmans' point out that the attraction of UK property for foreign funds could possibly increase if the UK were to join the European Exchange Rate Mechanism, thus reducing volatility.

Social and demographic changes

A property investment has value only if there is occupational demand. Over time the type of property in demand changes, due partly to social and demographic changes. Currently the demographic trends in the UK show a declining under 18 population and a large increase in the numbers aged between 45 and 59. In addition family sizes are getting smaller with a large growth in the proportion of one-parent families. All this has implications not only in the obvious sector of residential property, but in the retail and leisure sectors, as the providers of goods experience changing demand for their products. Indirectly, demographic profiles influence the availability of workers and this affects employment patterns and hence commercial property requirements. The recent increase in the numbers of part-time workers associated with working mothers may lead to employer companies seeking to locate business accommodation closer to residential areas or schools. The need for crèche facilities as well as leisure facilities nearby may also become of increasing importance.

Social and wealth trends, such as increased leisure time, higher real disposable incomes and the growth of the 'eating out' habit, have a pronounced effect on peoples' demands for and use of property reflected in effective tenant demand. Unless planning policies are flexible and able to react at speed to such changes in demand, and inevitably they cannot, disproportionate value changes will occur creating opportunities for the astute.

Technology change

No textbook on property would be complete without mention of the impact of technology change which affects the building, design and user requirement. We have already discussed the premature obsolescence which has been the fate of office buildings lacking the physical flexibility to accommodate the raised floors needed for computer cabling. The advent of microcomputers has also had a profound effect on the methodology of management for it has enabled quantitative approaches to be adopted to matters such as risk evaluation. It has also enhanced record keeping and data processing giving the manager quicker and more accurate retrieval of information in the form best suited to his needs and hence, in theory at least, facilitating better decision-making. For the rest of this chapter we examine in more depth certain aspects of the above.

TENURE PATTERNS

In the past the management attitudes towards property have been dominated by British institutional investors. Recently this pattern has begun to change with many overseas investors, notably American and Japanese, being attracted to invest in this country. In addition many occupying lessees are themselves subsidiaries of multinational organizations and it has now reached the point where the policies imposed by their head offices is affecting leasing patterns.

This pattern of investment policy is of course not one way; many UK companies are extremely active in property markets abroad and such activity is bound to increase with the advent of 1992 at which time trading restrictions between the member countries of the European Economic Community will be lifted.

In the light of the above we consider it is now essential for managers of UK property portfolios to have at least a rudimentary knowledge of property markets and leasing patterns in other countries. Of particular relevance is the United States of America, but the major European countries, the Far East and Australia are also of interest.

Accordingly, information was gathered from surveyors practising in different parts of the world regarding leasing patterns elsewhere. A summary of our findings, which inevitably are more detailed for some countries than others, is set out below and the key points are tabulated in Table 12.1.

United States of America

The property market

The first point that must be appreciated about the property market in North America is that it is extremely fragmented. To some extent this is inevitable due to the enormous geographical size of the country. What is perhaps more relevant is the differing laws relating to fiscal controls, tenure and land use enforced in each state. Capital gains tax and the treatment of foreign investors are federal matters but all states have the power to impose their own forms of taxation.

With respect of tenure, in general there is no equivalent to the Landlord and Tenant Act provisions, and in many states the tenant has no statutory protection upon lease expiry although this is not universally the case. Residential lettings too are sometimes unprotected by statute although in New York and some other states security of tenure and some rent controls are imposed. The degree of protection is, however, normally less than in the UK.

As a consequence of this low level of institutional funding and the oversupply of some properties, notably offices, the leasing patterns are the result of local market forces rather than any institutional influence.

UK and other foreign investors have been active in the States during

Table 12.1 Commercial leasing patterns (a general summary overview)

Country	Lease duration (years)	Statutory Renewal Right	Rent review frequency (years)	Basis of review	Repair liability external/internal structure	
UK	25	Yes	5	OMV	Tenant	Tenant
Australia	3–5	No	2	OMV Retail: CLI or turnover	Landlord	Tenant
Belgium	9	No, except retail	Annually 3	CLI with OMV every 3 years	Landlord	Tenant
France	9 with 3 yr Break	Yes	3	Construction Cost Index OMV at renewal for offices	Landlord	Tenant
Germany (West)	10	No	Variable	CLI or OMV	Landlord	Tenant
Holland	5 or 10	Yes	Annual	RPI and OMV at renewal	Landlord	Tenant
Italy	6	Yes	Annual	75 per cent of RPI	Landlord	Tenant
Portugal	Annual	Yes	Annual	Government Index	Landlord	Landlord with recovery
Scandinavia	⅔–10	Yes	Annual	CLI and OMV at renewal	Landlord	Tenant
South Africa	5 or 10	No	5	OMV & Annual CLI Retail: CLI or turnover	Landlord	Tenant
Spain	5 or 10	No	Annual	RPI	Landlord	Tenant
Switzerland	5 or 10	No	Annual	RPI	Landlord	Tenant
USA	5 to 10	Not universal	–	Retail, mainly on turnover rents	Landlord	Landlord with recovery

Key: OMV: Open Market Value.
      CLI: Cost of living index – calculation of this varies from country to country.
Source: Various.

the last decade attracted by the favourable currency exchange rates, an advantageous tax system and substantially higher yields than were obtainable in the UK. With the advent of UK investors has come some pressure to introduce UK-style leases, but the majority of let properties are subject to short, comparatively simple agreements such as those described below. Another factor which is at play with regard to leasing patterns are accountancy practices which favour the creation of short leases. For this reason many American occupiers, wherever the property is located, are obliged by company policy to take only short leases or leases with a tenant's break clause.

Term

The term is frequently five to ten years, reflecting a tenant desire for flexibility. Break clauses giving the landlord the power to relocate the tenant upon three months' notice are common; these give the tenant the right to surrender if he does not wish to be relocated.

Rent and rent review

Rents are paid monthly in advance and are not normally subject to review, even for terms up to ten years, demonstrating comparatively weak letting markets. Where the landlord does succeed in writing in a review the basis may be either to open market value, a percentage thereof, or it may be indexed.

With retail property, turnover rents are frequently found; the lack of security of tenure provision meaning that the landlord has the freedom to obtain possession at the end of the lease from any lessee whose turnover appears unsatisfactory.

Repair clauses

Leases in the US are described as being let either on a gross, net, double net or triple net terms. Basically 'triple net' equates to a full repairing and insuring liability; under double net the landlord insures; whilst with gross the landlord retains total responsibility for the building.

As a complete contrast to the 'institutional' lease of the UK, the US commercial lease will typically be on gross terms with the landlord providing comprehensive services including porterage, heating, landscaping. To an extent this is born of necessity due to the large number of multi-let buildings, but it does also reflect a reluctance on the part of the lessee to become involved with the care of the buildings. The cost of providing services and of carrying out maintenance are frequently claimed back in full by way of a service charge, or in part by an indexing charge allowing the landlord to increase the rent by the amount of any increase in servicing costs over a base figure.

Assignment

Assignment and subletting clauses normally mirror UK arrangements with landlord's consent being required.

User

User clauses are commonly drawn on fairly wide lines with the use being restricted in general terms and prohibiting only such uses as would affect the insurance or be regarded as immoral or illegal.

Summary

Whilst generalizations are always dangerous, the American property investment market is less sophisticated and developed than its British counterpart; the lack of government intervention combined with a fiscal policy which in the past acted as an incentive to new building has resulted in simple 'tenant-orientated' leases. Some indicators show a possible move towards longer leases on full repairing and insuring (FRI) terms, but it cannot yet be considered an established trend.

France

Although established investment markets in provincial towns such as Lyon and Marseilles do exist, Paris dominates the French property investment market and within Paris the office sector is undoubtedly of greatest importance.

A striking difference between Paris and London or indeed, large American cities, is the age of the infrastructure much of which dates back to the beginning of the twentieth century. Not only did Paris escape large-scale bomb damage during the Second World War, but redevelopment since then has been limited. The reasons for this are complex but must be attributable in part to the tight planning controls and to the prescence of 'flying freeholds' which are common and lead to difficulties in site assembly.

Until June 1987 there was also a tax on developments in Paris exceeding certain specified plot ratios but this disincentive has now been removed, albeit with a threat of reimposition in the future.

The lifting of this tax and the relaxing of certain planning controls has recently led to an increase in development activity, particularly by institutions.

Lettings of commercial property are governed by the Civil Code, which dictates that leases should be for a minimum term of nine years, unless the agreement is for less than two years, a 'bail précaire' as it is known. Similarly to England, upon lease expiry the tenant has the right to a new lease in most circumstances; the landlord's right to refuse being on such grounds as redevelopment, or own occupation.

The commercial letting market extends to offices, shops and industrial but the investment market in town centre shops has in the past been extremely limited and offices are still the dominant sector. This is due partially to the controls placed on rent, which are indexed to the 'INSEE' (cost of construction index). As a result rents are artificially low and the market tends to be one dominated by leasehold transactions at premiums. There is now an interest in out-of-town shopping centres and investors such as Norwich Union have been actively involved in the development of such schemes. Here the problem of rent reviews dictated by indexing are overcome by the use of turnover rents. The typical lease terms for offices are as set out below:

Term

Commonly nine years, but the lessee has the right to break the agreement at every third year, to coincide with the rent review.

Rent and rent review

Rents are payable in advance and and in general are reviewable every three years. At review the rent can rise according to a 'ceiling coefficient' based on the 'INSEE' cost of construction index. If, however, the index would result in a figure above the open market value the amount chargeable is restricted to the open market value. Upon lease renewal office rents revert to open market values but shop and industrial units are again subject to the 'ceiling coefficient' The result of this has been artificially low rents as noted earlier. If the ceiling rises by more than 25 per cent in three years tenants may call for a review.

Repair

Most leases are on internal repairing terms, which is consistent with much European practice. Service charges may claw back for the landlord some of the repair costs but this is not unversally the case.

Assignment user clauses

These clauses follow the general pattern of assignments being allowed with landlord consent, but users being fairly tightly restricted.

Summary

The French legal and planning systems have placed constraints upon development and on the landlord and tenant relationship in such a way that institutional investment has been affected, shopping in particular being less attractive than in the UK. Recent indicators show an increasing interest in foreign investment activity, although this is still largely concentrated in the office sector.

West Germany

With an established record of economic growth and low inflation, Germany would appear to be an attractive environment for investors. There is an established institutional property market, but involvement has been traditionally only with 'ready-made' investments rather than in development and this remains the case.

The market activity centres round the retail and office sectors, with industrial property being very largely owner occupied, although there is now some letting activity. The residential and leisure sectors have some institutional funds committed to them but they do not form important parts of many portfolios.

Lease terms

Length of lease

Normally for ten years but the lessee frequently has an option to renew. There is no statutory right for the lessee to have a new lease thereafter.

Rent and rent reviews

Rent is payable monthly in advance, and although some leases allow for reviews to Open Market Value, the more usual arrangement is for the rent to be indexed to a cost of living index with provision for the rent to fall as well as rise. Legal restraints prevent landlords from indexing on an upwards only basis. Turnover rents are found in some retail situations but they are not favoured by institutional investors and are uncommon. The period between rent reviews varies.

Repair

In common with other European Countries, leases are almost always on internal repairing terms only, with the landlord retaining responsibility for the exterior and structure. The tenant pays a service charge monthly with the rent but this only covers the costs of maintenance and services, not repairs.

Assignment/user

Similar clauses to those found in French leases prevail.

Scandinavia

In Scandinavia, as in Germany, the property investment market tends to be restricted to offices and shops due to the high proportion of owner occupation in the industrial sector. The dominant players in the market are the insurance companies and property and construction companies rather than pension funds. The size of the market is small to date and it is of recent origin, but it is growing rapidly in size and sophistication.

There is legislation which parallels the Landlord and Tenant Act as far as commercial lettings are concerned but, as with the UK, they do not impinge greatly on the workings of the free market.

Lease terms

Term

Leases may be only two to three years on up to a general maximum of ten years. Generally at the end of the term the lessee has a statutory right to a renewal.

Rent reviews

Rents are payable either monthly or quarterly in advance. They are indexed annually to a cost of living index. At the end of the lease they are reviewed to the 'open market' rental value. In Denmark the rent is reviewed every other year to market rent be that up or down.

Repair

As would be expected with short leases, the landlord retains liability for all external repairs and decoration as well as liability for the structure. Service charge arrangements allow the landlord to recover back some at least of the repair costs.

Assignment and user clause

Assignment clauses tend to give the landlord an absolute discretion over consent to assignment or subletting. The user clause on the other hand is often less specific than its British counterpart.

Other European countries

Other European countries such as Belgium, Holland, Italy, Portugal, Spain and Switzerland all have active property markets though the level of activity and sophistication varies from country to country. Spain and Portugal in particular are seeing a rapid development of their market with much foreign interest. In Spain this is due in part to recent relaxation of very strict rent controls on commercial property. British investors as well as those from Japan are now actively involved with the retail market in Spain and British retailer presence now exists.

Legislation too is varied, but in all the above mentioned countries with the exception of Spain commercial lessees do have the right to renew their leases upon expiry. Since the lifting of restriction in Spain there is in general no artificial rental ceilings.

Lease terms

Leases are of varying lengths from annual agreements in Portugal; five or ten years for Spain, Switzerland and Holland; six yearly in Italy and nine-yearly in Belgium. The common theme is thus of short-term agreements, albeit with renewal rights.

Rents and rent reviews

In none of these countries has UK-style rent review patterns developed, all standard leases being regulated by some type of annual indexing arrangement. In the case of Italy the reviews are restricted to 75 per cent of the increase in the RPI, elsewhere full cost of living increases are permitted. In Belgium the rent is reviewed to the open market every third year, and in Holland an open market review takes place at renewal.

Repair

In none of these countries are the lessees generally expected to accept liability for structural and external repairs. Indeed in Portugal the lessor is responsible for all outgoings albeit with the ability to collect the cost of internal repair via a service charge. Elsewhere internal repair is generally a lessee's obligation.

Australia

The physical isolation of Australia from the traditional centres of property investment activity may in the past have created an essentially domestic market, but this is certainly not the case now. Foreign investors and multinational companies are active in both development and investment although there is currently legislation which prevents foreign investors from taking 100 per cent equity in standing investment properties without an official 'waiver' of the regulation. No such restriction applies to development projects.

Although an investment market exists in all property sectors, the industrial sector tends to have a high incidence of owner occupation. There is an established market in the residential sector which is too restricted by legislation in many countries to attract investors, and in leisure which elsewhere apart from USA is still in its infancy as an investment vehicle.

Leases

Despite the strong prescence of institutional investors these have had little influence on the type of lease commonly granted, details of which we set out below. Some pressure for the introduction of UK-style leases is beginning but we understand that to date this has not had any market impact.

Term

The most usual term is for three to five years, but residential property is normally let on annual agreement. Options to review are sometimes written in but there is no statutory security of tenure.

Rent and rent reviews

Rents are payable in advance, and generally are reviewed biennially to open market rent. Shops, however, are either let on turnover rent or often reviewed annually based on the consumer price index. Residential rents are likewise subject to annual review.

Repair

With commercial property the lessee is normally liable for internal repair. External repairs and the structure are the lessor's responsibility. Service charges are sometimes levied to cover the full cost of all landlord expenditure but in other cases the service charge is restricted merely to increases in maintenance and cost of service provision.

Assignment/user

Assignment is usually permitted subject to the landlord's consent, such consent not to be unreasonably withheld.

User clauses vary; they may specify an actual use or be couched in general terms only.

South Africa

Our information regarding South Africa is limited and indeed the political regime makes it an area where foreign investment is declining. However, there is an institutional property market, originally British led, in all main commercial sectors and residential property.

The leasing pattern does not, however, follow the British one, nor do the tenants enjoy the same security of tenure provisions. Leases indeed mirror more closely those found in Europe with five-year leases on internal repairing terms being the norm. Rent reviews are five-yearly to full market rent but with annual cost of living escalation clauses built in. Retail property is, however, often let on turnover arrangements.

Conclusions

In compiling the above, the main points of which are summarized in Table 12.1, it became clear that the UK is isolationist as far as its leasing pattern is concerned. We have seen elsewhere in the book how the 'clear' lease has evolved due quite largely to the influence of the institutions and their desire to rid themselves of 'hands on' management responsibility and obtain a certain easily measured income. This, of course, has only been possible in a climate of strong tenant demand, itself partially a product of our stringent planning controls.

In other countries there are also established and strong investment markets, with similar institutions playing key roles, but nowhere is there influence so significant. There are also many instances where tax and planning laws impose severe restrictions on development, although it is true that in countries such as the USA this does not apply. Despite these similarities, however, no other country has seen the emergence of the twenty-five-year full repairing lease; and nowhere else are terms comparable in length granted. Rent reviews too, operate differently in the UK, where complex legal battles are frequently fought. In many other countries an annual indexation to protect the real level of income is mixed with a renewal at a market level.

Despite these differences, in other countries institutional investment markets do function with investors seemingly being prepared to accept a much closer involvement with their buildings and a less certain income flow.

We are not advocating that any one leasing pattern is necessarily preferable; obviously the whole background to the letting must be considered as well as the investment climate. However, with the inevitable

increase in international and multinational involvement in property investment, resulting not only from 1992 and its impact on Europe but other
global considerations, we anticipate a possible trend towards some more
uniform approach.

In the responses to our survey, several agents reported the gradual desire
on the part of lessors to move the responsibility for outgoings on to lessees,
this being the case particularly in Australia and America. On the other
hand, in the UK there is a body of opinion that supports a case away from
the universal adoption of the twenty-five-year standard FRI (full repairing
and insuring) lease. The case against the clear lease clearly hinges on the
lack of flexibility it gives the landlord, the possible loss of rental income
in times of high rental growth and the problems of delay that it creates for
redevelopment. There are also signs in the UK commercial market that
tenant requirements, which may dictate shorter leases, are beginning to
have an impact on the market.

In addition the case has been convincingly argued by a Royal Institution
of Chartered Surveyors' (RICS) working party on the maintenance of
commercial tenanted property, that to put the burden of repairs upon the
tenant can result in poor design detailing with an emphasis being placed on
initial cost with little consideration of costs in use.

In conclusion therefore we maintain that for good management an
open view should be adopted, with investors prepared to consider other
countries' practices and see what lessons, if any, are applicable to their
own letting arrangements.

THE USE OF QUANTITATIVE MEASUREMENT TECHNIQUES

As part of our research for this book we spoke to fund managers and
property professionals regarding the questions of performance measurement and risk evaluation. Prior to undertaking this research we were of
the opinion that quantitative techniques were not widely used although we
were uncertain as to whether the cause related to ignorance, complacency
or because they were not convinced that their use would improve the quality
of decision-making. In the final analysis it is, of course, the usefulness
of the techniques to the decision-maker which should be the controlling
factor.

From our discussions it became obvious that the use of risk techniques
such as we explain and advocate in Chapters 6 and 7 is still strictly
limited although performance measurement is now widely carried out
by institutional investors. We also undertook a questionnaire survey
of specifically targeted managers regarding their use of performance
measurement and risk evaluation techniques. Whilst the sample size of
seventy was not large, and we accept that any questionnaire can pose
more questions than it answers, the level of response (64 per cent) was

encouraging. The results reinforced our previously-held opinions and below we summarize the findings.

Methods of performance measurement

All those who responded to the questionnaire use some method of measurement with the internal rate of return (IRR) being the most widely adopted. It was interesting to note that some fund managers appear to be unaware that the time-weighted rate of return (TWRR) and the money-weighted rate of return (MWRR) are two separate measures.

Performance targets

Again the universal response was that managers do look at other performance measures when evaluating property although some look on the alternatives as 'guides' sooner than targets. Here the consensus ends. The range of alternatives used as a benchmark, or target, varies from a specially-created target fund, to the indices produced by large firms such as Jones, Lang and Wootton and Weatherall, Green and Smith, to those of Wood Mackenzie and Investment Property Databank. As expected, the use of gilts as a benchmark is widespread. What is interesting to note is the variation in gilts chosen. Whilst some managers just indicated gilts, others specified either index-linked, or long-dated or in some cases medium-dated stock.

The use of equity indices appears to be less favoured, although some managers do use the FT SE100 index.

Frequency of performance review

We have pointed out in this book that the time-scale over which returns are measured (that is, the time horizons of investors) has shortened in recent years with investors who traditionally were prepared to take a long-term view becoming preoccupied with short-term returns. In view of this it did not surprise us that all responses indicated a review of performance on an annual basis, with many carrying out quarterly reviews. As one fund manager expressed it 'it never stops'.

Assessment of risk

It was in this area that we received some of the most interesting responses, as the level of understanding and use obviously varied dramatically. Whilst some respondents were prepared to admit that they do not measure risk at all and relied on the 'seat of the pants' approach, several others expressed the view that they were aware of the need to adopt quantitative techniques which were 'under review at the present time'.

Of the managers who were attempting to evaluate risk, the use of a risk adjusted discount factor or 'risk premium' is the measure most commonly utilized. However, others demonstrated an extensive knowledge and use of techniques such as modelling, simulation and sensitivity analysis, and two managers questioned are considering the application of portfolio theory and Capital Asset Pricing Model to property.

The comments of one manager are particularly interesting as they summarize much current thinking on the matter and succinctly highlight some of the difficulties inherent in the practical application:

> In respect of risk measurement, performance measurement and asset allocation we are actively aware of the following:
>
> 1 Asset allocation in respect of past performance is in no way correlated to future performance.
> 2 Before one is able to apply CAPM one must first accept the proposition that the UK commercial market is strong and efficient.
> 3 The individuality and illiquidity makes commercial property investments unsuited to 'equity fund' active/passive managements.

In conclusion we argue that the trend to more quantitative measures is established and the case for future research in this area is demonstrated, a view shared by Baum and Crosby (1988) who say 'much work remains to be done, however. We will wish to know more about investors' criteria for equated yield choice, their attitude to risk, and whether it is based upon portfolio or single asset principles. . . .'

INVESTMENT VEHICLES

In Chapter 2 we detailed the advantages and disadvantages of property as an investment. Among the most significant of its drawbacks are:

(a) The lotting problem.
(b) Illiquidity.
(c) The need for management.
(d) The complexity of financing developments.

During the early 1980s when property was experiencing a period of low comparative returns, attention was given to possible ways of overcoming these inherent difficulties. One of the outcomes has been proposals for unitization.

Unitization can be defined as the multiple ownership of a single property and plans exist for a unitized property market (UPM) to be launched. To date only one property has been so offered.

The basic idea of shared ownership of property is not revolutionary or new in any way. The chief difference between unitization and conventional joint ownership lies in the scale of the sharing and the basic motivation for the deal. Traditionally ownership is shared by people or organizations known to each other, for example, joint tenancy of a house or the ownership is split in 'layers' to satisfy investment and occupational needs, as in a landlord and tenant relationship. In each case the relationship between the parties is governed by legal contract and in neither case is there any possibility of extending the ownership to a large number of institutions or individuals.

A partnership may also own land, but the definition of a partnership as a 'relationship which subsists between persons carrying on a business in common with a view to profit' (Partnership Act 1980) is sufficiently restricted as to render the partnership an unsuitable vehicle for multi-ownership.

Property Bonds, too, are a form of shared ownership in that the pooled premiums paid by many individuals are invested in property. They have not in general acted as a satisfactory property medium because they are generally illiquid, investors have no say in the type of investment undertaken and their performance has often been distinctly mediocre.

During 1985 various proposed routes to unitized property were devised and in December of that year the RICS published a report on the unitization of real property, welcoming the prospect of a unitized property market (UPM) and identifying the following social and economic advantages that they thought unitization could bring:

1 Stimulate regional investment in large socially desirable urban renewal projects.
2 Enable groups of smaller investors and, in due course, the general public to participate in a wider market to which they presently have limited access.
3 Create a vehicle which would supplement the involvement in the market of the major investment institutions.
4 Introduce liquidity into the market to the benefit of all classes of investor.
5 Open a wider range of property investment opportunities and enable an investor to spread risk through a tax neutral vehicle.

The three routes described in the report, and still under discussion are:

(a) Single Asset Property Companies (SAPCO).
(b) Single Property Ownership Trusts (SPOTs).
(c) Property Income Certificates (PINCS).

Single Asset Property Companies (SAPCO)

The SAPCO is in essence a normal property company but one where the constitution is worded so as to restrict the investments made to one property. The first proposal for a SAPCO was made in 1986, at which time the Stock Exchange refused the listing as it had not then formulated rules for unitized property. Accordingly when S&W Berisford set up Billingsgate City Securities, whose only asset was the single tenanted Montagu House in Lower Thames Street, London EC3, it was launched on the Luxemburg Stock Market. The launch was a complex arrangement comprising deep discount mortgage bonds and preference shares.

Although it attracted great publicity at the time, not all the shares were taken up and many were left with the underwriters. The subsequent history of Billingsgate has not been encouraging to advocates of unitization. Trading the shares has been sluggish and at a discount relative to asset value. The value of the building has increased substantially since launch and at the time of writing the original freeholders, Berisford, who retained two-thirds ownership of the building, are in the process of buying back the shares with a view to winding up the company. If they do succeed in doing so it may well deter others from similar ventures.

Other objections to SAPCOs apart from their short, ill-starred history, include the following:

(a) shares in property companies tend to be volatile,
(b) the shareholder has no effective influence on management policy,
(c) there is potential double capital gains tax on the sale of the asset and the sale of the shares.

Single Property Ownership Trusts (SPOTs)

This is the route that was favoured by the RICS. The mechanism is simple, with reliance on a trustee holding title to the property and with a trust deed detailing how the property should be managed and the rights of the unit holders.

The intention is that income from the property is passed to the unit holders who hold a technical legal interest in the property.

In essence, therefore, it is similar to a property unit trust, which is an unauthorized trust open only to institutional investors. As such it required legislative approval which was given in s.76 of the Financial Services Act 1986. This section provides that a single property scheme may be offered to the public only if arrangements have been made for units in it to be dealt with on a 'recognised investment exchange'.

After discussions with the Stock Exchange details for listing were approved and may be summarized as follows:

(a) The scheme must own a freehold or a long leasehold interest of at least

110 years in a single property.

(b) A single property is defined as a single building or a group of adjacent or contiguous buildings with or without ancillary land and managed as a single enterprise.

(c) The scheme's activity must be restricted solely to the management of the scheme for at least the next five years.

(d) The property must be let so that expected annual income should cover expected outgoings.

(e) The property must have a value of at least £10m.

(f) The scheme may be refused for listing if the debt/equity ratio is considered to be unacceptably high, thus excluding any highly geared properties.

(g) The list particulars must include a full report and history of the building.

(h) Surveys are to be carried out every three years and independent valuations undertaken with every further issue of securities.

(i) All potential conflicts of interest by promoters, managers, or directors must be disclosed.

(j) Rents must be fully distributed after allowing for deductions for operating and service charges and sinking fund provision.

Although the way is therefore clear from a legislative and market-place viewpoint, SPOTs have not yet come to the market due to fiscal difficulties. In order that the trust is tax transparent (that is, that the taxation burden on income and capital gain is dictated by the investors own circumstances) legislation was required. The Finance Act 1987 provided the Treasury with powers to make regulations concerning the tax treatment of SPOTs. To date, despite discussions with the Treasury, no regulations have been made which enable tax transparency to be obtained. Without this the proposals for SPOTs are unlikely to progress.

Property Income Certificates (PINCs)

The PINC, which has been devised by agents Richard Ellis and County Bank Ltd, did not require the framework of the Financial Services Act. In essence PINCs are more complex than SPOTs or SAPCOS. They comprise two parts:

1 An income certificate, giving the holder a contractual right to receive a share of a property's rental income flow.

2 An ordinary share in a specially created management company responsible for day-to-day management of the property.

The two parts are permanently stapled together so that the investor in effect has a contractual right to a share in the property's income sooner than a legal interest in the land. It is envisaged that any property launched under the PINC arrangements will not be a 100 per cent flotation; instead it is intended that the freeholder will retain a substantial stake in the property.

Although the promoters of PINCs had planned for the first property to be offered in 1987, the scheme (like SPOTs,) ran into fiscal difficulties with the Department of Trade and Industry regulations. Currently these have not been resolved so that, like the other vehicles, the future is far from clear, or even optimistic.

In summary it can be said that the perceived benefits of unitization are:

(a) The ability for small investors to partake in direct property investment, without detriment to their diversification policies.

(b) Following from this is the ability for a small investor to be able to invest in prime properties, previously beyond his pocket.

(c) Many individual developments are so large that both long-term and short-term funding present difficulties, with financiers being reluctant to accept the full risks attached. Syndication presents one solution, unitization another.

(d) High risk projects often encounter financing difficulties. As the overall risk with unitized properties is shared between many investors, in theory it should be possible to undertake projects normally rejected as of unacceptably high risk, including those with a high 'social benefit' content.

(e) With a unitized property, shares or units in the building can be traded in much the same way as shares or unit trusts. This would overcome the liquidity problem.

(f) Some large properties trade at a discount due to the limited number of potential purchasers with adequate funds. If such properties could be unitized it might increase their asset value by removing the quantum discount.

(g) Because the management of a unitized building would be entrusted to a management company, the investor of units would not be involved in the day-to-day management aspects which act as a deterrent to investors who lack property expertise.

Against these benefits, however, must be balanced the drawbacks, some of which are listed below:

(a) Many experts consider that if and when a UPM is launched the assets will trade at a discount in much the same way as property company shares. This view is substantiated by the Billingsgate experience. If this were to be the 'norm', then the avoidance of 'discount for size' argument is invalidated.

(b) One of the aims of unitization is to encourage investment in high risk, secondary schemes or in economically depressed areas. However, it appears that this is unlikely; unitized schemes will have to be 'promoted' and it is hard to see that such high risk schemes will succeed in attracting funds.

(c) One of the major attractions of property is its low volatility. Because units will be capable of being traded easily and quickly they are likely to suffer rapid price fluctuations. Unitized property will be volatile in nature. A survey of major investors in 1988 (unpublished dissertation by R. Wyard, Kingston Polytechnic) indicated that, of the institutions contemplating investment in a UPM, approximately 50 per cent would view such assets as equities rather than property. This lack of consensus would not appear to bode well for the proposed market.

(d) Many critics argue that in the time-lag since the schemes were first planned in 1988, developments in funding techniques have moved so far so fast that many of the basic reasons for a UPM have now gone.

(e) The management of a unitized property would be undertaken by a management company. However, management decisions such as refurbishment and redevelopment require funding, and the quality of management is fundamental to the performance of a property.

The question remains therefore as to how far the unit holders would be able to participate in management decisions and indeed whether they would have any sanctions against poor managers. This problem would appear to be least in the case of PINC.

The raising of funds for development would most likely be funded from new issues of units or by conventional borrowing with the charges being offset against rental income. In the case of a property nearing the end of its economic life, or in need of capital injection, the share price could be depressed substantially.

(f) The problems of insider dealing on the Stock Exchange have received considerable publicity. Although the rules of listing for unitized property aims to prevent any such problems, insider dealing and insider knowledge are likely to present dangers which it will be difficult to guard against adequately.

(g) Fiscal difficulties still remain to be solved. The delays experienced in actually bringing a UPM into existence combined with the poor performance of Billingsgate are such that there is a natural nervousness on the part of investors.

Despite the drawbacks, the potential advantages remain and it remains to be seen whether the UPM becomes a reality in the UK. Perhaps investors, who are showing caution regarding the concept, will look at the success of similar schemes in the USA and Australia to see if any lessons can be learnt.

CONCLUSION

In this chapter we examined some of the factors which are influencing the future of property portfolio management in the UK. As technological change occurs at a seemingly ever increasing rate, so do the demands placed upon the manager of a property portfolio.

No longer can the property market be viewed in isolation. It is an integral part of the investment market and as such there is a move towards exposing property to similar analyses to those undertaken in other investment sectors. This, combined with the development of microcomputers, has led to the heightening of the debate regarding how best cross media comparisions can be undertaken. In the search for greater comparibility other forms of ownership such as unitization will continue to be explored, now that legal barriers have been removed, as and when market conditions dictate.

The debate is not yet ended, but from our survey work it is clear that the level of awareness is high, and that DCF appraisal techniques for performance measurement, together with some level of risk analysis, is beginning to become established at least at institutional level.

Not only is property considered in terms of a diversified UK portfolio, it is now perceived in international terms. This is evidenced by the flows of money in, notably in the form of bank lending by overseas banks, and by the interest in overseas property by British institutions. Currently the UK has an 'isolationist' policy to the letting patterns of commercial properties and a stronger tradition of letting than many other countries. The reasons for this lie within the historical backgrounds, as well as different legal and planning provisions. Whether the gathering international influence will affect such patterns remains to be seen, but some market indicators show that changes are slowly starting to take place.

Case study: The Hale Leys Shopping Centre, Aylesbury, Buckinghamshire

Purpose

The purpose of this case study is to provide a practical illustration of the creation of a property investment. It is based on fact and traces the process from its initial inception to the time of the first rent review.

Because it is a factual example, for reasons of confidentiality, certain stages are covered in outline rather than detail. It is hoped that despite this it serves to highlight the basic requirements for the creation of a satisfactorily performing property investment, namely a blend of innovation, co-operation, technical expertise and attention to detail.

THE HALE LEYS SHOPPING CENTRE, AYLESBURY, BUCKINGHAMSHIRE

Location

Aylesbury is situated in the centre of an agricultural area and grew originally as a market town serving its agricultural hinterland. The town is the largest in the district of Aylesbury Vale and is roughly equidistant from Oxford to the south-west and Milton Keynes to the north. It can therefore be regarded as a subregional centre with a mainly rural catchment area.

The site

The Hale Leys Shopping Centre was developed as a result of an initiative by the British Airways Pension Fund, Aylesbury Vale District Council and Laing Properties plc, who acted as developers. The site is located in the centre of Aylesbury bounded to the north by High Street, to the south by Market Square and to the south-east by the Civic Centre car park. The site, before development, comprised mainly vacant backland crossed by a right of way known as Hale Leys Passage which linked Market Square with the High Street. Plan 1 (Figure A1) shows the location of the site on a schematic of land uses in Aylesbury. Immediately to the south-west of the site and Market Square is the Friars Square Shopping Centre which was developed by Hammersons in the 1960s.

This centre is typical of its period, mainly of concrete construction and with the ground level open to the elements. Not surprisingly the centre at the time of writing was the subject of a proposed refurbishment. The Hale Leys site links this centre with the High Street to the north-east and one of the main objectives of the local authority's support for the scheme was to achieve a cohesive shopping centre by promoting Hale Leys as the link between the two major existing shopping areas of the town.

The planning background

At the time of development there was no approved structure plan for the County of Buckinghamshire. However, the written statement which was submitted to the Secretary of State for approval in 1977 contained three stated policies in respect of shopping. These were:

(a) New Town centre shopping development should meet the demands of customers without access to private cars.
(b) New shopping developments should be an appropriate use of the land well related to existing car parking and would not involve the provision of additional infrastructure.
(c) Demand for new shopping should be available and evidenced by consideration of the catchment population.

The district council's local plan was in the course of preparation in 1978 and had not progressed to the public participation stage. However, the council had taken pains to publicize the proposal and in the Aylesbury Town Map, which was approved by the Minister of Housing and Local Government in 1961, the majority of the site was zoned as shopping with the exception of the United Reformed Church and the Bank Gardens, both of which occupied very small site areas. A small part of the site was designated as a conservation area at the same time as most of the town centre in 1969 but no individual buildings on the site were listed.

With local authority support and planning policies which allowed retail development the site was an attractive proposition for developers so long as it could be assembled and major retailers could be attracted. Site assembly again involved the local authority in taking initiatives to promote the scheme.

Site assembly

A substantial part of the site had been owned for many years by Guardian Royal Exchange Assurance Company. Other principal landowners were the

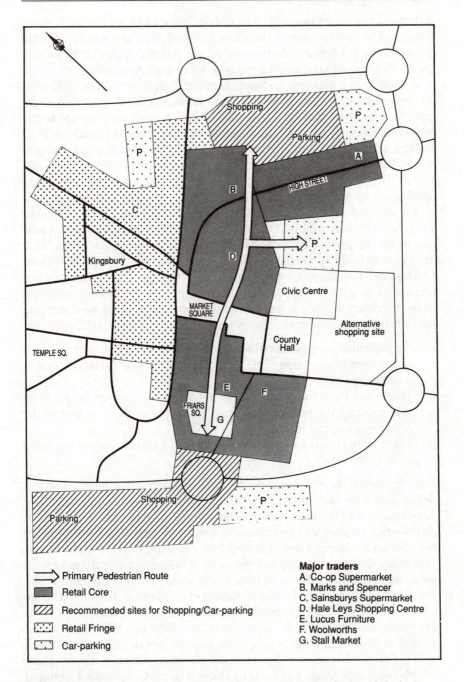

Primary Pedestrian Route
Retail Core
Recommended sites for Shopping/Car-parking
Retail Fringe
Car-parking

Major traders
A. Co-op Supermarket
B. Marks and Spencer
C. Sainsburys Supermarket
D. Hale Leys Shopping Centre
E. Lucus Furniture
F. Woolworths
G. Stall Market

Figure A.1 Plan 1: The site location of Hale Leys Shopping Centre, Aylesbury, Buckinghamshire

Aylesbury Brewery Company (part of Ind Coope) and the United Reform Church. The district council themselves owned backland which provided access to Market Square. At the time of site assembly from 1978 onwards the district council land was occupied by a Borough Assembly Hall.

In addition two shops on the frontage to the High Street, numbers 20a and 20b owned by Clays of Buckingham and Phildar (UK) Ltd, were brought into the scheme to provide a wider and more appropriate entrance to the proposed shopping centre. Guardian Royal Exchange originally showed interest in developing the site themselves and Laing Properties plc had also discussed the scheme with the insurance company as possible developers. In July 1977 Guardian Royal Exchange, through agents, made a planning application for the development of 'a shopping precinct and church hall' on the site and this was approved by the district council on 12 December 1977. In 1978 there followed the promotion of three compulsory purchase orders by the district council. These were made in respect of the land in the ownership of Guardian Royal Exchange, the United Reformed Church and two shops on the High Street frontage. The remaining site areas were acquired by agreement. In the statement of reasons submitted to the Secretary of State in support of the compulsory purchase order, the council stated the following reasons for the development being necessary:

(a) An important environmental site in a conservation area was in a cleared and unsightly condition. The council stated it was anxious to see it redeveloped sympathetically.
(b) There had been little increase in net retail floor space in the town centre during the previous ten years whilst the spending power of the catchment had increased.
(c) There were structural benefits in linking two major existing shopping areas in the town.

In the statement of reasons the council also stated that its plans with a development partner to carry out the scheme were well advanced. The developer named in the document is Guardian Royal Exchange's agent but Aylesbury Vale District Council were aware at the time that it was possible the insurance company would not wish to carry out the development. By promoting the compulsory purchase order on Guardian Royal Exchange's land, they were ensuring that they could force the development of the site with an alternative developer should the Guardian Royal Exchange withdraw. All the land comprised in the compulsory purchase orders was eventually acquired from the landowners and, following the withdrawal of Guardian Royal Exchange, Laing Properties plc began serious discussions with the district council as prospective development partners. A subsequent full planning application was made by Damond Lock Grabowski, Chartered Architects, acting for Laing Properties plc on 18 March 1980 and full planning consent was granted on 29 May 1980.

Scheme concept

The scheme as designed by the developer's architects, comprised twenty-one shop units, two major stores, a public house, offices on the frontage to the High Street and management accommodation. A simple enclosed mall with a glazed roof linked the High Street and Market Square and connected into the existing multi-storey car park immediately to the east of the site. Bank Gardens was retained as a landscaped garden providing an entrance to the car park. The mall was ventilated by natural means with the assistance of reversible fans for temperature control.

The anchor tenants who would occupy the three major stores are located at the centre of the development and at first floor level there is a vehicle gyratory system. This provides the storage areas for all the shop units in the centre. The church tower fronting the High Street was retained for use as staircase access to the office block above the shop units, mall entrance and vehicular entrance. As a design detail all the windows in the tower were filled with engraved and coloured glass illustrating scenes from various aspects of Aylesbury life. The centre was designed structurally on a reinforced concrete frame with pad foundations and the main central unit, eventually let to Boots, was designed on a steel frame with cladding panels for the walls. The shop units were provided with load-bearing division walls supporting lightweight roof construction and providing beams so that local openings could be formed between adjacent units if these were let in combinations of one or more.

Catchment area and lettings

The 1981 census shows that Buckinghamshire had a population of 567,979 which had increased by 19.3 per cent from 1971. Almost a quarter of the population was aged 16 and under. Of those in work, social class II (intermediate occupations) had the greater representation with a similar number of people being classified under social class III (skilled manual occupations). The unemployment rate was running at 6.0 per cent at the time, 15.3 per cent private households had at least one child under 5 but a significant percentage of the population was living alone (17.1 per cent of households). The picture that emerges from a study of the catchment area is of a preponderance of old people and young married couples but with 18.7 per cent of people in the age group 45–65.

The approach of Laing Properties, the council's proposed development partner after 1979, was to identify three tenants who would act as a major attraction for the centre. Boots the Chemists, Martins the Newsagents, together with Mothercare, had all expressed an interest at this time in taking the three main units in the centre. This combination of anchor tenants is a variation on having a major supermarket as an anchor store. The combination is often selected as an alternative to one major store in subregional town centre shopping development where the catchment area population comprises middle income groups with an emphasis on families with children. Another example where this approach has been used is the Swan Centre in Eastleigh, Hampshire, which is being developed by a partnership agreement between Shearwater Estates and Eastleigh Borough Council. Here it is proposed that the centre will be anchored on Boots, Mothercare and W. H. Smith.

With the three major anchor tenants identified and located at the focus of the centre, a range of comparison shops selling products not available at the time in Aylesbury were targeted as potential occupiers of the remaining twenty-one units. The Friars Square centre, adjacent to Hale Leys, has a popular central market and at basement level a wide range of stalls including fresh food retailing. It was therefore not considered necessary to incorporate fresh food retailers in the Hale Leys scheme tenant mix. Pedestrianization flows were already established between the High Street and Market Square and the new centre was able to take advantage of this and the pedestrian draw of the Friars Square centre. The letting strategy therefore concentrated on fashion trades, electrical goods and jewellery with lively shop fronts encouraged. To avoid dead frontages it was not proposed to let to banks or building societies, although a travel agent, Thomas Cook, was eventually included in the scheme.

The developer/local authority agreement

Following the promotion of the compulsory purchase order, the grant of planning permission, agreement on scheme concept, and the identification of the anchor tenants, the developer, Laing Properties and the district council signed an agreement. This was made on 14 July 1980.

The agreement, in fact a contract, allowed the developer to occupy the site under licence during the development period and on completion to take a long ground lease from the council. The form of lease was incorporated into the agreement. The council benefited by means of a ground rent calculated as a share in the rents of the scheme and there were clauses which sought to give the council a measure of control over scheme changes and lettings as these would materially affect the value of its interest. The agreement with ground lease ran to some 15,000 words and it is instructive to consider how it illustrates the differing incentives of the two partners to the scheme.

The district council had a long-term interest in the success of Hale Leys both from the point of view of ground rent increases and civic pride. The developer in one sense had a similar incentive but his interest in reality was short term as he was in the process of arranging long-term funding with an institution which would probably mean that he would assign his leasehold interest on completion of the scheme. The agreement between council and developer sought to reconcile these differing incentives and to allow the developer a way of withdrawing from the scheme if the anchor tenants should fail to sign pre-let agreements. The main provisions relating to the agreement and ground lease were as follows:

1 The developer would pay a minimum ground rent during the development period which was calculated by reference to the estimated annual rack rent of the development less 6.5 per cent of the development cost. If this figure was less than £150,000 then this sum would be payable.
2 Upon completion of the development the council would grant the developer a ground lease of ninety-nine years with the developer's option to renew for a further twenty-six years.
3 The rent payable under the ground lease was £533,870 plus 50 per cent of the amount by which annual rents exceeded this figure.
4 The period of development was specified at 3.5 years unless extended by *force majeure* or because the council was late in acquiring necessary land from third parties.
5 Reference is made in the agreement between the council and developer to approved plans. Any variation to these plans would require the prior approval of the council if 'substantial charges' were envisaged or a new planning consent required. The council's approval was not to be unreasonably withheld.
6 The acquisition of Crown Passage by the council was crucial to the scheme and the developer was allowed to withdraw (under the agreement) if the council were unsuccessful in acquiring this land.
7 The developer was also allowed to withdraw if pre-lets could not be arranged for the two largest anchor stores and either the third largest store or the public house.
8 The agreement specified that occupational tenants would lease the buildings at open market rents and all lettings would be arranged on good estate management principles. The council was allowed to object to any proposed letting within seven days but only if strong reasons were given.
9 The developer was allowed to assign his leasehold interest without approval by mortgage or charge but the lease provided for the developer to offer the leasehold interest back to the council if he wished to assign for any other reason. There was a similar offer back provision if the council wished to dispose of its interest.
10 Rights of inspection of the works were provided for the council both during construction and after completion.
11 The council's share of the equity in the form of rent would be recalculated yearly during the lease thus ensuring that the council benefited from rent reviews in the occupational leases.

The agreement and lease therefore attempted to ensure that the interests of both parties were met. Risk to the developer was reduced by allowing him to withdraw from the scheme if the pre-lets did not materialize. There is no stronger evidence of the importance of pre-let anchors to the viability of shopping development. The council's rights to approve variations or lettings were limited to being able to object to changes or lettings only if there was an indisputable case for doing so.

The funding agreement

Having secured an agreement with the council, the developer had to ensure that long- and short-term funding was available. By an agreement dated 4 March 1981, the Airways Pension Fund Trustee Limited provided both short- and long-term funding for the scheme. The funding agreement gave the funder considerable powers to control the activities of the developer. At the end of the letting period the developer was paid a capital sum calculated by deducting a percentage of the short-term cost plus interest rolled up from the capital value of the scheme. The multipliers of YP figures were stated in the agreement. The developer thus had an incentive to let the centre at the highest possible rent, but to ensure that its long-term interests were met the agreement provided for approvals, rights and preconditions in favour of the pension fund as follows:

1 A condition of funding was that pre-let agreements were entered into with Mothercare, Boots and Martins. This is further evidence of the importance of obtaining anchor tenants to secure funding for a scheme.
2 Approved plans and specifications were attached to the agreement. The developer was able to make minor amendments to these, with the approval of the fund not to be unreasonably withheld. The fund retained the right to disallow any major amendments.
3 The scheme architect, Damond Lock Grabowski, and contractors were both specified in the agreement. The type of contract was also specified. Any changes to architect, contractor or contract had to be approved by the fund and approval was not to be unreasonably withheld.
4 An end date for practical completion of the development was stated as 1 June 1983 but this could be extended by circumstances outside the developer's reasonable control.
5 A model lease for the occupational lessees was specified in the agreement and the fund reserved the right to approve lettings together with the type of tenants' shop front and percentage of service charge.
6 Rights of inspection throughout the course of the works were reserved for Airways' structural engineer and the developer's architect was obliged to 'consult with' the fund's structural engineer before issuing a final

certificate. No rights were provided for the fund to formally approve the issue of the final certificate.

7 The important matter of 'as built drawings' being provided for the Fund was covered in the agreement.

Operation of the Funding Agreement

The agreement between the developer and council and the later agreement between developer and fund both seek to protect the interests of those parties to the scheme who were not directly involved as developers. In all agreements of this type, however, there is always some margin between the written word and practical management action. Although strong rights of approval were incorporated into the agreements and ground lease it was in the interests of all parties that the development should be completed and successfully let. If from time to time the developer failed to seek the appropriate approvals or failed to follow some other item in the agreement this was unlikely, in practice, to lead to serious repercussions for him.

The funding agreement with the pension fund was finally made some time after the start of the building contract. Up to that time the developer funded the scheme from his own resources although he was later reimbursed by the pension fund. The funding market for schemes of this nature was buoyant but there was a risk to the developer that he would be obliged to complete the scheme without the involvement of the pension fund.

Construction

The contractor, Walter Lawrence and Son Ltd, took possession of the site on 17 November 1980 and the developer's architect was appointed supervizing officer. As is not unusual in these cases, the contractor took possession of the site nine months before the contract was finally signed although the intention of the parties were made clear in a letter of intent. Quantity surveyors, L. C. Wakeman, and structural engineers, Deakin Callard and Partners, were known by reputation to both the developer and architect and were also appointed. During the course of construction no major changes to the scheme were necessary although there were constructional problems regarding water penetration from the service deck into some of the units. The solving of these problems resulted in the practical completion of the scheme being phased over the period 8 January – 11 November 1982.

The dates specified in the contract for completion of the three major stores were met and these tenants were able to commence shopfitting and stocking to programme. For the remaining units, however, considerable delays resulted from the problems of water penetration and the last shop accepted by the architect as practically complete, Unit 19 let to Thomas Cook, was accepted fourteen weeks after the date specified in the contract.

At the time of the centre opening for trading, some six weeks before Christmas 1982, many of the units were being fitted out by tenants, but at the time of the official opening, by the Princess of Wales, in March 1983, the centre was trading well with retail units occupied.

The office block on the frontage to the High Street was eventually let to six tenants and the last unit was not occupied until December 1984. Where phased occupation takes place, as at Hale Leys, the anchor tenants, who are usually the first in occupation, will wish to open in the months approaching Christmas when trade is strongest. However, they will also wish to open in a centre which is fully let with an appropriate tenant mix of complimentary traders. The balancing of traders' requirements with contracting and subcontracting problems is always problematical in shopping development and required careful management at Hale Leys.

Leases and lettings

Plan 2 (Figure A2) shows the lettings in the centre which were all agreed between January 1982 and January 1983. Zone A rents varied from £18.06 p.s.f. to £31.47 p.s.f. Not surprisingly shops which were closer to the focus of the centre tended to be let for higher zone A figures, but the figures are somewhat distorted by the irregular shapes of some of the units, for example Units 18 and 4 on Plan 3. The office block was let at rents between £6.25 p.s.f. and £7.55 p.s.f. to five local firms. Letting agents for the scheme were Hale and Partners of London, although halfway through the development Leonard Green were appointed joint agents. This was not the result of a marketing decision but because a key agent from Hale and Partners joined Leonard Green at that time. The offices were let by Platt and Meade of Aylesbury.

As in all lettings, the form of draft lease specified by the pension fund was varied on occasions in matters of detail. Furthermore, lettings to the three anchor tenants and the brewery were well advanced before the fund was involved. The main provisions of the preferred lease, which is for a twenty-five-year term, place the following obligations on tenants:

1 Rent payable by quarterly payments in advance.
2 A penal rate of interest '4 per cent above base rate' for unpaid rent.
3 To pay all outgoings including insuring the demise.
4 To pay a service charge calculated on the basis of weighted average floor space.
5 To repair all parts of the demise.
6 To decorate and clean.

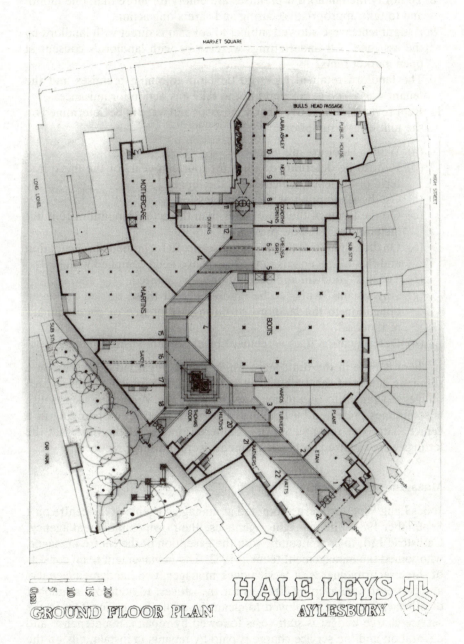

Figure A.2 Plan 2: Hale Leys Shopping Centre Letting Plan

7 Fitting out works were carried out as an obligation to the landlord (thereafter rentalized at rent review).

8 To notify the landlord if premises are empty for more than one month and to take appropriate securing and caretaking action.

9 Assignments were allowed subject to covenants direct with landlord by the assignee. All underlettings were to be with landlord's consent at open market rents.

10 The landlord retained rights to develop adjoining premises and the tenant was asked to covenant not to take any action for nuisance.

11 Rent reviews were at five-yearly intervals and were to be determined on the following assumptions:

(a) Willing landlord and tenant.

(b) Rent to be determined either for fourteen years or the unexpired term of the lease, whichever is the longer.

(c) On the assumption of vacant possession.

(d) On the terms of the lease other than the actual amount of rent but including rent review provision.

(e) On the assumption that the premises are fit for immediate occupation and that all covenants in the lease have been complied with.

(f) Tenants' goodwill and occupation to be ignored.

(g) Any tenants' works to be ignored except those carried out as an obligation to the landlord or during a rent free or concessionary rent period.

(h) Determination if no agreement by expert not arbitrator.

There is little in the draft lease which can be regarded as unusual in a shopping centre of this type except perhaps that there is no clause which obliges the tenant to occupy and use the premises. A positive user clause is sometimes preferred by landlords to ensure continuity of trading in a centre. Turnover rents were not considered, indeed at the time that the lettings were finalized such arrangements were unusual practice.

Management of the centre

Jones Lang Wootton were appointed as managing agents of the centre on 1 September 1981. The managing agents use their own employment agency, Cathstead Ltd, to appoint staff, with the exception of the centre manager, who joined the management team in 1982. The management team consists of three security guards, a service deck manager, two handymen/cleaners and two part-time evening cleaners for the offices. In addition, a number of other cleaners are employed to clean the mall. The major item in the service charge budget is staff costs followed by repairs, maintenance and decoration and the service charge is paid by tenants in instalments on the modern quarter days of 1 April, 1 July, 1 October and 1 January. The amount of the service charge budget is first approved by the pension fund and the fund's representative also meets with the centre management at least once per quarter to inspect the development. The service charge covers the following items:

1 Insurance
2 Water supply
3 Electricity
4 Gas
5 Cleaning materials
6 Refuse collection
7 Staff costs
8 Uniforms
9 Repairs, maintenance and decoration
10 Plan equipment, maintenance, acquisition and hire
11 Lift maintenance and repairs
12 Boiler maintenance and repairs
13 Fire equipment, including sprinklers
14 Management office expenses
15 Floral decorations
16 Promotion and advertising
17 Sinking fund

Since the centre opened and up to the time of writing there have been two assignments of retail units. The first assignment was Unit 8 which was originally occupied by a local menswear trader. This unit was then assigned to a ladies accessories trader which was part of the House of Fraser and subsequently reassigned to Next, a fashion multiple. Unit 18 was assigned to Bright Lights from Curry's when this company was taken over by Dixons. Neither of the two retail assignments which have taken place gives the head lessor of the centre any cause for alarm as the character of the centre, quality of the tenants and the tenant mix have been maintained or improved as a result. One of the tenants in the office block failed early in the life of the centre and the fund accepted a surrender before reletting.

The first rent reviews fell to be determined in July 1987 and nine retail units and the public house were due to be reviewed at that time. There was a lack of open market evidence in Aylesbury and no units were vacant at Hale Leys to establish open market rents. All the leases specified open market rents but it is a curious feature of lettings in shopping centres that the level of rent is often determined, not by those tenants trading in the centre, but by those trading outside it. A letting of a vacant unit to a tenant not already trading in the centre establishes a true market rent and is much to be desired by landlords. In spite of the lack of open market lettings the first round of rent reviews have been agreed at rents which are on average equivalent to £41.40 p.s.f. Zone A. Zone A equivalents at first letting averaged £25.58

p.s.f. and the comparison shows an annual compound growth rate in rental values of just over 10 per cent. Evidence at the time of writing is that no retail tenants at the centre have expressed a wish to assign and trading continues to be buoyant.

The head lessees of Hale Leys appear well satisfied with the retail investment that they helped to create. Retail rental growth was good over the first five years of trading and the tenant mix has been stable with few assignments or surrenders. Most importantly the anchor tenants appear to be trading well and profitably. The only reason why the fund would disinvest from property in Aylesbury is if very substantial sums were needed for refurbishment and these are not predicted at the present time. In the future the retail focus of Aylesbury will be strengthened by the refurbishment of Friars Square and the proposed retail development of the Upper Hundreds to the north of the High Street. This will involve the construction of a multi-storey car-park and a variety store as well as standard shop units. Hale Leys can be considered as an example of a subregional shopping scheme which is a result of a successful partnership between council, fund and developer. It is typical of the type of smaller shopping development which was completed in the mid 1970s and is proving a worthwhile long-term investment by both the British Airways Pension Fund and Aylesbury Vale District Council.

Law Society Royal Institution of Chartered Surveyors Model Rent Review Clause – Variation C

This extract forms part of the model forms of Rent Review Clause published on behalf of the Law Society and the R.I.C.S.

Determination in default of agreement to be either by arbitration or by independent valuer acting as expert (at the landlord's option) with alternative provisions for (a) upwards only review and (b) upwards or downwards review [*see Introduction*]

. . . yielding and paying to the landlord yearly rents ascertained in accordance with the next four clauses hereof without any deduction by equal quarterly payments in advance on the usual quarter days the first payment (being an apportioned sum) to be made on the date hereof

CLAUSE 1

Definitions

In this lease 'review date' means the . . . . day of . . . . in the year 19. . . . and in every . . . . . . year thereafter and 'review period' means the period starting with any review date up to the next review date or starting with the last review date up to the end of the term hereof

CLAUSE 2

The yearly rent shall be:
(A) until the first review date the rent of £. . . . . and

Provisions for review of rent in upwards only review

(B) *(i) during each successive review period a rent equal to the rent previously payable hereunder or such revised rent as may be ascertained as herein provided whichever be the greater*

OR

For revision of rent in upwards or downwards review

(B) (i) during each successive review period such revised rent as may be ascertained as herein provided and
(B) (ii) in the event of a revised rent not being ascertained as herein provided the rent payable for the relevant review period shall be the rent payable immediately prior to the commencement of such period

CLAUSE 3

Ascertainment of amount by arbitrator or by independent valuer at the landlord's option

Such revised rent for any review period may be agreed at any time between the landlord and the tenant or (in the absence of agreement) determined not earlier than the relevant review date at the option of the landlord either by an arbitrator or by an independent valuer (acting as an expert and not as an arbitrator) such arbitrator or valuer to be nominated in the absence of agreement by or on behalf of the President for the time being of the Royal Institution of Chartered Surveyors on the application of the landlord (in exercise of the said option) made not earlier than six months before the relevant review date *but not later than the end of the relevant review period* and so that in the case of such arbitration or valuation the revised rent to be awarded or determined by the arbitrator or valuer shall be such as he shall decide is the yearly rent at which the demised premises might reasonably be expected to be let at the relevant review date

(A) On the following assumptions at that date:

(i) That the demised premises:

(a) are available to let on the open market without a fine or premium with vacant possession by a willing landlord to a willing tenant for a term of [10] years or the residue then unexpired of the term of this lease (whichever be the longer)

(b) are to be let as a whole subject to the terms of this lease (other than the amount of the rent hereby reserved but including the provisions for review of that rent)

(c) are fit and available for immediate occupation

(d) may be used for any of the purposes permitted by this lease as varied or extended by any licence granted pursuant thereto

(ii) That the covenants herein contained on the part of the landlord and the tenant have been fully performed and observed

(iii) That no work has been carried out to the demised premises which has diminished the rental value and that in case the demised premises have been destroyed or damaged they have been fully restored

(iv) That no reduction is to be made to take account of any rental concession which on a new letting with vacant possession might be granted to the incoming tenant for a period within which its fitting out works would take place.

(B) But disregarding:

(i) any effect on rent of the fact that the tenant its sub-tenants or their respective predecessors in title have been in occupation of the demised premises

(ii) any goodwill attached to the demised premises by reason of the carrying on thereat of the business of the tenant its sub-tenants or their predecessors in title in their respective businesses and

(iii) any increase in rental value of the demised premises attributable to the existence at the relevant review date of any improvement to the demised premises or any part thereof carried out with consent where required otherwise than in pursuance of an obligation to the landlord or its predecessors in title except obligations requiring compliance with statutes or directions of Local Authorities or other bodies exercising powers under statute or Royal Charter either (a) by the tenant its sub-tenants or their respective predecessors in title during the said term or during any period of occupation prior thereto arising out of an agreement to grant such term or *(b) by any tenant or sub-tenant of the demised premises before the commencement of the term hereby granted so long as the landlord or its predecessors in title have not since the improvement was carried out had vacant possession of the relevant part of the demised premises*

CLAUSE 4

IT IS HEREBY FURTHER PROVIDED in relation to the ascertainment and payment of revised rent as follows:

Further provisions as to arbitration

(A) (In case of arbitration) the arbitration shall be conducted in accordance with the Arbitration Acts 1950 and 1979 or any statutory modification or re-enactment thereof for the time being in force with the further provision that if the arbitrator nominated pursuant to Clause 3 hereof shall die or decline to act the President for the time being of the Royal Institution of Chartered Surveyors or the person acting on his behalf he may on the application of either the landlord or the tenant by writing discharge the arbitrator and appoint another in his place

As to independent valuation

(B) (In the case of determination by a valuer)
(i) the fees and expenses of the valuer including the cost of his nomination shall be borne equally by the landlord and the tenant who shall otherwise each bear their own costs and

(ii) the valuer shall afford the landlord and the tenant an opportunity to make representations to him and

(iii) if the valuer nominated pursuant to Clause 3 hereof shall die delay or become unwilling, unfit or incapable of acting or if for any other reason the President for the time being of the Royal Institution of Chartered Surveyors or the person acting on his behalf shall in his absolute discretion think fit he may on the application of either the landlord or the tenant by writing discharge the valuer and appoint another in his place

As to memoranda of ascertainment

(C) When the amount of any rent to be ascertained as hereinbefore provided shall have been so ascertained memoranda thereof shall thereupon be signed by or on behalf of the landlord and the tenant and annexed to this lease and the counterpart thereof and the landlord and the tenant shall bear their own costs in respect thereof

As to interim payments and final adjustments
upwards only review

(D) (i) If the revised rent payable on and from any review date has not been agreed by that review date rent shall continue to be payable at the rate previously payable and forthwith upon the revised rent being ascertained, the tenant shall pay to the landlord any shortfall between the rent and the revised

rent payable up to and on the preceding quarter day together with interest on any shortfall at the seven day deposit rate of . . . . BANK such interest to be calculated on a day-to-day basis from the relevant review date on which it would have been payable if the revised rent had then been ascertained to the date of actual payment of any shortfall and the interest so payable shall be recoverable in the same manner as rent in arrear

OR

(D) (i) If the revised rent payable on and from any review date has not agreed by that review date rent shall continue to be payable at the rate previously payable and forthwith upon the revised rent being ascertained the tenant shall pay to the landlord any shortfall between the rent and the revised rent or as the case may be the landlord shall pay to the tenant any excess of the rent paid over the revised rent payable up to and on the preceding quarter day together with interest on any shortfall or as the case may be any excess at the seven day deposit rate of . . . . BANK such interest to be calculated on a day-to-day basis from the relevant review date on which it would have been payable if the revised rent had then been ascertained to the date of actual payment of any shortfall or any excess and the interest so payable shall be recoverable in the same manner as rent in arrear or as the case may be as a debt

(ii) for the purposes of this priviso the revised rent shall be deemed to have been ascertained on the date when the same has been agreed between the landlord and the tenant or as the case may be the date of the award of the arbitrator or of the determination by the valuer

(E) If either the landlord or the tenant shall fail to pay any costs awarded against it in the case of an arbitration or the moiety of the fees and expenses of the valuer under the provisions hereof within twenty-one days of the same being demanded by the arbitrator or the valuer (as the case may be) the other shall be entitled to pay the same and the amount so paid shall be repaid by the party chargeable on demand.

As to notice by the tenant to trigger landlord's application

(F) Whenever a revised rent in respect of any review period has not been agreed between the landlord and the tenant before the relevant review date and where no agreement has been reached as to the appointment of an arbitrator or valuer nor has the landlord made any application to the President for the time being of the Royal Institution of Chartered Surveyors as hereinbefore provided the tenant may serve on the landlord notice in writing referring to this provision and containing a proposal as to the amount of such revised rent (which shall not be less than the rent payable immediately before the commencement of the relevant review period) and the amount so proposed shall be deemed to have *been agreed by the landlord and the tenant as the revised rent for the relevant review period and sub-clause (D) (i) hereof shall apply accordingly unless the landlord shall make such application as aforesaid within three months after service of such notice by the tenant. Time shall be of the essence in respect of this provision.*

References and selected further reading

1 THE INVESTMENT MEDIA

Baum, A. and Crosby, N. (1988) *Property Investment Appraisal*, London, Routledge.

Baum, A. and Mackmin, D. (1989) *The Income Approach to Property Valuation*, 3rd edn, London, Routledge.

Curry, S.J. (1985) *Investment: Question and Answers*, London, Financial Training Publications Ltd.

Darlow, C. (ed.) (1983) *Valuation and Investment Appraisal*, London, Estates Gazette Publications Ltd.

Debenham, Tewson and Chinnock (1989) *Money into Property*, Debenham, Tewson and Chinnock.

Enever, N. (1986) *The Valuation of Property Investments*, 3rd edn, London, Estates Gazette Publications Ltd.

Fraser, W.D. (1984) *Principles of Property Investment and Pricing*, London, Macmillan.

Fraser, W.D. (1985) 'Gilts' yields and property's target return,' *Estates Gazette*, 273, 1291–4.

Goff, T.G. (1986) *Theory and Practice of Investment*, Oxford, Heinneman.

Scarett, D. (1984) *Property Management*, London, E. & F.N. Spon.

Stapleton, T. (1986) *Estate Management Practice*, London, Estates Gazette Publications Ltd.

Wingfield, R.G. and Curry, S.J. (1981) *Success in Investment*, London, John Murray.

2 PROPERTY AS AN INVESTMENT

Assets Valuation Standards Committee (1982) *Guidance Notes on the Valuation of Assets*, 2nd edn, Royal Institution of Chartered Surveyors.

Baum, A. (1989) *Property Depreciation and Obsolescence*, Unpublished thesis, University of Reading.

Baum, A. and Crosby, N. (1988) *Property Investment Appraisal*, London, Routledge.

Baum, A. and Mackmin, D. (1989) *The Income Approach to Property Valuation*, 3rd edn, London, Routledge.

Bowcock, P. (1978) *Property Valuation Tables*, London, Macmillan.

Bowie, N. (1983) *Depreciation, Who Hoodwinked Who?*, London, Estates Gazette Publications Ltd.

Butterworth's *Tax Guides* (Annual).

Brown, G. (1987) 'A certainty equivalent expectations model for estimating the systematic risk of property investment', *Journal of Valuation* 6, 32.

Darlow, C. (ed.) (1983) *Valuation and Investment Appraisal*, London Estates Gazette Publications Ltd.

Davidson, A.W. (compiler) (1989) *Parry's Valuation Tables*, 11th edn, London, Estates Gazette Publications Ltd.

Enever, N. (1986) *The Valuation of Property Investments*, 3rd edn, London Estates Gazette Publications Ltd.

Fraser, W.G. (1984) *Principles of Property Investment and Pricing*, London, Macmillan.

Fraser, W.D. 1985 'Gilt yields and property's target return', *Estates Gazette* 273, 1291–4.

Greenwell, W. *et al.* (1976) 'A call for new valuation methods', *Estates Gazette* 238, 481–4.

Jones Lang Woottoi (1987) *Risk and Asset Allocation: Implications of Portfolio Strategy*, Jones Lang Wootton.

Jones Lang Wootton (1988) *The Allocation of Property Assets*, Jones Lang Wootton.

McIntosh, A.P.J. and Sykes, S.G. (1985) *A Guide to Institutional Property Investment*, London, Macmillan.

Marshall, P. (1979) *Donaldson's Investment Tables*, Donaldsons.

Mellows, A.R. (1978) *Taxation of Land Transactions*, 2nd edn, Butterworth.

Rees, W. (ed.) (1988) *Valuation – Principles into Practice*, London, Estates Gazette Publications Ltd.

Rose, J.J. (1977) *Rose's Property Valuation Tables*, The Freeland Press.

Richmond, D. (1985) *Introduction to Valuation*, 2nd edn, London, Routledge.

Salway, F. (1986) *A Study of Depreciation in Offices*, Centre for Advanced Land Use Studies.

Stapleton, T. (1986) *Estate Management Practice*, 2nd edn, London, Estates Gazette Publications Ltd.

Trott, A. (1980) *Property Valuation Methods, Interim Report*, Polytechnic of the South Bank/ Royal Institution of Chartered Surveyors.

3 INVESTMENT PROPERTY SPECIFICATION

Britton, W., Davies, K., Johnson, T.A. (1989) '*Modern Methods of Valuation*', 8th edn, London, Estates Gazette Publications Ltd.

Chartered Surveyors Weekly (1986) 'Fund managers' choice', *CSW*, 20 November.

Darlow, C. (ed.) (1983) *Valuation and Investment Appraisal*, London, Estates Gazette Publications Ltd.

Debenham Tewson and Chinnocks, *Money into Property* (Annual).

Fraser, W.D. (1984) *Principles of Property Investment and Pricing*, London, Macmillan.

Healey and Baker (1986) *The Workplace Revolution*, Healey & Baker.

Healey and Baker, *Quarterly Investment Reports*, Healey & Baker.

Healey and Baker, *Property Rent Indices and Market Editorial*, (Annual).

Hillier Parker (1986) *Shopping Centre Refurbishment*, Hillier Parker Research.

Hillier Parker (1988) *International Property Bulletin*, Hillier Parker.

Institutional Investment in Property – Current Requirements and Criteria, papers from a Henry Stewart Conference 14 October 1988, Henry Stewart Publications.

Investment Property Databank, *The Annual Review*, IPD.
Jones Lang Wootton (1987) *Risk and Asset Allocation: Implications of Portfolio Strategy*, Jones, Lang Wootton.
McIntosh, A.P.J. and Sykes, S.G. (1985) *A Guide to Institutional Property Investment*, London, Macmillan.
Morgan, P.G. and Walker, A. (1989) *Shopping Centre Development*, London, Estates Gazette Publications Ltd.
Morley, S., Marsh, C., McIntosh, A.P.J. and Martinos, H. (1989) *Industrial and Business Space Developments*, London, E. & F.N. Spon.
Rees W. (ed.) (1988) *Valuation – Principles into Practice*, 3rd edn, London, Estates Gazette Publications Ltd.
Richard Ellis, *Quarterly Review*, Richard Ellis.
Stapleton, T. (1986) *Estate Management Practice*, London, Estates Gazette Publications Ltd.

Legislative Measures and Official Publications

Agricultural Holdings Acts 1948, 1986, HMSO.
Housing Acts 1980, 1985, 1988, HMSO.
Landlord and Tenant Acts 1927, 1954, 1985, 1987 and 1988, HMSO.
Law Commission (1989) *Commonhold*, HMSO.
Offices, Shops and Railway Premises Act 1963, HMSO.
National Agricultural Land Classification, Ministry of Agriculture, Fisheries and Food.
Northfield (1979) *The Report of the Committee of Inquiry into the Acquisition and Occupancy of Agricultural Land*, Cmnd. 7599.
Rent Act 1977, HMSO.
Use Classes Order 1987, HMSO.

Journals

Chartered Surveyor Weekly, annual reviews and centrefolio reports.
Estates Gazette, annual reviews and special reports.
Estates Times, special supplements.

4 PROPERTY INVESTMENT AND DEVELOPMENT, 1945–88

Burden and Campbell (1985) *Capitalism and Public Policy in the U.K.*, London, Croom Helm.
Cox, A. (1984) *Adversary Politics and Land*, Cambridge, Cambridge University Press.
Darlow, C. (ed.) (1983) *Valuation and Investment Appraisal*, London, Estates Gazette Publications Ltd.
Fraser, W.D. (1984) *Principles of Property Investment and Pricing*, London, Macmillan.
Lloyds Bank Review, April 1977, no. 124, Lloyd's Bank.
Marriott, O. (1967) *The Property Boom*, London, Pan Piper.
Plender, J. (1982) *That's the way the Money Goes*, London, André Deutsch.

5 INVESTORS AND PORTFOLIO RETURNS

Barber, C. (1988) 'Performance evaluation', *Estates Gazette*, 27 August 1988.

Baum, A. and Crosby, N. (1988) *Property Investment Appraisal*, London, Routledge.

Darlow, C. (ed.) (1983) *Valuation and Investment Appraisal*, Estates Gazette Publications Ltd.

Fraser, W.D. (1984) *Principles of Property Investment and Pricing*, London, Macmillan.

Fraser, W.D. (1985) 'Gilt's yields and property's target return', *Estates Gazette* 273, 1291–4.

Fraser, W.D. (1986) 'Property's risk and the enigma of yield trends in the 1980's', *Estates Gazette* 277, 706–10

Frost and Hager (1986) *A General Introduction to Institutional Investment*, London, Heinemann.

Greenwell, W. *et al.* (1976) 'A call for new valuation methods', *Estates Gazette* 238, 481–4.

Hall, P. (1984) 'The measurement of property investment performance,' *Journal of Valuation* 3, 376–83.

Hager, D.P. and Lord, D.J. (1985) '*The Property Market: Property Valuation and Property Performance Measurement*, London, Institute of Actuaries.

McIntosh, A.P.J. and Sykes, S.C. (1985) *A Guide to Institutional Property Investment*, London, Macmillan.

Newell, M. (1985) 'The rate of return on a measure of performance', *Journal of Valuation* 4, 130–42.

Trott, A. (1980) *Property Valuation Methods*, Interim report, Polytechnic of the South Bank/Royal Institution of Chartered Surveyors.

Wolman, C. (1986) 'Pension fund investment', *Financial Times Supplement* 17 February 1986.

6 RISK AND THE INDIVIDUAL INVESTMENT

Arnison, C. and Barrett, A. (1986) 'Valuation of development sites using the stochastic decision tree method', *Journal of Valuation* 3, 126–33.

Baum, A. (1987) 'Risk explicit appraisal: a sliced income approach', *Journal of Valuation* volume 5, 250–67 and volume 3.

Baum, A. and Crosby, N. (1988) *Property Investment Appraisal*, Chapter 8, London, Routledge.

Byrne, P. and Cadman, D. (1984) *Risk, Uncertainty and Decision-making in Property Development*, London, E. & F.N. Spon.

Darlow, C. (ed.) (1987) *Valuation and Development Appraisal*, Chapter 4, Estates Gazette Publications Ltd.

Fraser, W.D. (1984) *Principles of Property Investment and Pricing*, London, Macmillan.

Fraser, W.D. (1985) 'Gilt yields and property's target return', *Estates Gazette* 273, 1291–4

Fraser, W.D. (1986a) 'Property's risk and the enigma of yield trends in the 1980s', *Estates Gazette* 277, 706–10.

Fraser, W.D. (1986b) 'The target return on UK property investments', *Journal of Valuation* 4, 119–29.

Fraser, W.D. (1986c) 'The risk of property to the institutional investor', *Journal of Valuation* 4, 239–60.

Hager, D.S. and Lord, D.J. (1985) *The Property Market, Property Valuations and Property Performance Measurement*, Institute of Actuaries.

Lumby, S. (1984) *Investment Appraisal*, Wokingham, Van Nostrand Reinhold (UK).

McIntosh, A.P.J. and Sykes, S.G. (1985) *A Guide to Institutional Property Investment*, London, Macmillan.

MacLeary, A.R. and Nanthakumaran, N. (eds) (1988) *Property Investment Theory*, Chapters 5 and 9, London, E. & F.N. Spon.

Royal Institution of Chartered Surveyors (RICS) (1990) *Statements of Asset Valuation Practice and Guidance Notes*, RICS.

Sykes, S.G. (1983) 'The assessment of property risk', *Journal of Valuation* 1,253–67.

7 RISK AND THE PORTFOLIO

Baum, A. and Crosby, N. (1988) *Property Investment Appraisal*, London, Routledge.

Brown, G. (1983) 'Making property investment decisions via capital market theory', *Journal of Valuation* 2, 142–60

Brown, G. (1987) 'A certainty equivalent expectations model for estimating the systematic risk of property investment', *Journal of Valuation* 6, 33.

Brown, G. (1988) in MacLeary, A. and Nanthakumaran, N. (eds) *Property Investment Theory*, London, E. & F.N. Spon.

Corner, D. and Mayes, D.G. (eds) (1984) *Modern Portfolio Theory and Financial Institutions*, London, Macmillan.

Fraser, W.D. (1986) 'The risk of property investments to the institutional investors', *Journal of Valuation* 4, 239–60

Hartigay, S. (1985) 'Selection of assets for a property portfolio using portfolio theory', *Journal of Valuation* 3, 272–83.

Hargitay, S. (1986) 'The portfolio problem in the property investment context', *Journal of Valuation* 3, 117–25.

Jones Lang Wootton (1987) *Risk and Asset Allocation: Implications of Portfolio Strategy*, Jones Lang Wootton.

Locke, S. (1985) 'Portfolio considerations in valuation: an introduction', *Journal of Valuation* 3, 317–23.

Locke, S. (1987), 'Performance assessment index and capital asset pricing models', *Journal of Valuation* 5, 230–49.

MacLeary, A. and Nanthakumaran, N. (eds) (1988) *Property Investment Theory*, London, E. & F.N. Spon.

Markowitz, H. (1959) *Portfolio Selection – Efficient Diversification of investments*, Newhaven, Conn., Yale University Press.

Moore, P.G. '*The Business of Risk*', Cambridge, Cambridge University Press.

Sweeney, F.M. (1988) '20 per cent in property – a viable strategy', *Estates Gazette* 8806, 26–8.

Wyatt, A. (1984) 'Real estate portfolio performance', *Journal of Valuation* 2, 342–55.

8 and 9 ACTIVE MANAGEMENT

Audit Commission (1987) *Property Management – Audit Commission for Local Authorities for England and Wales*, London, HMSO.

Audit Commission (1988a) *Local Authority Property – An Overview*, London, HMSO.

Audit Commission (1988b) *Local Authority Property – A Management Handbook*, HMSO.

Avis, M., Gibson, V. and Watts, J. (1989) *Managing Operational Property Assets*, Reading, Reading University.

Benson, C. (1988) 'The corporate view of the investment surveyor', Paper given for I.C.C. conference, Institution and College Conferences.

Braham, M. (1985) *Commercial Leases*, London, Collins Professional and Technical Press.

Brech, E.F.L. (ed.) (1975) *The Principles and Practice of Management*, London, Longman.

Britton, W., Connellan, O.P. and Crofts, M.K. (1989) *The Economic, Efficient and Effective Management of Public Authority Landed Estates*, Kingston, Surrey County Council Kingston Polytechnic.

Britton, W., Davies, K. and Johnson, T.A. (1989) *Modern Methods of Valuation*, 8th edn, London, Estates Gazette Publication Ltd.

Centre for Advanced Land Use Studies (CALUS) (1970) *Urban Property Management*, Reading, CALUS publications.

Centre for Advanced Land Use Studies (CALUS) (1983) *Commentary on a Commercial Lease*, Reading, College of Estate Management.

Darlow, C. (ed.) (1983) *Valuation and Investment Appraisal*, London, Estates Gazette Publications Ltd.

Fox-Andrews, J. (1978) *Business Tenancies*, London, Estates Gazette Publications Ltd.

Fraser, W.D. (1988) in MacLeary, A.R. and Nanthakumaran, N. (eds) *Property Investment Theory*, London, E. & F.N. Spon.

Macintosh, A.P.J. and Sykes, S.G. (1984) *A Guide to Institutional Property Investment*, London, Macmillan.

Marriott, O. (1967) *The Property Boom*, London, Pan Piper.

Mew, S.R. (1989) *Pension Funds and Insurance Companies: a study of differences in attitude towards direct property investment*, (unpublished dissertation).

Rees, W.H. (ed.) (1988) *Valuation – principles into practice*, 3rd edn, London, Estates Gazette Publications Ltd.

Royal Institution of Chartered Surveyors (RICS) (1986) *The Maintenance of Commercial Property – a Working Party Report*, RICS.

Royal Institution of Chartered Surveyors (RICS) (1990), *Statements of Asset Valuation Practice and Guidance Notes*, 3rd edn, RICS.

Scarrett, D. (1984) *Property Management*, London, E. & F.N. Spon.

Stapleton, T. (1986) *Estate Management Practice*, 2nd edn, London, Estates Gazette Publications Ltd.

Thompson, F.M.L. (1968) *Chartered Surveyors – the Growth of a Profession*, London, Routledge & Kegan Paul.

Thorncroft, M. (1965) *Principles of Estate Management*, London, Estates Gazette Publications Ltd.

Williams, D. (1985) *Landlord and Tenant Casebook*, London, Estates Gazette Publications, Ltd.

Williams, D. (1986) 'Repairs update', *Estates Gazette*, 5 April 1986.

Williams, D. (1987) '"Repair" reconsidered', *Estates Gazette*, 25 April 1987.

Williams, D. (1987) 'Landlord and Tenant Acts', *Estates Gazette*, 15 August 1987.

Williams, D. (1987) *A Casebook on Repairs*, London, Estates Gazette, Publications Ltd.

Williams, D. (1989) 'Landlord's remedies for disrepair', *Estates Gazette* 23 September 1989 and 30 September 1989.
Williams, D. (1989) 'Does the 1954 Act apply?' *Estates Gazette* 26 November 1989.
Williams, D. (1989) 'Business tenancies – 1954 Act update', *Estates Gazette* 26 November 1989.
Williams, D. (1989) 'Law Commission proposals for reform', *Estates Gazette* 26 November 1989.
Williams, D. (1989) 'Service charges on commercial premises', *Estates Gazette* 11 November 1989.
Wootton, B. (1987) 'Institutional asset and property portfolio management, paper given for conference 'The Dawning of the Age of Property Management and investment', Profex Conferences.

Useful journal reading
The Estates Gazette
The Journal of Property Management (Henry Stewart Publications)
The Journal of Rent Review and Lease Renewal (Henry Stewart Publications)

10 REDEVELOPMENT AND REFURBISHMENT

Cadman, D. and Austin Crowe, L. (1972) *Property Development*, London, E. & F.N. Spon.
Darlow, C. (ed) (1987) *Valuation and Development Appraisal*, Estates Gazette Publications Ltd.
Debenham, Tewson and Chinnock (1986) *Unitisation of Large Properties: Portfolio Diversification Potential*, Debenham, Tewson and Chinnock.
Fraser, W.D. (1984) *Principles of Property Investment and Pricing*, London, Macmillan.
Harvey, J. (1987) Urban Land Economics, London, Macmillan.
Healey and Baker (1988) *Prince Property Yields 1977–88*, Healey & Baker.
Hillier Parker (1986) *Shopping Centre Refurbishment*, Hillier Parker Research.
SEL Report and Accounts, 1987

11 FUNDING AND THE DEVELOPMENT PROCESS

Barnes, M. (1983) 'How to allocate risks in construction contracts, *International Journal of Project Management* 1(1)
Fraser, W. D. (1984) *An Approach to Major Projects*, Major Projects Association.
Gibbs, R. 'Raising finance for new development', *Journal of Valuation* 5, 343.
McIntosh, A.P.J. (1987) *Finance for Property Development*, unpublished paper.
Ratcliff, J. (undated) *Project Management for Property Development*, Polytechnic of South Bank, Dept. of Estate Management, occasional paper.

12 INTERNATIONAL INFLUENCE AND CURRENT TRENDS

Austin, R.S. (1986) 'The Paris office market', (3 articles) *Estates Gazette*, 278.
Barkshire Committee (1986) *The Unitised Property Market – A Discussion Document*, The Barkshire Committee.
Barter, S.L. (ed.) (1988) *Real Estate Finance*, London, Butterworth.
Baum, A. and Crosby, N. (1988) *Property Investment Appraisal*, London, Routledge.
Blakely, P. (1988) 'Property trusts in Australia', *Estates Gazette*, 280, 1429.

Chambers, S. (1988) 'American property: investment in the USA during the 1980s', *Estates Gazette*, 8833.

Debenham, Tewson and Chinnock (1986) *Unitisation of Large Properties: Portfolio Diversification Potential*, Debenham Tewson and Chinnock.

Duxbury, P. (1988) 'Property unitisation', *Chartered Surveyor Weekly* 5 May.

Erdman, E. (1989) *Investment Commentary*, Edward Erdman Research.

Hillier Parker (1988) *International Property Bulletin*, Hillier Parker.

Hood, A. *et al.* (1987) 'Report on FIABCI Congress 1987', *Estates Gazette*, 282, 974–94.

Lewis, D. (1988) Investing in US Real Estate (5 articles) *Estates Gazette*, 8809.

Royal Institution of Chartered Surveyors (1985) *The Unitisation of Real Property*, RICS.

Royal Institution of Chartered Surveyors (1986) *The Unitisation of Commercial Property*, a supplementary report, RICS.

Schiller, R. (1988) 'Office decentralisation – lessons from America,' *Estates Gazette* 8814, 20–22.

Sinclair, N. (1987) 'Unitisation of properties', *Law Society Gazette* 13 May, p.1394.

The Revolution in Property Financing, Conference papers by various contributors, Henry Stewart Publications 1987.

Index

acquisition policy 198–204; active management 200–1; comparability 203; finance availability 200; in-house or retained agents 201–2; location and tenant demand 203; method of return measurement 199; minimum return 199; occupational requirements 204; portfolio composition 204; portfolio effect 203; portfolio shape 200; prime or secondary 203; risk 200; tenure 202; time return horizon 204

active management 173; acquisition policy 200–1; commercial lease 174–96; performance 197–221

adjustment techniques, risk 150–7; certainty equivalent 153–5; sliced income approach 155–7

aesthetics and design 44, 207–8

agents, property management 201–2

Agricultural Holdings Acts (1948, 1986) 90–1

agricultural property 90–3

architects 227–8, 260

Arnison, C., and Barrett, A. 148

assignment clauses 180; Australia 274–5; France 270; Germany 272; Scandinavia 272; USA 269

Association of Consulting Engineers (ACE) 260

Audit Commission 205

Australia 273–5

Avis, M., Gibson, V., and Watts, J. 205

banks: fixed or restricted interest

rates 246–7; as investment 10; and redevelopment funding 235–6

Barber, Anthony 108–9

Barnes, Martin 258

Baum, A. 1–3, 36, 48–9, 52, 56–7, 126, 153–4, 169

Belgium 267

Berisford, S & W 280

Betterment Levy 208

Bowcock, P. 66

Bowie, N. 57

Brech, E. F. L. 197

Brixton Estate 235

Brown, G. 59, 161, 169

building management 26

building societies 10

Building Societies Act (1986) 9

building value, and site value 222–4

Burden and Campbell 104

Butterworth's *Tax Guides* 66

campus developments 88–90

capital asset pricing model (CAPM) 164–70; application to property 168–70; use of 167–8

Capital and Counties 73, 186

capital gains taxation 61, 209

capital security and growth 2–3; property 63

capital value risk 131–2

capitalised 'top slice' leaseback 241–2

Centre for Advanced Land Use Studies (CALUS) 178

certainty equivalent 153–5

change 263–5; foreign investment 264; social and demographic 265;